MOSCOW-PEKING AXIS

Strengths and Strains

MOSCOW-PEKING AXIS
Strengths and Strains

By

HOWARD L. BOORMAN
ALEXANDER ECKSTEIN
PHILIP E. MOSELY
BENJAMIN SCHWARTZ

Foreword by ARTHUR H. DEAN

⚬∾⚬

Published for the
COUNCIL ON FOREIGN RELATIONS
by
HARPER & BROTHERS
New York
1957

MOSCOW-PEKING AXIS: STRENGTHS AND STRAINS

Copyright, 1957, by Council on Foreign Relations, Inc.
Printed in the United States of America

All rights reserved, including the right to reproduce this book or any portion thereof in any form.

For information address Council on Foreign Relations, 58 East 68th Street, New York 21

SECOND PRINTING

American Book–Stratford Press, Inc., New York

Library of Congress catalog card number: LC 56–7909

Published in Great Britain and the British Commonwealth, excluding Canada, by London: Oxford University Press

COUNCIL ON FOREIGN RELATIONS

11104

FOREWORD

by Arthur H. Dean

TODAY the Moscow-Peking axis represents a formidable and inscrutable force in world politics. Its combined power, which straddles two continents, is felt far beyond its own borders. Its impact, present and potential, upon relations among nations is bound to be far-reaching.

Are the Chinese Communists completely dominated by Moscow? Are they potential rivals to the Soviets? Is there friction? Or is there the probability of friction between them? Will the more numerous Chinese, under the leadership of Mao Tse-tung, take over leadership of the international Communist movement? Since it may be assumed that one of our foreign policy objectives should be to bring about, if we can, possible strains in the Sino-Soviet alliance, should we try to "push them together" or "pull them apart," and, if so, "how?"

This dilemma is posed, for example, by the question of our embargo on trade with Communist China. Those who advocate the continuance of the embargo in order to aggravate the economic strains, and, consequently, the political strains within the Sino-Soviet alliance believe in "pushing them together." Those who believe in "pulling them apart" advocate the removal of trade controls and the lessening of political conflicts on the ground that they hurt our own allies more than the Communist Chinese, are rather insensitive instruments to accomplish the desired objective, and can hardly be expected to bring about a collapse of the Chinese Communist regime or appreciably to affect the economy of the Soviet bloc. They also believe that their removal may serve to lessen Communist China's dependence upon the U.S.S.R. and provide opportunities for non-Communist powers to influence the course of its foreign policy, but that, because of its ambitious economic program, Communist China appears unlikely to risk embarking on Titoism unless it can hope to obtain from alternative sources essential industrial and technological requirements for its economic expansion.

While our military power, if properly maintained, can, and I strongly believe, will, deter the Soviet leadership from embarking on a general war, one that would be accompanied by widespread destruction, the cold war, long continued, may cause some of our less fortunately situated friends to examine a good deal more closely the precise worth to them of their military alliances with us. This reappraisal may seem to them the more urgent, now that the true nature of the struggle with the Soviet Union and international Communism appears to be undergoing a significant transition, and it becomes even clearer that the long-range Communist objective to encompass the downfall of the free world by subversion and infiltration remains unchanged.

Gradually there is emerging in the West a consciousness that the civilization to which we are all accustomed, the one from which we draw our ideals, is being confronted on all sides by new ideas and new forms of government. In formulating a creative and imaginative foreign policy for the American people, all of this has great significance, and, in our natural optimism that all is right with the world, we must not overlook unpleasant and ugly facts, rely too much on ideas drawn from the past, fail to perceive the new problems created by changes in the status of former colonial territories, or be too negative in our approach to world problems.

The British have withdrawn from India, Ceylon and Burma, and, apart from the recent British-French episode, from the Suez Canal Zone; the Dutch from Indonesia; the French from Indochina; the Federation of Malay States and the Straits Settlements are about to vote on their independence within the Commonwealth or outside; and the Treaty Ports in China are no more.

Having regained control of Manchuria and taken over
North Korea, the Chinese Communists, in cooperation
with their ally, Ho Chi Minh, have taken over North
Vietnam, are infiltrating Laos and Cambodia, are threatening South Vietnam, Thailand and Burma, and have made
serious inroads into the political life of Indonesia, where
rumors of an impending coup have been frequent. Apparently, the Communist leaders are on more cordial terms
with Prime Minister Nehru than are we, his visit here not-
withstanding.

In the Middle East new and independent states are pressing for fulfillment of their intensely nationalistic aspirations. Syria is being subjected to Communist infiltration,
the British-French invasion of Egypt is likely to have
far-reaching consequences, and our new Middle East policy
remains to be implemented. Africa, the sleeping giant, is
slowly awakening. The Gold Coast, Morocco, Tunisia,
Libya and Sudan have achieved their independence.

The role of the United Nations is changing rapidly,
especially since it now has eighty members, many of them
newly independent nations.

The days when an American Secretary of State could
deal effectively with the peace of the world through the
chanceries of Europe, the British Commonwealth, Latin
America and Japan are over.

Whether or not we choose to extend diplomatic recognition to one of its partners, it would be folly not to realize
the ominous impact of the Moscow-Peking axis on the
security and prosperity of the Western world. Ever since
President Eisenhower stated clearly that we would not attack the Chinese mainland or support Chiang Kai-shek in
so doing, Mao Tse-tung has held the peace of Asia in his
own hands. Will he choose to tolerate it, or will he attack
Formosa or the offshore islands? Will he seek to intimidate
Japan, once the scourge of China, or to woo it? Meanwhile
Japan writhes discontentedly, its expanded population
held within the confines of its own volcanic islands,
badgered by the Soviets into reluctantly entering a peace
treaty with them, prevented from trading with the Chinese

mainland through its voluntary adherence to the United
Nations embargo, and wooed in every way by the Soviets
and by the lure of trade with the Communist Chinese.

What of Communist China?

—After overrunning mainland China in 1949, the Chinese
Communists proceeded step by step to bring the disparate
segments of the sprawling economy under the intimate
control of the planning authorities, and then to launch
their first Five-Year Plan, proclaimed in 1953 but fully
elaborated only in 1955. In its essence, the Plan is pushing
the development of heavy industry at the expense of all
other factors and forcing through the collectivization of
the villages more rapidly than was done by Stalin in Russia, as a means of extracting an increasing share of the
farm output to support the industrial, export and military
goals of the leadership. Government policy is devoted to
keeping consumption at the lowest possible levels compatible with political stability—keeping the regime in power
while maximizing the rate at which internal control is extended.

In industrial development, power and transport, level
of literacy and availability of skills, Communist China was
at a much lower state of development in 1949 than was
—Russia in 1900. Thus, despite its ambitious industrial program, it has a much longer road to travel toward the goals
of industrialization, and the obstacles are greater. So far,
however, its forceful, brutal, efforts appear to be having a
certain measure of success though there may be serious
famine in China in the near future. Denied access to other
sources of foreign loans and investments, Communist
China is today completely dependent on the Soviet Union
and its satellites for the outside help which is essential to
its initial stage of industrialization.

The trade of mainland China with what now constituted the Soviet bloc, negligible before World War II,
now comprises an overwhelming share of its foreign trade.
Indeed, the embargo enforced on Communist China as a
result of its aggression in Korea has brought about a far
greater dependence on the Soviet bloc than would other-

wise be the case. In turn, this relationship puts a substantial, though probably not excessive, strain upon the machine-tool sector of the Soviet economy and forces it to exchange high-priority machinery for low-priority foodstuffs and other consumer goods.

Whether a Communist China, freed from its complete economic dependence on the Soviet Union, would become less hostile politically toward the West is highly debatable. Certainly, the mere reduction or removal of trade controls would not go far to help Communist China achieve its ambitious industrial goals, for it could not count on receiving any large long-term credits or aid from outside the Soviet bloc. Furthermore, any concessions on our part for which we do not extract an enforceable *quid pro quo* would merely be taken by the Chinese as a sign of weakness.

Mindful of the tragic mistakes made by Stalin and others in Poland and Hungary and in China as early as 1927, as well as the break with Tito and the reluctance of Stalin to cast the People's Republic of China in a co-starring role, the new Soviet leadership now appears to be giving Mao-Tse-tung and his deputy Chou En-lai a maximum of cooperation with a minimum of interference, and it recognizes the People's Republic as its principal ally in Asia. The Soviet press avoids all criticism of the way in which Chinese Communism has developed, and the Chinese Communist leadership is accorded higher honors than any other non-Soviet party. Although events in Hungary and Poland are being followed by Communist China's leaders with much interest and with sympathy for the principle of satellite independence from Moscow, Peking appears to endorse Soviet actions nevertheless. Probably it is even more interested than the Soviet Union in maintaining internally the state of affairs euphemistically characterized as the "cult of personality," in view of the importance to it of Mao's continued and unquestioned authority during the present period of reconstruction of mainland China's society.

In 1949, soon after the new government in China had been formed, Mao Tse-tung made his first and, so far, only pilgrimage to Moscow, to see Stalin. Five years later, Khrushchev and Bulganin journeyed to Peking, to attend the celebration of China's national holiday, on October 1, 1954. Step by step, the Russians have withdrawn from Port Arthur and Dairen, have ceded their rights in the Sino-Soviet joint-stock companies, and have transferred to China their claims to the Chinese Changchun railway.

In terms of the total national economy of the United States, the American economic and financial stake in China in 1949 was a minor one, in contrast with British interests and investments, and one which, in time of crisis, could be sacrificed without disastrous consequences. Further, the amount of direct political pressure which Peking can bring to bear upon the United States is negligible. America's response to Communist China's intermittent and unconvincing gestures toward "normalizing" their relations is more likely to be nurtured by the hopeful optimism characteristic of domestic opinion in this country than by either the inherent vigor of the political propaganda shown by Peking or the actual facts with respect to the Peking regime. Being unable to threaten the United States directly, Communist China's present goal can only be to disrupt by indirect means the political influence and military power of the United States in the Far East and the Middle East.

The most troublesome Far Eastern issue between Communist China and the United States is Taiwan. Both powers view the Chinese Nationalist Government as a Chinese government on Chinese soil and thus as an operating, albeit exiled, alternative to the Communist government on the mainland. The United States accepts, and Communist China deplores, the fact that Nationalist China is a Chinese government with a recognized international status, a place in the United Nations, and a seat on the Security Council. Despite some recent blandishments, Peking basically regards the Nationalist regime as a "nest of traitors," to be annihilated at some convenient time. The rest of non-Communist Asia—indeed, much of the rest of the world—is interested in Taiwan only to the extent that the struggle over it may increase the danger of war, and they regard its continued survival as largely an American problem.

There appears to be slight prospect of evolving a solution which would be either pleasing or persuasive to all the parties directly or indirectly concerned. However, unless we direct ourselves positively to saving Taiwan for the Nationalist Chinese and for the inhabitants of Taiwan, who are strongly oriented to the free world, a policy of drift may lead to subversion and thus to its falling into Communist hands.

The general strategic objective pursued by Mao Tsetung with Moscow's support has been to consolidate the position of Communist China as the dominant power of Eastern Asia. His government has pursued this objective relentlessly throughout three years of exhausting military conflict in Korea and six years of continuing political warfare directed against both the West and the rest of Asia.

The Chinese Communists have made every effort to conciliate and control the Moslems within their own borders, particularly in Sinkiang, and are pressing forward to integrate both this region and Inner Mongolia under Communist control backed by large-scale settlement of Chinese in the new oil fields of the Gobi desert. Through its "own" Moslems Peking seeks to strengthen its ties with the Moslem countries, including India, Indonesia and Pakistan, the Arab countries, and many parts of Africa, where Islam is making many new converts today. Indeed, the West, entranced by the headlines given to a few of the anti-Communist speeches there, seems largely to have failed to grasp the long-term significance of the Bandung Conference, in terms of Peking's active efforts to win over the peoples of Asia and Africa and in terms of the expanding role of the Asian-African bloc in the United Nations.

Mao is keenly aware of the lasting, uncomplaining qualities of the Chinese people, of its infinite capacity for stoical endurance and nerveless waiting. He believes strongly in the irresistible capacity of the Chinese, in periods of strong and energetic central government, to expand their influence in Asia. Can he also convince the rest of Asia that the emergence of a strong and unified China, under Communist leadership, as the predominant power in Asia is in their best interests?

In the past few years, Western observers have been preoccupied with the difficult problem of forestalling Communist expansion in Asia. The striking increase in the capacity and willingness of Communist China actively to push the expansion of its own sphere of political influence as well as that of international Communism, which may prove to be more important to the future of Asia than the recent impact of self-conscious nationalism, is sometimes inaccurately assessed. Over nearly a century the West had been accustomed to dealing with an aging and virtually powerless imperial China. Now it confronts a young and vigorous China, which is prepared to run great risks in order to assert both Chinese and Communist influence in Asia.

Although the United States is the target for Peking's most vitriolic denunciations, the Communist leaders in Peking know that modern China's greatest problem is modern Japan and its greatest opportunities lie in Southeast Asia. For its part, Peking must attempt to delay or prevent Japanese rearmament, to restrain or disperse Japanese influence in Asia, and to wean Japan from its present alignment with the United States. In pursuit of these goals, it must attempt to influence the politics of Japan, the economy of Japan, and the people of Japan.

From Peking's standpoint, an anti-Communist state in South Korea with strong American support is at best a nagging annoyance and at worst a dangerous threat. However, it is in Southeast Asia, with its large overseas Chinese population—a vast arc of territories extending from Burma, through Thailand, Malaya, Indochina and Indonesia to the Philippines on the east—that Communist China sees its long-term sphere of influence. Here it can find rich surpluses of rice, rubber, tin, copra and oil. Here is an important segment of the human resources of Asia, stirring in reaction against three centuries of Western domination.

Here are the ingredients of revolution: poverty, ignorance, agrarian discontent, extreme nationalism, cultural confusion, and intellectual restlessness. Surveying the rich human and material resources of Southeast Asia, which the Chinese call *Nan-yang,* or "South Seas," the Communist authorities in Peking are determined to seize again China's traditional leadership in Eastern Asia.

The West would be foolhardy to ignore the fact that Communist China is, and will continue to be, an increasingly important force in the world. Whatever Peking's present relative weight within the Sino-Soviet alliance, its role within the Communist bloc will grow in importance. Outside powers must reckon with the likelihood that, if peace is maintained, the general community of belief and purpose underlying the Sino-Soviet alliance gives prospect of its being a reasonably durable and highly effective union. In any case, its importance to Soviet policy would be increased if or as any of the satellites in Europe succeed in detaching themselves from Moscow's complete control.

The main problems which confront the United States today, in its relations with the Sino-Soviet alliance, were subjected to an intensive examination by a Study Group of the Council on Foreign Relations during the winter of 1955-56. In accordance with Council practice, the Group included persons expert in the study of the politics and economics of China and Russia, and others with broad experience of policy-making and policy study. Its discussions were centered around five analyses, each prepared by a leading expert. These papers, which have been revised by their authors during the last months of 1956, have been brought together in the MOSCOW-PEKING AXIS.

Howard L. Boorman has surveyed "The Political Impact" of the Sino-Soviet Alliance. As one part of his work in the Foreign Service, Mr. Boorman established and conducted for several years a special bureau at Hong Kong for the study of developments in Communist China. He is now the Director of the Research Project on Men and Politics in Modern China at Columbia University.

Alexander Eckstein, the author of the "Moscow-Peking

Axis: the Economic Pattern," is a member of the Russian Research Center and a research associate in the program of Chinese Economic and Political Studies at Harvard University. He has devoted the past ten years to intensive study of the Soviet, satellite and Chinese Communist economies.

Benjamin Schwartz, who has written the chapter on "Ideology and the Sino-Soviet Alliance," is the author of *Chinese Communism and the Rise of Mao*. He is a master of the complexities of Communist ideology, both Soviet and Chinese, and of tracing its intimate connections with policy.

"The Borderlands and the Sino-Soviet Alliance" sums up many years of close attention by Mr. Boorman to developments in the areas lying between the main centers of the Russian and Chinese civilizations and their changing impact on Sino-Soviet relations.

Philip E. Mosely, who writes on "The Moscow-Peking Axis in World Politics," is Director of Studies at the Council on Foreign Relations and was formerly Director of the Russian Institute of Columbia University. During World War II, he was Chief of the Division of Territorial Studies, a section of the Department of State which prepared many background and policy analyses for use in the postwar settlement, and between 1943 and 1946 he was engaged in several major negotiations with representatives of the Soviet government. Mr. Mosely has also served as general editor of the volume.

The five studies, now offered to a wider public, have benefited greatly from the detailed and knowledgeable criticisms to which they were subjected in the meetings of the Study Group. Each author, of course, speaks only for himself, not for the Council Study Group as a whole, or its individual members.

The members of the Study Group, in addition to the authors, were: Robert Amory, Jr., A. Doak Barnett, Brigadier General T. J. Betts, Everett N. Case, Harlan Cleveland, Herbert Feis, George H. Greene, Jr., William J. Jorden, Walter H. Mallory, Dean Rusk, Lt. Colonel John

D. Sitterson, Jr., Richard L. Walker, and C. Martin Wilbur.

Having had the pleasure of serving as Chairman of the Group, I have been asked to write a Foreword. Needless to add, it does not purport to express any viewpoint but my own. In it I have attempted to jot down some of the problems raised by the Moscow-Peking axis and to sketch their impact upon American foreign policy.

It is in the hope of providing a fuller understanding of the workings of the Sino-Soviet alliance, and of the pitfalls which lie ahead for American policy, that these five studies are now presented to a wider public. They will, I hope, help to stimulate more intensive discussions of the purposes and operations of American policy toward the Moscow-Peking axis and to lead to the strengthening of the political, economic and spiritual resources of the free world in line with the dynamic character of the American people.

CONTENTS

Tables

Appendices

MOSCOW-PEKING AXIS

Strengths and Strains

CHAPTER ONE

THE SINO-SOVIET ALLIANCE: THE POLITICAL IMPACT
by Howard L. Boorman

THE ERUPTION of Chinese Communist power in Eastern Asia has led to a radical shift in the world balance of power. As early as 1950, it was apparent that the new and compulsive political entity which styles itself the People's Republic of China was to be the heart of an extraordinarily difficult problem in world politics. The protracted war in Korea and the Communist conquest of northern Vietnam have confirmed the strategic imbalance created by the recrudescence of Chinese power in Asia. Neither the armistice agreements which put an end to hostilities in these two areas nor the persistent efforts of non-Asian nations to bolster present barriers to Communist expansion in Asia have yet given hope that a new situation of balance and stability between the contending forces has been attained.

Nor can the problem be understood by analyzing its purely Chinese dimensions in isolation. Communist China is firmly allied with one of the two strongest military and industrial powers in the world, and it has, in general, pursued its national and international objectives in coordination with the Soviet Union. Communist China has also come to play an increasingly significant role within the coalition of the world's two great Communist powers athwart the Eurasian land mass. Formerly it was possible and profitable to discuss the Soviet impact on the Western world. Now one must ponder the still broader problem: the Sino-Soviet impact on the world.

Is the Moscow-Peking axis unbreakable? What is Communist China's role within the Sino-Soviet alliance? Will mainland China find Russian backing sufficient to help it achieve its own lusty desires and ambitions?

Answers to these broad questions must be sought if the non-Communist world is to formulate effective policies for meeting the most ruthless challenge of our day. Viewed in perspective, the emergence of the Sino-Soviet alliance as the most dangerous coalition in the world has been neither abrupt nor accidental. If its intrusion into the world's consciousness has been jarring, the development itself is actually the result of a series of particular events—sometimes unnoted or misinterpreted by contemporary observers—which have gradually merged into a reasonably distinct total pattern. Thus, to understand the potentialities of the Moscow-Peking axis we must review what is now known of relations between the Russians and the Chinese Communists during the past few years, and we must examine how far the general aims of Chinese Communist foreign policy and the specific requirements of the alliance coincide or diverge.

PEKING AND MOSCOW

Russia and the Chinese Communists before 1949

Two decades ago, after the Chinese Communists had carried out their epoch-making Long March from Kiangsi to the remote hills of northwest China, reliable information about their relations with the Russians became exceedingly elusive. Mao's followers displayed a careful orthodoxy in their theoretical statements and a respectful deference toward Moscow, and they executed a thoroughgoing program aimed at building up a tightly disciplined Communist party along strict Leninist lines. Yet, in retrospect, one cannot point to a large body of concrete data bearing upon the political or personal contacts of the Chinese Communist leaders with Stalin and the contemporary top leadership of the Soviet Union.

Even later, following the Japanese surrender in 1945 and the emergence of Mao Tse-tung and his followers from the caves of Yenan, the Communist march to total power in China left behind few clues as to the precise nature of Russian support or influence. In fact, in this respect the years between 1945 and 1949 are particularly obscure, even for the specialized student of relations between the Soviet and Chinese Communist Parties.

There had been collaboration in Manchuria between the Russian units which appeared there after the war against Japan had been won in the Pacific and the Chinese Communist forces which speedily made their way overland to that critical arena of conflict. Yet the extensive Russian removal of important industrial equipment from an area which was so soon, as it turned out, to come under complete Communist domination raises the question as to the degree of confidence with which the Russians viewed their Chinese counterparts in the immediate postwar period. A few years later, in the discussion groups organized in China to implant the new revolutionary creed, there was no question more difficult for a Chinese Communist political commissar to answer satisfactorily than the query: If the Russians are really such good fellows and such superior disciples of Marx and Lenin, why did they behave like a mob of hoodlums in Manchuria in 1945-46?

During the years following the Japanese surrender, when the Chinese Communists were fighting their way to power, their own political line with respect to the Soviet Union was both consistent and correct. Their radio station in northern Shensi paid dutiful homage to Moscow, and Liu Shao-ch'i's essay, *On Internationalism and Nationalism,* published in November 1948, supported the Soviet stand in the Tito apostasy of that year. It is debatable whether the Chinese Communists had organized their diplomatic assumptions into a coherent whole as early as the end of 1948, at a time when they were still preoccupied with the military aspects of the civil war then being fought in China. In any case, it seems clear that the senior leaders of the Chinese party viewed their orientation toward Moscow as both necessary and, in terms of their own interests, highly desirable. In July 1949, even before the establishment of the new National Government in Peking, Mao Tse-tung formally outlined the Chinese Communist position with respect to Sino-Soviet relations. His "lean-to-one-side" speech announced forthrightly that the new regime would base its policies on close cooperation with the Soviet Union, not with the non-Communist "imperialist" world.

Until 1949, while the Chinese Communists were fighting for victory, the Soviet attitude toward the National Government of China was ambiguous. At the official level, it was scrupulously proper. The Russians continued to maintain formal diplomatic relations with the National Government, the sworn enemy of the Communists in China. At the operational level, the Soviet attitude was cynical and enigmatic. As late as 1949, the Soviet ambassador in China continued to negotiate with the National Government over important economic and transportation concessions in Sinkiang, apparently with a view to obtaining for Russia a special position in the province during the very months when the Chinese Communist armies were driving rapidly into the northwest.

The scanty evidence regarding conversations and agreements between the Russians and the Chinese Communists during 1947-49 is both incomplete and contradictory. It is relatively simple to sketch the broad outlines of the design, but difficult to fill in the fine detail. Possibly official Soviet representatives in China were not always *au courant* of developments in the Communist-controlled areas of the country in which they were stationed. And it is probable that Stalin, much farther removed from the rapidly changing circumstances in the hinterland of China, was not adequately prepared for the new political situation which was then being created by the startling military advance of the Chinese Communist armies as they drove southward and westward from Manchuria.

Certainly the balance in the Sino-Soviet Communist Party relationship was now drastically altered from what it had been a generation before, in the 1920's, when the Chinese Communist Party was young, inexperienced, and firmly under Moscow's direction. By 1949, Chinese Communism had grown into a vigorous and self-confident force which, if not yet fully mature, was clearly enjoying the brash assurance of late adolescence. It possessed a tightly knit political organization, then numbering over 3 million members, and a battle-toughened army of over 1.5 million men. During the two decades when it had been growing to this stature, the Communist Party of China had probably been less under direct Soviet control than Communist parties elsewhere. Its revolutionary armies were native to the soil and had not required active support from the Soviet Red Army to plan their campaigns or win their battles. By 1949, the Chinese Communist leaders possessed a background of practical political and administrative experience in their own country far more extensive than that which the leaders of the Bolshevik revolution in Russia had possessed in 1917 or even in 1921.

Stalin and the New Ally in Peking: 1949-1953

The Central People's Government of the People's Republic of China was formally established on October 1, 1949. The Soviet Union at once accorded it recognition, and the large Russian embassy on Legation Street, closed since the Chinese Communist occupation of Peking, reopened for business. Early in October, N. V. Roshchin—who had served as Soviet ambassador to the National Government of China as recently as May 1949, when he departed for Moscow—arrived in China again as the first foreign diplomat accredited to the new Communist regime there. Mao Tse-tung, in turn, dispatched the first Chinese Communist ambassador to Moscow.

The establishment of formal diplomatic relations and the exchange of official representatives, while noteworthy, were nevertheless routine. Neither these developments nor the tidy political slogans which poured unceasingly from Peking could provide adequate answers to the basic security and ideological problems involved in the new phase of contacts between the Russians and the Chinese Communists. It was left to Mao Tse-tung himself to travel to the Soviet Union to discuss these issues personally with Stalin. Mao's mission to Moscow underscored the fact that, for a prominent Communist, he was still in a decidedly irregular position. Ruler of the most populous Communist nation, he had never visited Russia, spoke no Russian, and had had relatively little contact with the Russians. His journey to negotiate with Stalin at the end of 1949, when the Soviet dictator was already seventy, was Mao's first venture outside his native China and, to date, his only pilgrimage to the Mecca of world Communism.

It was doubtless an extraordinarily difficult period of negotiation for the two Communist leaders in Moscow, for both were tough political realists, not vague theorists. It is probable that Stalin, increasingly rigid in his later years, viewed Mao Tse-tung as an Asian and an inferior. Mao, for his part, knew very well that Stalin's failure, two decades earlier, to understand the realities of the Chinese political situation had led Moscow in 1927 to issue unrealistic directives to the Chinese Communists and had resulted in staggering Communist losses at the hands of the Kuomintang. Whether Stalin and Mao reviewed the past or discussed the theory and practice of Communist revolution in Asia is uncertain. All the effusive propaganda about Sino-Soviet friendship could not, however, conceal the probability that the negotiations must have been devoted, essentially, to hardheaded practical bargaining. Mao Tse-tung stayed in Moscow for nine weeks—from December 16, 1949, until February 17, 1950—at what was one of the most important Communist conferences of the postwar period.

On February 14, 1950, a joint communiqué announced the conclusion of three new Sino-Soviet agreements, signed in the Kremlin by the late A. Y. Vyshinsky, then the Soviet Minister of Foreign Affairs, and Chou En-lai, the Chinese Communist Foreign Minister.

The first was the Sino-Soviet Treaty of Friendship, Alliance, and Mutual Assistance, the foundation stone of the new alliance between the two major Communist powers. This treaty is valid until 1980 and may be further extended by mutual consent. Its focus is Asia; its nucleus is a military alliance ostensibly directed against defeated Japan. In it, Moscow and Peking agree to take all necessary measures to prevent the resumption of aggression on the part of Japan "or any other state that may collaborate with Japan directly or indirectly"—a clear reference, in this context, to the United States. If either Communist China or the Soviet Union is attacked by Japan "or any state allied with it" and thus becomes involved in a war, the other party will immediately render military and other assistance by all means at its disposal.

The second agreement covered the respective rights of the Russians and the Chinese Communists in Manchuria, the major border area in which both have significant strategic interests. It stipulated:

That the principal railroad network in Manchuria, the Chinese Changchun railway, would continue to be operated under joint Sino-Soviet administration (as had been provided earlier in the agreement signed between Moscow and the National Government of China in August 1945).

That the important naval base, Port Arthur, would also continue to be "jointly used," with Russian troops garrisoned there (as they had been since 1945), and would be employed to support joint military operations in the event of war with Japan or any country allied with Japan. Both of these arrangements—that concerning the Chinese Changchun railway and that concerning Port Arthur—were to be terminated upon the conclusion of a peace treaty with Japan or at the end of 1952, whichever came earlier.

That the administration of Dairen, the principal port at the southern end of the Chinese Changchun railway, was confirmed as belonging entirely to the Chinese. Since 1945, it had been under Soviet control.

The third agreement dealt with Russian financial assistance to Communist China. The Russians granted a credit which, at the official rate, amounted to U.S. $300 million, at an interest rate of one per cent per year. This credit arrangement covered the five-year period from 1950 through 1954, with one-fifth, or U.S. $60 million, to be made available annually. Communist China was to use this loan to pay for deliveries of industrial and railway supplies from the Soviet Union: equipment for electric power stations, metallurgical and engineering plants, mining equipment, railway and other transport equipment, rails, and "other materials for the restoration and development of the national economy." China was to repay the credit in ten equal annual installments, the first at the end of 1954 and the last at the end of 1963.

At the same time, the Soviet and Chinese Communist governments exchanged notes covering two other matters. The treaty and other agreements concluded on August 14, 1945, between the Soviet Union and the National Government of China were now declared null and void, and the independent status of the Mongolian People's Republic (Outer Mongolia) was guaranteed by both governments.

The developing alliance between the Soviet Union and Communist China was extended by other agreements signed in the spring of 1950. These provided for the establishment of a network of Sino-Soviet joint-stock companies to operate in the borderland areas of China:

Two companies to undertake the exploitation of nonferrous and rare minerals, and petroleum in Sinkiang (Chinese Turkestan), the vast province in the far northwest of China adjacent to Russian Central Asia;

A civil aviation company to operate flights between

Peking and the Soviet Union via Manchuria, Outer
Mongolia, and Sinkiang;

A company to build and repair ships at Dairen, the
commercial port adjacent to Port Arthur in southern
Manchuria.

And, in the spring of 1950, the two Communist allies completed initial negotiations on trading arrangements under
which the Soviet Union was to supply industrial equipment while Communist China would, in return, export
raw materials.

The forging of the Moscow-Peking axis was thus well
begun before the outbreak of the Korean war in mid-1950
and the ensuing Chinese Communist intervention, in October. From 1950 through 1952, the government in Peking
was in the difficult position of having to push through its
initial programs of political unification and economic rehabilitation at home, while at the same time deeply involved in a costly and risky military engagement in Korea.
Viewed from one standpoint, the Korean war was useful
to the Communists in China, for it permitted them to
consolidate domestic controls and mobilize human and
material resources more rapidly than would otherwise have
been politically feasible. In the midst of a war, internal
opposition, or even criticism, could be dealt with as trea-
son committed in favor of the "imperialists." By mid-1952,
however, there were indications that the rulers in Peking
were more anxious to push forward with their internal
development programs than to continue what were for
them increasingly pointless military operations which were
also placing a severe strain upon scarce resources.

The war in Korea served to test Sino-Soviet relations.
The alliance provided substantial Russian assistance to the
modernization of the Chinese Communist forces. It also
furnished a useful deterrent to more ambitious proposals,
such as the bombing of Chinese bases in Manchuria, on
the part of the United Nations forces.

Caution suggests that the interpretation of the diplomatic history of the Korean war be left to the future,

since the present evidence is as overabundant as it is incomplete. Sino-Soviet relations during the Korean conflict
are, in many respects, still a riddle. At times, Russian and
Chinese moves seemed perfectly timed to present a common Communist front. Yet there were instances in the
United Nations negotiations where, it would appear, the
Russians failed to take complete advantage of tactical
opportunities favorable to them and made only inconclusive gestures toward advancing Chinese interests. Certain it was, in any event, that Communist China felt by
mid-1952 that the point of diminishing returns had been
reached in Korea.

Further high-level political discussions between the
Russians and the Chinese were now required. The most
pressing problem was the joint consideration of issues outstanding under the agreements of February 1950 on the
Chinese Changchun railway and Port Arthur. Thus, in
the early autumn of 1952, a delegation headed by Chou
En-lai flew to Moscow for new negotiations with the Soviet
leaders. In mid-September, an official communiqué outlined the areas of agreement. The Soviet government was
to transfer to China, with full title and without compensation, all Russian rights in the joint management of the
Chinese Changchun railway and all property belonging
to it. A second exchange of notes declared that the Chinese
government "suggests and asks the Soviet government to
agree to postpone the withdrawal of Soviet troops from the
jointly-used Chinese naval base of Port Arthur" until
peace treaties had been concluded between the Communist governments and Japan. This exchange of notes, in-
corporating Peking's "request" and Moscow's "agreement," was retroactively made a component part of the
Sino-Soviet Treaty of 1950.

Implementation of these revised arrangements proceeded on schedule. The transfer of the Manchurian rail
network from joint Sino-Soviet to full Chinese control was
carried out at a formal ceremony in Harbin at the end of
1952. This was a significant event in the Communist bloc,
as it marked one of the first instances in Stalin's post-1945

career when the Russians had voluntarily relinquished valuable economic rights once they had been acquired. While giving up its control over the principal railway in Manchuria, Moscow tightened and prolonged its hold on the important Far Eastern naval base of Port Arthur. In view of the generally unsettled situation in the Far East and the continued military stalemate in Korea, it is possible that Communist China, possessing only a tiny naval force of its own, may have felt in the autumn of 1952 that the continued garrisoning of Soviet forces there was actually desirable from the standpoint of its national security. The terminology of the notes exchanged was nevertheless of interest in indicating the deliberate care apparently taken to demonstrate that the extended stay of Russian forces in Port Arthur was at China's request and by China's grace. The net result, in any event, was that the Soviet Union continued to maintain its own military and naval establishment at a major base within Chinese territory.

The negotiations of August and September 1952 also touched upon the issue of Outer Mongolia. The three governments—"with a view to strengthening their mutual economic and cultural ties"—worked out a tripartite Sino-Soviet-Mongol agreement on the construction of a new strategic rail link, through the Mongolian People's Republic, to connect the rail systems of the Soviet Union and Communist China. This agreement, concluded in 1952, was not announced publicly by the Communists until two years later, in October 1954.

It seems likely that Chou En-lai's negotiations in Moscow must also have dealt with the Korean war, which was dragging into its third year with no clear indication of an armistice, and with no slackening of Communist military commitment in Korea. There was, however, no public mention of this subject, nor of Sino-Soviet economic relations, although it was clear that the issue of long-term Russian assistance was of pressing concern to the Chinese Communists as they prepared to move into their first Five-Year Plan of "large-scale economic construction," scheduled to begin in 1953. Indeed, after Chou En-lai and some of his delegation had returned to Peking late in September 1952, other experts and advisers who had accompanied him to Moscow stayed behind, apparently to continue detailed economic negotiations which lasted well into the following year.

An event of major significance in the Communist world at this time was the Nineteenth Congress of the Communist Party of the Soviet Union, held in October 1952. The first since 1939, this Congress was an important general gathering of Communist parties, with many sending their most senior leaders to Moscow for the occasion. The Communist Party of China was represented by Liu Shao-ch'i, who offered the official greetings of the Chinese party to the Congress at the session of October 8.

That Mao Tse-tung should have selected Liu Shao-ch'i to speak for the Chinese Communist Party at the Soviet party Congress was not surprising, for Liu had clearly established his pre-eminence as deputy to Mao in the realm of party affairs in China. This was Liu's first trip to Moscow since the distant days when he had studied there as a neophyte of the Comintern from 1920 to 1922, and it would be interesting to speculate on his personal impressions and reactions to the changes which had taken place in the Soviet capital. On his 1952 trip Liu remained in Moscow for slightly over three months. Yet his return to Peking in mid-January 1953 was accompanied only by the briefest of official announcements which told nothing except that he had been met at the airfield by virtually the entire membership of the Political Bureau of the Chinese Communist Party. Nor did Peking make any subsequent statements regarding his trip, the subject of his negotiations, if any, with the Russians, or the degree of success of his mission. That this visit, the most extended stay in Moscow of any key member of the Chinese Communist Political Bureau since 1950, was devoid of significance is doubtful. There would seem little reason—aside from medical consultation—for a senior Communist with the manifold responsibilities which Liu had in Peking to linger in the Soviet Union for over fourteen weeks except for the purpose of conducting serious discussions. The fact that his extended sojourn in Moscow took place during the final months of Stalin's life offers grounds for speculation. But the visit was, and remains, an enigma.

Many aspects of the relations between Moscow and Peking during the Stalin period are still obscure. It is not clear, for example, how far Stalin may have attempted to go in penetrating the internal control apparatus of the Chinese Communist dictatorship. It is, however, reasonably clear that he was reluctant to cast the People's Republic of China in what might be construed to be a co-starring role on the international Communist stage.

But if the director was aging and obdurate, Communist China—the youthful aspirant from the East—was both resilient and realistic, confident that its very energy would ensure general recognition in the end. Whatever Mao Tse-tung's private estimates may have been during these years, he apparently felt it important during the final weeks of Stalin's life to lay public emphasis upon the essential solidarity of the Sino-Soviet bloc in checking any "aggressive moves of imperialism" in the Far East; upon the lack of strain in Moscow-Peking relations; and upon the continuing Russian support for Peking in the pursuit of the basic —still unattained—national goals of China.

New Leaders in the Kremlin and Mao's China: 1953-1956

The death of Stalin in March 1953 introduced a distinct note of uncertainty into the relations between the two major powers of the Communist bloc. The outward propaganda manifestations, however, continued to be characterized by stress upon political and ideological unity, and the general atmosphere of amity was punctuated by persisting protestations that the Sino-Soviet bloc was impregnable, unbreakable, and invincible. No other non-Chinese figure in modern times has, through his death, occasioned the overwhelming, unspontaneous Chinese attention which Stalin called forth. There was an official mourning meeting in Peking, with over half a million people present, and a required five-minute period of silence throughout the country. Peking automatically produced a special essay, signed by Mao Tse-tung and dedicated to Stalin, entitled *The Greatest Friendship*. It was noteworthy that Mao himself did not hasten to Moscow, an omission which some observers interpreted as an assertion, both to the Russians and to the world at large, of the heroic personal stature of the leader of the only successful major Communist revolution in Asia. However, like many of his less prominent compatriots, both Communist and non-Communist, Mao Tse-tung has a strong aversion to air travel, and, in view of the necessity for prompt action, his decision not to fly to the Soviet capital may have been a routine one.

From the outset, it appeared that the post-Stalin leadership in Moscow, perhaps in some degree concerned during its first days in power over the possible actions of Mao Tse-tung, had concluded that the most realistic attitude was to leave no doubt of his continuing status as the principal Soviet ally in Asia. The new Russian regime made a definite attempt to treat the Chinese with cautious politeness and signs of public respect. At Stalin's funeral, Chou En-lai, who headed the official Chinese Communist delegation, was given precedence over all other non-Russian Communist leaders and was placed on a virtually equal footing with the top-ranking members of the Soviet party and government. He walked abreast of Khrushchev, Beria, Malenkov, Voroshilov, Kaganovich, Bulganin and Molotov behind Stalin's bier—a most unusual honor for the Russians to accord to a foreign Communist at a Soviet function. In the funeral speeches, the Russian leaders made a clear distinction between "the great Chinese people" and the "countries of people's democracy," the phrase used in referring to the satellite states in Eastern Europe. Both by their statements and by their treatment of Chou En-lai, the new Russian rulers indicated that they regarded the Sino-Soviet coalition as the key to their Far Eastern policy.

In the realm of formal interstate relations with Communist China, Moscow also attempted to start with a clean slate. Immediately after Stalin's death, the Russians announced the appointment of V. V. Kuznetsov to be a Deputy Minister of Foreign Affairs and simultaneously Soviet ambassador in Peking. He replaced A. S. Panyushkin, former envoy in Washington, who had been appointed to the Peking post in mid-1952 under Stalin, but who in March 1953 had been in China for only about three months. Kuznetsov was known as an energetic individual, a metallurgical engineer by training, who had had varied experience in industrial organization and management and in trade union work in the Soviet Union, as well as in the World Federation of Trade Unions. He was the first Russian chief of mission assigned to Peking since 1949 who had not previously been accredited to the National Government of China, either in Chungking or later in Nanking. One might speculate about the reactions of the Chinese Communists to the fact that Stalin, during his lifetime, had sent as diplomatic representatives to Peking men who had earlier been accredited to the very government in China against which the Chinese Communists had fought so long and so hard. It was clear, in any case, that Moscow's assignment of a Deputy Foreign Minister to Peking definitely raised the status of the Soviet embassy there.

At the end of March 1953, as Kuznetsov left for Peking in the company of Chou En-lai, Moscow announced three new Sino-Soviet agreements "recently" concluded there. These were:

A protocol on trade between Communist China and the Soviet Union for 1953;
A protocol to the original credit agreement of February 14, 1950;
An agreement on Soviet assistance to Communist China in the expansion and construction of power stations.

The first of these, the trade protocol for 1953, was a routine agreement, renegotiated annually since 1950. The second agreement, on credit, and the third, on power stations, were the initial indications of increased Russian economic and technical assistance, which was subsequently announced in more detail later in the year. It appears probable that these March 1953 agreements were interim in nature. Their signing may have been hastened by the political desirability of making some concrete pronouncement as soon as possible after Stalin's death in order to forestall any doubts which might arise either among the Western nations or within the Communist bloc about the firmness of the Sino-Soviet coalition.

The broad questions of long-term Russian aid to China and of Communist policy toward the Korean war remained open. By 1953, the stimulation of sustained economic growth on the mainland of China had been set as a major policy goal of the Peking regime. Support from the Soviet Union was thus essential, for any large-scale assistance to Peking's development programs had to come almost exclusively from the U.S.S.R. and from the partially industrialized satellites in Eastern Europe.

Only four days after returning from Stalin's funeral, Chou En-lai put forward a new proposal for the resumption of the Korean negotiations, which had at that point been stalemated for several months. Chou's timing in making this proposal so soon after his return from Moscow, where he must have discussed the Korean war with the new Russian leaders, cannot have been fortuitous. The Communist bloc, aware that the new administration in Washington contemplated no essential change in United States policy toward Korea, appears to have been more genuinely desirous of an armistice after Stalin's death than it had been earlier. In essence, Chou's proposal for the disposition of the prisoners of war differed little from the United Nations resolution, based on the formula suggested by India, which the Communists had rejected outright only three months before.

With the change in Communist tactics, however, it was the March 30 proposal by Chou En-lai which, after continued patient negotiations by the United Nations at Panmunjom, provided the basis for the agreement on the exchange of prisoners of war, signed on June 8, and for the armistice agreement, finally concluded on July 27, 1953. The Communists failed to follow up on several incidents, such as the release of the North Korean prisoners by Syngman Rhee in late June, which they might easily have utilized as pretexts to suspend or break off negotiations, had they been so inclined.

Thus Peking secured one major objective: the cessation of the war in Korea with its severe drain on Chinese resources. It was clear during these months that, domestically, the Peking regime was having only moderate success in its first steps toward industrial expansion. Yet Sino-Soviet economic negotiations still dragged on in Moscow. Already well into the first year of their vaunted Five-Year Plan, the Chinese Communists were apparently without a clear conception of the final results of these negotiations or of the level of long-term Russian aid which could be anticipated.

The summer of 1953 brought one development of particular interest in the Soviet Union. In July, a Chinese Communist Industrial and Agricultural Exhibition was held in Gorky Park in Moscow. On the closing day, a delegation of the senior rulers of the Soviet Union visited the Chinese exhibition. Every member of the new Presidium of the party as constituted immediately following Stalin's death was in attendance (except Beria who had already been purged). The fact that all top Russian leaders (Malenkov, Molotov, Khrushchev, Voroshilov, Bulganin, Kaganovich, Mikoyan, Saburov, and Pervukhin) deigned to spend over an hour at a Chinese Communist exhibition was itself of interest. Of greater potential significance, however, was the little noted Soviet statement issued at the exhibition and at once described by Peking as "an inspiring expression of confidence in the ability of the Chinese people in their large-scale economic construction." Addressing themselves to the people of Communist China, the Russian rulers declared:

Dear comrades: You may confidently feel assured of the ever friendly and active support of the various peoples, the Communist Party, and the Government of the Soviet Union in the cause of the socialist transformation of the People's Republic of China.

This was a far more straightforward pronouncement of official Russian support for Communist China and its ambitions than the laconic messages which normally issued from Moscow during Stalin's lifetime.

Shortly thereafter, in September 1953, Peking announced that the Soviet Union would by the end of 1959 assist China in the construction or renovation of 141 "large-scale enterprises." This Russian assistance constituted a carefully worked out set of arrangements referring to specific installations in China which the Russians themselves, as well as the Chinese, presumably considered important. The tenor of the September 1953 announcement suggested that a substantial amount of detailed staff work must have been carried on over a period of several months and that the Russian contribution to this planning, in view of the lack of experience of the Chinese, must have been considerably larger than that of the Chinese. Doubtless there were differences in viewpoint between Moscow and Peking, differences which could have been resolved only by hard bargaining. Possibly the Russians were unwilling to guarantee as high a level of economic and technical aid as the Chinese desired. But it was apparent that both governments were realistic enough to appreciate the advantages inherent in safeguarding the political strength of the Sino-Soviet coalition.

Late in 1953, a new Soviet ambassador, the third within a single year, arrived in Peking.[1] He was Pavel F. Yudin. The new ambassador, whom the Chinese Communists punctiliously referred to as Academician Yudin, was known principally as a high-ranking Marxist-Leninist theorist. He had been editor of the Cominform journal

[1] Kuznetsov, who was replaced, returned to Moscow on assignment to the Ministry of Foreign Affairs. In March 1955 he was promoted to be a First Deputy Foreign Minister.

and had visited Communist China briefly as a lecturer late in 1950. On December 15, 1953, Yudin presented his credentials to Mao Tse-tung, whose *Selected Works* he had reviewed favorably in *Pravda* the year before. It was of interest that the new chief of the Russian embassy in Peking was a party intellectual rather than a career diplomat, a general, or an engineer. As though to provide the proper setting for Academician Yudin, Communist China was, during this period, laying great stress upon Soviet support in the theoretical realm as well as in the material sphere of economic and military aid. All cadres were studying appropriate sections in the *Short History* of the Communist Party of the Soviet Union in order to draw inspiration from the official account of how the Russians had gone ahead so rapidly in the industrial development of their country.

At the end of the year, a special Russian delegation headed by I. F. Tevosyan, the Soviet Minister of Metallurgical Industry, flew to Peking to witness the launching of new installations at the Anshan Iron and Steel Company in Manchuria, marking the completion of three out of the 141 Soviet-aided projects. Anshan, developed by the Japanese during their occupation, is the most important center of steel production in Communist China. Peking had laid great emphasis upon its rehabilitation, and apparently it wished to have Russian officials from Moscow witness the recently completed results: a heavy rolling mill, a seamless tubing mill, and a new blast furnace.

Moscow's attention to its principal Asian ally continued to increase during 1954. Two specific cases may be cited in which—considering the attention normally given to protocol matters by both Moscow and Peking—it appeared that the Russian leaders were making conscious bows in the direction of Communist China. On February 14, an unusually large group of the most senior Russians (Malenkov, Khrushchev, Bulganin, Kaganovich, Mikoyan, Saburov, Pervukhin, and others) attended a reception given at the Chinese Communist embassy in Moscow in honor of the fourth anniversary of the signing of the 1950 Sino-

Soviet Treaty. The Russian attendance was especially striking at that time, as the Chinese ambassador was absent from his post. Two weeks later, an official dinner was given in Moscow for the editor of the Peking *People's Daily*, the organ of the Central Committee of the Communist Party of China, who had been invited to the Soviet Union by the editorial board of *Pravda*. While the Chinese editor was not even a member of the Central Committee of the Chinese party and could not conceivably be ranked as a major political figure in Peking, virtually the entire top leadership of the Communist Party of the Soviet Union attended the farewell banquet given for him at the Kremlin on February 27.

During the second half of 1954, Chinese prestige in the Communist world continued to climb. At the Geneva Conference in the summer, Foreign Minister Chou En-lai went far in establishing Peking's point that the settlement of Asian problems would inevitably involve Western negotiations with Communist China. And in the autumn of 1954, a large Russian delegation, headed by Khrushchev and Bulganin, paid an official visit to Peking. The results of the new conversations between the Russians and the Chinese Communist leaders, as announced in mid-October 1954, represented a further advance for the Chinese and a further re-enforcement of the Moscow-Peking axis. Had there previously been doubt on the question, it now appeared even more unlikely than before that either Moscow or Peking would, in the near future, embark upon fundamentally incompatible international policies. In the political and military spheres, as in the economic, there would be continuing close coordination.

The new agreements between the Communist powers, as worked out in Peking, were the subject of two joint government declarations and a number of official communiqués.

The first declaration dealt with Sino-Soviet relations and Communist foreign policy. It affirmed that the two governments were "in full agreement" with respect to both Sino-Soviet cooperation and "all questions concerning the international situation." Recalling the 1950 Treaty of Friendship, Alliance, and Mutual Assistance, scheduled to bind the two nations until 1980, the declaration confirmed the determination of the two governments to consult on all questions touching the "common interests" of the Soviet Union and the People's Republic of China, with a view to achieving "unity in action directed to safeguarding the security of the two states and maintaining peace in the Far East and throughout the world."

The declaration also announced that there would be general coordination of policy and approach between Moscow and Peking on Asian problems. It endorsed the "five principles" on which Nehru and Chou En-lai had previously agreed, and set forth Communist attitudes toward Indochina, Taiwan, Korea, and Southeast Asia.

The Geneva Conference, which brought about the cessation of military operations in Indochina and created the possibility of regulating the situation in Indochina in accordance with the legitimate national rights of the peoples of that area, showed the significance for the cause of peace of the participation in the discussion of pressing international issues of the Great Powers who, under the United Nations Charter, bear the primary responsibility for maintaining international peace. It also showed that the policy of the United States' ruling circles of preventing the People's Republic of China from taking its rightful place in the United Nations is utterly untenable.

Such a policy of the United States and its direct acts of aggression against the People's Republic of China, particularly its continued occupation of China's territory of Taiwan and its military and financial support to the Chiang Kai-shek clique, the enemy of the Chinese people, are incompatible with the task of maintaining peace in the Far East and easing international tension.

The two Governments consider it an abnormal situation that Korea continues to be divided into two parts, contrary to the natural aspirations of the Korean people for a united, peace-loving, democratic Korean state. In view of the fact that the unification of Korea is one of the important tasks, the fulfillment of which would have great significance for the consolidation of peace in the Far East, the two Governments consider it necessary to convene in the nearest future a conference on the Korean question, with the wide participation of the countries concerned.

The People's Republic of China and the Soviet Union strongly condemn the formation of the Southeast Asia aggressive military bloc, because this bloc is based on the imperialist designs of its sponsors, which are directed in the first instance against the security and national independence of the Asian countries as well as against the interests of peace in Asia and the Pacific region.

The two Governments consider it necessary to declare that the People's Republic of China and the Soviet Union will continue to base their relations with states in Asia and the Pacific region and with other states on the strict observance of the principles of mutual respect for sovereignty and territorial integrity, non-aggression, non-interference in each other's internal affairs, equality and mutual benefit, and peaceful co-existence, thereby opening up wide possibilities for the development of fruitful international cooperation.

A second declaration dealt with the relations of the two Communist powers with Japan. Reiterating previous strong criticisms of American policy, it asserted that the United States had "imposed" upon Japan the peace treaty signed at San Francisco in September 1951 and other agreements which ran counter to the Potsdam Proclamation of 1945, and that Japan thus remained in the position of a "semi-colonial country." The present situation, it stated, had evoked a "legitimate apprehension" in Asia that Japan might be utilized to carry out "schemes of aggression" which would run counter both to "the interests of the Japanese people themselves and to the task of maintaining peace in the Far East." The declaration also voiced the Communist hope that the Japanese would be able to free themselves from "dependence" upon the United States and establish "normal relations" with other countries, "first and foremost with their neighbors." Specifically, the governments of both the Soviet Union and Communist China announced their readiness to take steps to normalize their positions vis-à-vis Japan and stated that

Japan would have their full support in establishing political and economic relations with the Soviet Union and Communist China.

At the same time, four joint Sino-Soviet communiqués were also released at Peking. The Russians agreed that Soviet armed forces would be withdrawn completely from Port Arthur and that the naval base there would be restored to full Chinese Communist control by the end of May 1955. By this step the Soviet government renounced the right, negotiated in September 1952, to maintain its forces there until the conclusion of peace with Japan.

As a further concession, the four Sino-Soviet joint-stock companies, established in 1950 and 1951, were transferred to exclusive Chinese Communist control. Beginning in 1955, the Russian shares in the operation of these companies were to be sold to the Chinese, who would pay for them "over the course of several years" by exports to the Soviet Union.

A new agreement on scientific and technical cooperation provided that the Soviet Union and Communist China would supply each other with technical data, exchange related information, and send specialists to give technical assistance and acquaint each other with the latest developments in the fields of science and technology. To carry out this cooperation, a Sino-Soviet commission would meet twice a year, alternately in Moscow and Peking.

Finally, a joint communiqué announced that the Soviet Union and Communist China had agreed on the construction "in the near future" of a railroad from Lanchow in northwest China through Urumchi, capital of Sinkiang province, to Alma Ata in the Soviet Union. The Chinese Communists had already begun laying rail on this line two years before, and Moscow now formally undertook responsibility for construction of the short portion of the line lying within Soviet territory, from Alma Ata to the Soviet-Sinkiang border, and for providing technical assistance to the Chinese in their construction of the portion within Chinese territory.

The October 1954 negotiations in Peking also led to revised economic and financial arrangements. The new agreement provided that the Soviet Union would grant an additional "long-term credit" to Communist China. At the same time, Moscow agreed to provide assistance for the construction of an additional 15 industrial projects, making a new total of 156, and to increase the supply of equipment for the 141 enterprises covered in the 1953 agreement.

At the time of the Khrushchev-Bulganin visit, a tripartite Sino-Soviet-Mongolian communiqué formally announced an agreement, actually concluded at Moscow in September 1952, for the building of another rail link, through Mongolia, to connect the rail systems of north China and the Soviet Union.

Both Moscow and Peking moved swiftly to implement these agreements, which, both in scope and phrasing, reflected a significant modification since Stalin's death of Russian attitudes toward Communist China. At the beginning of 1955 the Russian shares in the four Sino-Soviet joint companies were transferred by sale to Communist China, thus liquidating Soviet interests in the exploitation of nonferrous minerals and petroleum in Sinkiang, in civil aviation, and in the shipbuilding company at Dairen. During May 1955, Chinese Communist troops moved into Port Arthur to replace the Russian units garrisoned there. Following the signing of the final protocol of transfer, on May 24, the senior Russian officers departed for Vladivostok, and Port Arthur reverted to complete Chinese control after nearly ten years of Soviet military occupation. In January 1956, the new railroad through Outer Mongolia was opened, providing an important channel of interior communication for the Sino-Soviet bloc. This line is of both military and economic significance, since it shortens by several hundred miles the rail connection between Moscow and Peking, previously effected over the circuitous and relatively vulnerable Manchurian rail network.

During 1955 and 1956 Soviet public statements consistently laid emphasis upon the importance of Russian solidarity with Communist China, chiefly by championing Peking's right to Taiwan and to China's seat in the United Nations.

On February 9, 1955, Bulganin denounced the United States for "aggravating the situation in the area of Taiwan," ignoring the "legitimate rights of the People's Republic of China, and trampling upon international agreements." He spoke of Taiwan as having been "seized" by the United States and expressed surprise that the United Nations had not condemned this "act of aggression."

The policy of the Chinese Government concerning that problem has evoked our complete approval and support. The People's Republic of China attracts the sympathy of the Soviet people and of all progressive mankind precisely because it is leading the struggle for a just cause, for the honor and independence of its country. In that noble cause, the Chinese people may count on the help of their faithful friend, the great Soviet people. . . .

On June 3, 1955, a joint Soviet-Yugoslav declaration called for "giving the People's Republic of China the representation to which it is entitled in the United Nations." Action to promote negotiation and disarmament would create

. . . an atmosphere . . . which would at the same time make possible a solution by peaceful means of such urgent problems of the first importance as . . . the satisfaction of the legitimate rights of the People's Republic of China with regard to Taiwan.

On July 18, at the "summit conference" in Geneva, Bulganin again spoke of the Taiwan situation and once more called for "recognition of the indisputable rights of China to its island." He recalled

. . . the well-known desire of the Government of the People's Republic of China to settle the Taiwan problem through direct negotiations between the United States and the People's Republic of China.

As to the seating of Communist China in the United
Nations, he called the existing situation "not only abnormal but inadmissable" and said that "this injustice
should be rectified, and the sooner that is done, the better."

At Rangoon, on December 6, 1955, Khrushchev sounded
the same note again:

Why have the American troops occupied the island of Taiwan and other near-by islands that are a part of the lawful
territory of the People's Republic of China?

No single Communist assertion may be taken as clear
evidence of long-term trends in Sino-Soviet relations, for
it may only reflect the tactical maneuvers of the moment.
The salient fact is not the specific Russian warrant that the
People's Republic of China can always count upon the
help of its "faithful friend, the great Soviet people," or
any variation on that theme. Rather it is the general tenor
of the joint pronouncements issued at Peking in October
1954, and the general emphasis in the more recent Russian
statements, issued not only in Moscow but in other parts
of the world as well, which are significant. All connote the
steady rise in importance and influence of Communist
China within the Sino-Soviet partnership.

The extent of Moscow's growing interest in China's industrial development within the Communist bloc was
again demonstrated in the spring of 1956, at the time of
the rapid trip through Asia of Soviet First Deputy Premier
Mikoyan. His two-day visit to China produced two new
Sino-Soviet agreements, announced on April 7, 1956, on
"further development of economic cooperation."

The first stated that the U.S.S.R. had agreed to provide
assistance for 55 industrial establishments, in addition to
the 156 projects for which it had undertaken to provide
aid in 1953 and 1954—a new total of 211 major enterprises.
This expanded program of Russian assistance, scheduled
to run from 1956 into the early part of Peking's second
Five-Year Plan (1958-62), marked a significant increase in
the number of Russian-supported projects in China and

reportedly represented, in terms of equipment and technical assistance, a value of about 2,500 million rubles (U.S. $625 million at official rates).

The second agreement called for the completion by 1960 of the Lanchow-Urumchi-Alma Ata railway, linking northwest China with Soviet Central Asia by way of Sinkiang. When completed, this 1700-mile line will connect China's rail network with the Turkestan-Siberian railway in the Soviet Union and will be of great long-range strategic significance. It will eventually provide a third connecting route, invulnerable to all except the longest-range aircraft, between the interior of China and the interior of Russia to supplement the existing Chinese Changchun railway through Manchuria and the recently completed line through Mongolia.

In retrospect, it is interesting to note that the China leg of Mikoyan's Far Eastern tour coincided with Peking's first official reaction to the political developments in Moscow stemming from the Twentieth Congress of the Soviet party, at which Mikoyan himself had been a principal spokesman at the desanctification of Stalin. The Chinese statement, *On the Historical Experience of Proletarian Dictatorship*, reviewed the question of Stalin's leadership in the world Communist movement in relatively cool and detached fashion, concentrating on theoretical rather than personal issues.[2] To date, the drastic dismantling of the Stalin myth in Moscow does not appear to have had serious political repercussions in Peking. It is true that significant Chinese political statements—such as Mao Tse-tung's essay, *The Greatest Friendship*, written in March 1953 on the occasion of Stalin's death—may prove embarrassing to the Chinese rulers. With respect to its own history, however, the Chinese Communist Party still maintains that it has successfully avoided the "cult of the individual" and that it has committed no basic error since Mao Tse-tung consolidated his effective control over two decades ago.

Actually, today the image of Mao Tse-tung in Asia is more comparable to the image of Lenin than to that of

2 *Jen Min Jih Pao* (People's Daily) (Peking), April 5, 1956.

Stalin. The party which Mao leads has apparently not been affected by the confusion which accompanied the death of the Soviet dictator three years ago, and Mao himself seems to have taken the posthumous denigration of Stalin in stride.

THE INTERNATIONAL IMPACT OF THE ALLIANCE

Any attempt to measure the strength of the Sino-Soviet coalition must look beyond the direct relations of the two major Communist states. A survey of the ties which bind Peking and the good earth of China across the very heart of the Eurasian land mass to European Russia and Moscow is not sufficient. There must be an even more complex calculation: an analysis of the shadow and substance of the alliance in the general context of world politics today.

The General Aim of Chinese Communist Foreign Policy

Since 1949, Peking's basic and continuing international objective has been to establish and maintain Communist China as the prime power of Eastern Asia. The broad strategic framework of policy for the pursuit of this goal has been constructed principally by a handful of veteran Chinese Communist leaders.

The career of the dominant figure of this group, Mao Tse-tung, indicates that he is both able and willing to take the long view of contemporary affairs. For two decades he waited in the countryside of China without being deflected from his domestic goal: total political power in China. Mao is aware of the lasting, uncomplaining qualities of the Chinese people; of their indomitable and tireless energy; of their infinite capacity for stoical endurance and nerveless waiting. But, if it is true, as some believe, that he regards himself as a man of destiny in Asia, he must be conscious that his personal intimations of immortality must be spread not only to the Chinese but also to millions of other Asians. To achieve a lasting place in the histories of his historically-minded compatriots, he must also convince the rest of Asia of the inescapable reality of his own vision: the emergence of a strong and unified China, under Communist leadership, as an Asian power of international proportions in the mid-twentieth century. Mao appears to be confident that the broad groundswells rolling out from that area of Eastern Asia inhabited by almost 600 million patient and persevering Chinese cannot in the end be ignored by China's neighbors, many of whom in centuries past bore tribute to Peking. One might suggest, therefore, that the ultimate goal of Peking's foreign policy is actually only a Communist adaptation of a very ancient Chinese tenet: the irresistible capacity of the Chinese to expand their influence in Asia in periods of strong and energetic central government.

In its strategic outlook, Peking is also influenced by its Marxist-Leninist image of the Western world. It sees the United States as the leading "imperialist" power and the most formidable immediate obstacle to the attainment of its international goals. Peking believes that the United States, as the pivot of the opposing coalition of non-Communist forces, is implacably bent upon blocking the rightful international claims of the People's Republic of China. Possibly, too, Peking feels that the United States, having naval and air bases in the Western Pacific and being equipped with nuclear weapons, may be a victim of a paranoiac hallucination: the eventual destruction of Communist China's national power.

But the United States, if now in Asia, is patently not of Asia. It is singularly invulnerable to the types of power which Communist China holds mobilized and available. Well equipped though it is with combat infantry troops, Communist China is not yet a world military power. It lacks the independent naval and air strength necessary to strike directly at American bastions in the Pacific, much less at the North American continent. Nor can mainland China exert significant economic pressure on the United States. Despite certain strategic materials formerly imported by the United States from China, the trade between the two countries was vital to neither. In terms of the total national economy of the United States, the American economic and financial stake in China was a minor one and, in contrast with British interests and investments in that country, it could easily be sacrificed in time of crisis. Also, the amount of direct political pressure which Peking can bring to bear upon the United States is negligible. American response to Communist China's intermittent and unconvincing gestures toward normal international relations is more likely to be decided by public opinion in the United States, optimistically intent upon finding simple solutions for complex problems, than by the inherent vigor of the political propaganda sown by Peking. Unable to strike directly at American power, Peking's present goal, therefore, can only be to threaten and disrupt the political influence and military positions which the United States holds among China's neighbors in the Far East.

The most troublesome issue involved in the Sino-American controversy is Taiwan. Yet critical and contentious as the problem of Taiwan is, its very existence serves to reenforce, not to alter, the long-term strategic outlook of Chinese Communist foreign policy. Indeed, it is paradoxical to observe that the United States and the People's Republic of China appear to embrace virtually identical assumptions with regard to the existence of the Chinese National Government. By both, it is viewed as a Chinese government on Chinese soil, once removed, possessed of a Chinese leader, a Chinese flag, and Chinese military forces. The United States approves, and Communist China regrets, the fact that it is a Chinese government with recognized international status and a place in the United Nations. Most important, neither denies that, as a non-Communist Chinese government, it stands as an alternative to the Communist government on the mainland. The political reality of Taiwan is an accepted fact; the political conclusions drawn from that reality are totally at variance. Peking necessarily views Taiwan with antagonism; Washington, with approval. Each regards the matter, essentially, as a Chinese domestic issue, with international implications. But the rest of non-Communist Asia, as indeed most of the rest of the world, is interested in Taiwan only to the extent that it may give rise to international complications and regards its continued survival as an American problem. There appears to be slight prospect of evolving a solution which would be either pleasing or persuasive to all the parties directly or indirectly concerned.

The Tactics of Chinese Communist Foreign Policy: 1949-1956

The general strategic objective formulated by Mao Tse-tung and his political associates in Peking—the consolidation of the position of Communist China as the dominant power of Eastern Asia—has remained constant through seven years of continuing political warfare aimed both at the West and at the rest of Asia. The tactical assumptions of Chinese Communist foreign policy have, however, varied significantly in accord with changing conditions, domestic and international.

The prime responsibility for China's foreign policy rests, in the tactical sphere, with Chou En-lai and the officials of the Ministry of Foreign Affairs. They conduct formal negotiations with other governments, both Communist and non-Communist. They are also charged, unofficially, with operations in the informal realm of cajolery and casuistry, of maneuvers and alarums—activities which, if frequently nebulous and sometimes inconclusive, play an important and disconcerting role in Chinese Communist diplomacy.

The tone of Chinese Communist tactical diplomacy has ranged from blunt belligerency to amiable compromise. Tactics have varied in accordance with differing conditions of pressure or stimulation in the West, differing conditions of response or resistance in Asia, and differing conditions of cordiality or evasion in Moscow. They have varied in accordance with the exigencies of Peking's domestic programs of economic rehabilitation, industrialization, and militarization. At times, Peking's tactics appear to have gained in subtlety even as its Minister of Foreign

Affairs has increased in sophistication through his contacts with the outside—non-Chinese, non-Communist—world. Year by year, Chou En-lai and his colleagues accumulate experience. The Ministry of Foreign Affairs of 1956 is not the Ministry of Foreign Affairs of 1950.

It is hazardous to attempt an interpretation of the totality of Chinese Communist foreign policy on the basis of any portion of that policy which may be manifested by any specific speech made in Peking. One can never be sure what portion of an utterance may be accepted at face value and what portion—consciously counterfeited for political or psychological effect, either within the Communist bloc itself or in Western countries—must be discounted. It would be disastrous to assume, as a general rule, that the Chinese Communists do not mean what they say. In many cases they do. In some, they do not. And in still others, they may be exercising a prerogative not generally associated with disciplined male revolutionaries: they may have changed their minds.

Perhaps, therefore, it would be more fruitful to attempt a limited estimate of Chinese Communist tactical attitudes toward specific areas in Asia: first, toward Japan, China's principal antagonist in the Far East; second, toward Korea and Indochina, areas where emerging Chinese Communist power has been involved, directly or indirectly, in conflict with Western power; and third, toward Southeast Asia as a whole, the area of long-term Chinese Communist pressure. In each of these areas, in varying ways, the tactics have manifested the two-pronged intent of Peking's broad attack: to consolidate and extend Chinese Communist power; to disrupt and weaken American power.

Japan. The United States may absorb the most consistent attention and the most vitriolic denunciation from the organs of Peking's propaganda machinery. But the authorities in Peking, both as Chinese and as Chinese Communists, know that modern China's enduring problem is modern Japan.

For several decades before the second World War, Japan was the modernized Asian nation without peer. The subsequent costly military attempt of Japan, not only to defeat the Western powers but also to conquer all the East, had repercussions more widespread, more complex, and more perverse than could have been imagined by those who originally framed the seductive slogan: "Asia for the Asians." Of all the powers involved in the affairs of Eastern Asia during the past half century, Japan, ironically, appears to have been the most effective contributor, directly, to the rise of Asian nationalism and, indirectly, to the spread of Communist influence in Asia.

Whatever degree of contempt the Chinese Communist leaders in Peking may feel toward their Japanese neighbors, they are only too well aware that disciplined Japanese infantry regiments, supported by a well-organized Japanese industrial system, fought stubbornly and cruelly for many years on Chinese soil. As Japan is known to be the only Asian power which has yet shown itself independently capable of fighting Chinese troops on Chinese terms —on the ground—it must be a major goal of Chinese Communist foreign policy to ensure that Japan, allied with the United States, does not again become a dangerous enemy. Thus, Peking has repeatedly emphasized since 1950 that the major purpose of the Sino-Soviet alliance is to prevent the re-emergence of Japanese military power in the Far East and, more important, to forestall the "resumption of aggression" on the part of either a rearmed Japan or "any other state which would unite with Japan in acts of aggression."

Politically, economically, and socially, modern Japan has been a more "advanced" nation than modern China. But in attaining its prewar position of supremacy and its high level of industrial and technical development in Asia, Japan utilized methods quite different from those now employed by Communist China. Japan, therefore, is not only a potentially dangerous enemy for Communist China; it is also a rival in the present competition for the cooperation of the other countries of Asia. Despite its zealous efforts at industrialization, Communist China still has only one basic product available for unrestricted export to its neighbors: a revolutionary ideology capable, under specific conditions, of capturing the loyalty of people in underdeveloped areas. Japan, however, offers a source of industrial products and experience, a reservoir of industrial techniques and technicians, of which the rest of Asia has a pressing need. Further, Japan furnishes—if in no other way than by its conquests, short-lived though they were—a concrete example that Communism is not the only path to first-rate international status in the twentieth century.

It is indeed a moot point whether the Chinese Communist authorities view Japan principally as a potential enemy power or as a potential complementary power, a non-Soviet source of assistance for China's industrialization. Sino-Japanese relations may take the pattern of possible cooperation as well as of possible competition.

However they view the problem of Japan, the Chinese Communists are sharply aware of the potentialities of Japanese power. They know that the energy of the Japanese has frequently tended to spill over from the crowded home islands. They have only had to lift their eyes beyond the borders of their own new nation to note the manner in which—since Japan ended its official postwar period of penance and occupation in 1951—Japanese diplomacy and trade, Japanese banking and shipping, Japanese scholarship and technology have again been slowly making their influence felt through Eastern Asia. Indeed, the fact of Japanese power has not only been recognized by Mao Tse-tung in Peking, but also by the United States, which has converted its major Asian enemy of only slightly over a decade ago into a major key to its present Far Eastern policy. Nor has Russia failed to note Japan's renewed importance. Through official negotiations with the legal government of Japan or through unofficial pressure upon the Japanese Communist Party, the Soviet Union seeks to neutralize the vitality of Japanese power, which now operates as a potential deterrent to Communist expansion along Russia's eastern flank.

For its part, Peking must attempt to delay or prevent Japanese rearmament, restrain or disperse Japanese influence in Asia, and wean Japan from its present alignment with the United States. In pursuit of these goals, it must attempt to influence the politics of Japan, the economy of Japan, the people of Japan, and, ultimately, the *yamato damashii*—the national soul—of Japan. If Peking cannot convert Japan to Communism, it will at least continue its attempt to convert Japan to a belief in the new leading role of Communist China in Asia.

Yet China's means of bringing effective pressure to bear upon Japan are relatively few, and Peking's tactical behavior in this area has often seemed ambiguous. It does not appear that, from the standpoint of the Chinese Communist Political Bureau, the Japanese Communist Party can be viewed as an instrument of major potency or reliability. Peking must, therefore, attempt to make direct overtures to Japan and the Japanese. The repatriation of Japanese nationals from Communist China—apparently a stock weapon in Peking's political arsenal—served as a preliminary gesture aimed at both the Japanese government and Japanese public opinion. The continuing flow of propaganda from the bookshops of Peking to the bookshops of Tokyo is bound to have some effect. And the question of trade between Japan and mainland China is an issue which may, to a limited extent, be translated from the theoretical clouds of international propaganda to the practical level of international trade, understandable to those Japanese who viewed the "China incident" as an investment venture rather than a military adventure and who may still be mesmerized by memories of the profits of the lucrative China trade.

In general, Peking's most consistent approach has been an attempt to gain the sympathetic attention of any Japanese individual or group potentially useful to Chinese Communist ends. Peking's target runs from one end to the other of the spectrum of Japanese sensitivities. It includes Japanese, who at a minimum, oppose all or part of the present Far Eastern policies of the United States; those who favor increased self-sufficiency in Tokyo's foreign policy; those who, for practical motives, desire a *rapprochement* with the Communist bloc; and those who, at a maximum, actually support the Far Eastern aspirations of the People's Republic of China. With so broad a target, it is inevitable that many arrows shot from Peking reach their mark. In divers ways, the Chinese can appeal to the sensibilities of Japanese who, for reasons personal no less than political, distrust the implications of the present American military role in Japan. At various times and in various ways, the Chinese Communist attempt to encourage anti-American and pro-Peking sentiment has either influenced or ensnared a motley variety of Japanese: businessmen and bankers, trade-union members, rebellious students, anti-militarists, Marxist-inclined intellectuals, yen-pinching budget-balancers, religious pacifists, feminists, leftist politicians, neutralists, sentimental humanitarians, and professional Japanese Old China Hands. It is too early to predict the extent to which Peking's poisoned barbs may, in the end, sap the strength of the sturdy, if neurotic, Japanese victim at which they are aimed.

Korea. In terms of geographic accessibility, there are two areas in Asia—Korea and Indochina—which China can threaten directly and from which it may feel threatened. In both, Communist China has been involved, directly or indirectly, in wars with the West. And, in both, the conflict must be measured not only in terms of the present dynamic ambitions of revolutionary Chinese Communism but also against the background of the centuries-old relentless assertiveness of Chinese power in Eastern Asia.

In the nineteenth century, profound Western ignorance of China's traditional tributary relations with these areas inevitably led to friction and conflict with the imperial authorities at Peking. In the past few years, Western preoccupation with the strategy of the struggle against Communism in Asia has tended to obscure the picture of the Eastern world as it is viewed by the Chinese despots now resident in the northern capital. While a century ago the West was fortunate in confronting an aging imperial China which was virtually impotent, it must now deal with a young and vigorous China prepared to go to great lengths to advance both Chinese and Communist influence in Asia.

Pyongyang today is again a focal point of Chinese influence in northern Korea; as early as the second century before the Christian era, it was also a base for one of the most powerful emperors of the Han dynasty in his campaigns to extend Chinese military control into Korea. For two millennia, Chinese power has intermittently exerted a strong, and sometimes dominant, influence in the Korean peninsula. In the twentieth century, the traditional Chinese concept that a strong China cannot permit an unfriendly Korea was greatly re-enforced by the unnerving fact that the emergent military and political power of Japan was able to bring all Korea under Japanese domination and then to conquer Manchuria and violate the integrity of China proper.

The strategic planners of the new regime established at Peking were confronted at once with a basic policy problem in the area nearest to China's most important industrial region. From Peking's standpoint, an anti-Communist state in South Korea, with American military (and especially air) support based in nearby Japan, was certainly a serious annoyance and, potentially, a dangerous threat. The advantages to China of controlling all of Korea were clear, and presumably the risks inherent in an attempt to extend Communist control to the entire peninsula were weighed against them.

We still know virtually nothing of the Sino-Soviet-North Korean negotiations which preceded the Communist attack in June 1950. We may only surmise that Mao Tse-tung must have been aware of, and presumably have approved, the planning for the operation. Yet there is no evidence now available indicating that Mao was committed in advance to throw his own troops into the conflict. This move was made only after the United Nations forces had smashed the North Korean armies and as they were moving toward the borders of Communist China, and the immediate threat may have been a more important direct incentive for Chinese intervention than the original machinations in Moscow. When Peking ordered Chinese Communist units into Korea in late 1950, it recognized the great hazards involved. The move exposed both Manchuria and mainland China to the immediate possibility of disastrous enemy air action. Even if it escaped such retaliation, Communist China committed itself to an extremely expensive war at the very time when it was attempting to press forward with its initial domestic political and economic programs.

The Korean conflict was inconclusive. It was, however, of great international importance to Peking, which has consistently manifested a concern with psychological issues in those areas of Asia where it does not exercise direct control. A Chinese military defeat in Korea would have meant the destruction of one of Peking's most effective weapons: prestige. As things turned out, Mao Tse-tung scored a significant psychological triumph. He was able to take advantage of the implications in Asia of one fact: if Communist China did not win a clear-cut victory in Korea, neither did the United States, the strongest industrial power in the world.

Further, the Korean war had important political repercussions within the Communist ranks. Before 1950, the influence of the Soviet Union was paramount in northern Korea. During the six years which followed, and especially since 1953, the influence of Communist China has registered major advances. There appears to be scant prospect that Peking will relinquish its present position in North Korea or its hope of eventually gaining control of South Korea.

Indochina. Indochina is another area upon which the Chinese may exert direct military and political pressure and from which they may feel themselves vulnerable. Northern Indochina has for centuries been exposed to active, although intermittent, Chinese influence, and the historical record indicates that no vigorous and unified Chinese government has ever been prepared to tolerate the continued existence there of any power potentially hostile to its national interests.

The requirements of traditional Chinese strategy in this southern sector, no less than the demands of contemporary Chinese revolution, were at once apparent to the Communist leaders in Peking. They were alert to the importance of the revolutionary political movement in Indochina, which owed its effectiveness in the struggle against French colonialism not only to its dedicated Communism but also to its mobilization of the energies of indigenous nationalism. Thus Peking bestowed its formal blessing upon Ho Chi Minh in January 1950, even before Moscow recognized the Communist regime in Indochina.

From Peking's standpoint, the military situation in Indochina in late 1950 may have appeared similar in some respects to that in Korea, for in both areas Communist military units were at war against Western military forces. Peking did, however, perceive significant differences between the two areas. Peking saw that the United Nations forces in Korea posed a major threat to the national security interests of Communist China, while the Western forces in Indochina were relatively weak and were making little headway against the indigenous Communist guerrilla forces. It noted that in Korea the Communist party ruled only half the country and was powerless in the remainder of the peninsula, while in Indochina the Communists led a widespread revolutionary movement and held power in many parts of the country. And there was still another essential consideration which must have appeared in Peking's intelligence estimates. While Manchuria, Communist China's most important industrial region, is immediately adjacent to Korea, the areas of Kwangsi and Yunnan in south China nearest Indochina are less important than Manchuria and also more mountainous and more easily defensible in the event of actual foreign invasion.

For Peking, Indochina was a theater of operations distinctly secondary in importance to Korea. At the same time, Peking paid close attention to the opportunities for extending its influence to the south. It rushed the 250-mile Laipin-Munankwan (formerly Chennankwan) railway to

completion in slightly over a year (September 1950-
November 1951) despite the fact that the line contributed
little to China's economic development. This railway—
running from central Kwangsi province in south China
through mountainous terrain to Munankwan, one of the
most important passes between China and Indochina—is
primarily of military and strategic importance. By linking
the principal rail network of mainland China with the
Indochina border, the railroad became a major Chinese
supply route for the Vietminh forces and a major channel
of communication and coordination between the Communists in China and those in Indochina. Despite its own
pressing armament efforts and its military requirements in
Korea, Communist China delivered military equipment
and supplies to the Vietminh and provided military advice
and training assistance. Liaison was greatly facilitated by
a linguistic factor: many of the Vietminh leaders speak
Chinese fluently. In the international sphere, Peking lent
political and propaganda support to the claims of Ho Chi
Minh in his "holy war" against the French.

Peking was fortunate in Indochina. It was able to con-
fine its contribution to limited material and moral assistance, and did not have to throw its own infantry forces
into the conflict as it had been obliged to do in Korea.
While it was clear that Communist China would not sit
quietly by in the event of a total Vietminh collapse, it
was equally clear that it had weighed the probable international consequences of a large-scale military intervention. So long as there was no threat of Western invasion of
Chinese territory from bases in Indochina, it mattered
little to Peking if the war went on indefinitely, especially
since events were working in favor of Ho Chi Minh's
cause. If more direct Chinese action became necessary, it
could be taken speedily.

The cessation of hostilities in Indochina after the agreements concluded at Geneva in the summer of 1954 appears
to have served Peking's provisional purposes. The division
of the area, without precipitating a world war, constituted
a significant victory for Communist China. Peking had

provided enough assistance so that the Chinese contribution was manifest to all, but not so much that the spec-
tators, either in Asia or elsewhere, could effectively allege
that the People's Republic of China had gained its success
solely by brute force. One cannot estimate the extent to
which Ho Chi Minh's immediate national interests in
Indochina may coincide with or diverge from Mao Tse-
tung's long-term international interests. But one may at
least predict that Peking will continue to have a major
influence in the political and military affairs of Indochina
and that it confidently believes that time is on the Communist side in the struggle against both Asian and Western non-Communists in that area.

Southeast Asia. It is in Southeast Asia, the vast arc of
territories running from Burma on the west to the Philippines on the east, that Communist China sees its long-
term sphere of influence. Here are rice, rubber, and tin.
Here is an important segment of the human resources of
Asia, stirring in reaction against three centuries of Western domination. Memory and desire are mixed in Southeast Asia; ancient tradition and modern nationalism are
intermingled. Here are the ingredients of revolution:
poverty, ignorance, agrarian discontent, nationalism, cultural confusion, and intellectual restlessness. Surveying the
rich human and material resources of the area known to
the Chinese as *Nan-yang,* the "South Seas," the Communist
authorities in Peking are determined to assert the fact
that the traditional cultural leadership of Eastern Asia is
once again in Chinese hands.

The very diversity of the lands and peoples of Southeast
Asia has led to a diversity of Chinese Communist assumptions with respect to specific problems and specific areas.
Peking's approach has varied in its treatment of those areas
which are contiguous to Communist China and of those
which are more distant and less subject to direct pressures.
Attitudes have varied toward those governments which
have formally recognized the People's Republic of China
and those, such as Thailand and the Philippines, which

have not. Tactics have varied between areas in which indigenous Communist activity is already contributing to
instability and those in which Communist activity is either
ineffectual or insignificant. And Peking's international
tactics in Southeast Asia have not only varied from place
to place; they have also shifted from time to time.

The Communist-sponsored Trade-Union Conference of
Asian and Australasian countries met in 1949 at Peking,
the new capital of the People's Republic of China. In
a major speech to the conference, on November 16, Liu
Shao-ch'i recited the Chinese Communist Party's cate-
chism on international relations and posed Communist
China as the model for all revolutionary (i.e. Communist)
movements in "colonial and semi-colonial areas" in the
East. He said:

> The path taken by the Chinese people in defeating imperial-
> ism and in founding the People's Republic of China is the
> path that must be taken by the peoples of all colonial and
> semi-colonial countries in their fight for national independ-
> ence and people's democracy.

Further, Liu Shao-ch'i outlined a blueprint for Commu-
nist-led revolutions in India, Burma, Malaya, Indonesia,
Indochina, the Philippines, and South Korea. He stressed
that, in furthering "liberation struggles" in these areas,
"armed struggle" should be carried on in the countryside,
while "in the enemy-controlled cities and areas, either
legal or illegal mass struggles" should be conducted to
coordinate with guerrilla warfare in the rural districts.
"Armed struggle," Liu Shao-ch'i emphasized, "can, *and
must,* be the main force in the people's liberation struggle" in "colonial and semi-colonial countries" of Eastern
Asia.

In the celebrations marking the thirtieth anniversary of
the founding of the Communist Party of China on July 1,
1951, Peking concentrated attention upon the international significance of the pattern of political revolution
which was exemplified in the establishment of the People's
Republic of China. Boldly Communist China announced:

The classic type of revolution in the imperialist countries is the October revolution.

The classic type of revolution in the colonial and semi-colonial countries is the Chinese revolution, the experience of which is invaluable for the peoples of these countries.

Liu Shao-ch'i's speech of late 1949 attracted great attention and was widely interpreted as a singularly candid statement of Peking's objectives and proposed operations in Southeast Asia. Similarly, the theoretical statements issued in mid-1951 were viewed by contemporary observers as a highly significant proclamation by Peking to the rest of Asia that its neighbors must follow the same pattern of revolution which had gained total control of China for the Communist party. Yet, in retrospect, these statements are principally useful for the light they cast upon the assumptions of the Chinese Communist leaders at particular times and under particular circumstances.

Liu Shao-ch'i's speech of November 1949 suggests what Mao Tse-tung—then in the full flush of military triumph on the mainland—hoped the Chinese Communist impact on Asia would be. The July 1951 statement that the Chinese Communist pattern of revolution had already—with or without formal Soviet approval—become in the minds of its makers a "classic type of revolution" for the unindustrialized areas of Asia reflects the attitude of a vigorous group of Chinese Communist leaders. Do they not perhaps feel that they are as much the descendants of the Emperor Wu of the Han dynasty as the heirs of Lenin?

Yet these statements, however much they may reveal of the temper of the Political Bureau in Peking, tell little of what has actually happened during the years since 1949. Aside from the Communist gains in Indochina, the "people's liberation struggle in colonial and semi-colonial countries" has not yet engulfed Southeast Asia. The recent reports of trouble on the Sino-Burmese frontier are inconclusive. It is not clear whether Peking's intent is to apply significant military pressure upon Burma in order to promote Chinese Communist political objectives within Burma, or only to reassert Chinese authority in a remote area where the international border has never been clearly defined.

Some observers view the communities of emigrant Chinese scattered through the *Nan-yang* area as instruments of Chinese expansionist tendencies and aspirations. To be sure, in Burma, Thailand, Indochina, Malaya, British Borneo, Indonesia, and the Philippines, there are important local Chinese communities potentially useful to Chinese Communist purposes. These overseas groups are unquestionably of some assistance in extending the political influence of Peking into the specific areas where they exist. They might aid in the forcible expansion of Communist China's military power into Southeast Asia should that be considered vital to Peking's interests.

The existence of the overseas Chinese, however, is hardly in itself evidence of Chinese imperialism. The Chinese in Southeast Asia are refugees who fled China's indigenous poverty to recoup or promote their family fortunes. A few have been extremely successful; they have accumulated great wealth and built complex networks of personal and financial influence. But these Chinese are not, on the whole, truly representative of the solid and self-centered heart of mother China. Their utility as potential leaders of Communist revolution is limited both by their own commercial acquisitiveness and by the fact that they are often heartily disliked by the local inhabitants for their clannishness, their energy, their shrewdness, and their dominant economic position. The record in Indochina over the past decade would suggest that actual extension of Communist political and military control there was pressed more effectively through use of the indigenous population than through manipulation of the unassimilated Chinese minority. On the other hand, the serious troubles in the British colony of Singapore, the major strategic crossroads of Southeast Asia, illustrate the exceedingly strong pressures which Peking may bring to focus there. The safest assumption is that Peking will attempt to utilize the overseas Chinese for its own ends whenever and wherever possible.

For several years Communist China has made special efforts to attract the most active and aggressive Chinese youth in Southeast Asia to seek their future and their fulfillment in the cause of Communist revolution. The authorities in Peking are fully aware of the positive utility of the young overseas Chinese, not only for their radical political enthusiasm but also, in practical terms, for their linguistic abilities and their experience outside China. Further, the authorities in Peking recognize the long-term importance of their influence: the steady withering of potential anti-Communist activity among overseas Chinese. If Peking is able, firmly and imaginatively, to capture and hold a significant portion of the overseas youth of China, it will have won a major victory for Communism in Asia.

It would be pleasant to be able to relax in a mood of easy optimism, confident that the Bandung Conference in the spring of 1955 represented a major triumph for the West in the East. Actually, it would be more realistic to assess Bandung as a victory for the developing maturity of Asia itself and of the new nations there, motivated by a deep, frequently exaggerated, desire to emphasize their Asian-ness and to assert their complete independence of colonialism and the white man. That Chou En-lai was the dominant individual figure at the conference does not occasion surprise. Chou was a symbol of the fact that, of all the Asian and African nations represented at Bandung, Communist China alone has prospects of becoming a major threat to the peace of the world.

At the end of 1949, Communist China surveyed its neighbors to the south in a mood of arrogant aggressiveness. Since Bandung, it appears to incline more toward cautious politeness. But there has been no evidence that Communist China has yet had any serious thought of abandoning its long-term strategic objectives in Southeast Asia, objectives generated both by its own psychological sense of manifest destiny and by the political compulsions of the Sino-Soviet alliance. And the smaller countries can hardly find consolation in the knowledge that the government in power in Peking is Asian, not Western.

Chinese Communist Foreign Policy
and the Moscow-Peking Axis

The international drives of the Chinese Communist regime, both material and ideological, are today greatly re-enforced by the alliance between Peking and Moscow. Yet the distractions—and headlines—of the day should not lead one to neglect China's own past or ignore its influence on the Communist China of today. In appraising the problems presented by the upsurge of Chinese Communist power it may be helpful to assume that Peking's foreign policy is an amalgam of both historical and contemporary ingredients. Essentially, this policy is derived from traditional Chinese patterns of thought and behavior, revitalized by the dedicated revolutionary *esprit* of Communism.

Throughout most of their recorded history, the Chinese have lived, acted, and reacted as the inhabitants of the center of the known world. The basic geographical setting of the Middle Kingdom was a significant factor in the evolution of the Chinese people. Great natural barriers and vast distances, separating the civilization of traditional China from other major centers of human life, bred a strong sense of ethnocentricity in the institutions and even in the language of imperial China. To be sure, isolation was seasoned with foreign intercourse. The movement of non-Chinese peoples and non-Chinese ideas in Asia had manifold repercussions upon the history of China. For over twenty centuries, however, China was the fertile cultural mother of all Eastern Asia, contributing far more to neighboring areas than it received from them. Korea and Japan, Mongolia, Turkestan, and Tibet in Inner Asia, Nepal and Bhutan, Burma, Siam, and Annam—all felt the powerful and pervasive force of the highly developed and self-confident civilization of the Chinese people. As recently as the mid-nineteenth century, all of China's diplomatic intercourse with peoples who dwelt outside the sphere of Sinic culture was regulated by a complex system of formal tributary relations. In the Chinese-centered universe, this tributary system defined the rights and responsibilities both of the outer areas and of the imperial authorities in the Middle Kingdom.

The sharp Western impact upon China in the modern period created an intolerable situation for the rulers of China. In the nineteenth century, the resulting irrepressible conflict placed China—a cultural imperialist by tradition—in the humiliating position of being a relatively weak and helpless power into which non-Chinese imperialist nations extended their influence and control. So far as China's foreign relations were concerned, the century marked a transition from the old system based upon tributary relations to a new system, based upon Western-imposed treaty relations, which operated to foster the gradual undermining by the West of the integrity of the Chinese empire.

The basic problem—the integration of China with the outside, non-Chinese world—has remained unsolved. The traditional system of tributary relations was, in essence, fully as "unequal," in reverse, as the Western system of treaty relations which supplanted it. And, for a century after 1840, an unfortunate conjunction of external pressures and internal weaknesses operated to defer, or indeed to prevent, any comprehensive reconciliation of conflicting viewpoints. Modern China and the modern world outside China have never truly met on a mature basis of mutual confidence and reciprocal respect.

Through reflective consideration of the historical context of China's central role in Asia, one may comprehend certain of the attitudes underlying Peking's foreign policy today. But to leave the issue there would be as slipshod intellectually as it would be disastrous strategically. Today, in the mid-twentieth century, mainland China is united and resurgent. It is now ruled by a new despotism which is revolutionary and Communist, not traditional and Confucian. The major distinction which sets the present Peking regime apart from strong Chinese dynasties of the imperial age is precisely the fact that it is Communist and that it operates in close alliance with the strongest Communist nation in the world. The impact of Commu-

nist China on Asia must, therefore, be studied as a unique
political phenomenon possessed of certain characteristics
not to be found in any of the great Chinese dynasties of
the past. Not only is Communist China a disciplined political and military power capable of exerting influence
upon non-Chinese areas in Asia; it is at the same time influenced by pressures from a powerful non-Chinese nation,
the Soviet Union.

The foreign policy of the government of the People's
Republic of China is a new and potent brew. Peking today represents a unified and dynamic mainland China under firm, centralized control. Peking today is heir both to
the psychological tradition of Chinese dominance and
superiority in Asia, and to the persisting failure of China
to adjust its role to the modern state system. On the other
hand, Peking also represents a Communist nation, motivated by Communist doctrine, acting in alliance with the
Soviet Union, and operating as the second most powerful
member of the Communist bloc. To the traditional Chinese *Weltanschauung*, Peking has now added a radical,
foreign element: Marxism-Leninism, with its sense of historical destiny, its ambiguous attitude toward traditional
Western values, and its strategic intentions concerning the
complete recasting of society throughout the world.

From the standpoint of the West, the outlook is not re-
assuring. If the Chinese—as Chinese—normally proved difficult to deal with in the past during periods when Chinese
national power was organized and effective, the Chinese
Communists—doubly endowed with self-assurance—are
certain to be doubly difficult today. The imperial rulers in
Peking regarded non-Chinese "barbarians" as subordi-
nates and inferiors. Consciously and deliberately, the
Chinese Communist rulers in Peking today regard non-
Communist barbarians as enemies. It would be blind to
ignore this essential fact, as it would be foolhardy to be-
little the implications of this Chinese Communist hatred
and distrust. The devotees of Communism, whether individual or corporate, feel that they are involved in a perma-

nent conflict with the non-Communist world. The struggle must go on relentlessly—although not necessarily overtly—until the victory of Communism is assured.

PEKING AND MOSCOW: THE TIE THAT BINDS

From the standpoint of the Communist world, it would appear that the general combination of ideological, military, political, and economic factors which shape the Sino-Soviet alliance provides a foundation of common interests and reciprocal practical benefits. Both Communist China and the Soviet Union find the present relationship not only expedient but necessary. Firm alliances—like lasting marriages—normally involve genuine mutuality of interest, not necessarily complete reciprocity of affection.

It is not surprising that the present Russian leaders regard the Sino-Soviet alliance as the essential element in their Far Eastern policy and accept Mao Tse-tung as their principal Asian ally in extending the citadel of world Communism. Mao and the Chinese leaders, *bona fide* Asians as well as Communists, are able to press the anti-Western attack in the Far East much more effectively than the Russians alone. The emergence of a Communist China which is, by Asian standards, militarily vigorous and powerful is advantageous to the Russians from the strategic standpoint. Communist China now provides the Russians with a unified and friendly ally on their Far Eastern flank. In addition, the troops and the machinations of Communist China act as a persistent threat to the Western powers and their interests in Asia, forcing their continued, indecisive commitment in that area and requiring them to make significant diversions of Western military resources from European and other theaters. And, so far as Moscow is concerned, the economic price of a willing and valuable ally is not inordinately dear.

Communist China, in turn, has had to rely upon the Soviet Union for political, economic, and military support. In the international sphere, Russian backing has been very important to Peking, which has neither representation in

the United Nations nor normal diplomatic relations with
the principal Western governments.

In its program of domestic economic development,
aimed at expanding its industrial base and military potential, Soviet aid has been indispensable. Without Russian advice and material assistance, the Chinese mainland
economy would probably have floundered more than it
has. From the Soviet Union, Communist China—deficient
in planning and technical personnel—receives advisers to
guide the mobilization of available domestic resources,
and engineers to speed its program of industrialization on
the Stalinist model. It obtains machinery needed to put
factories into production, transport equipment vital to
distribution—basic capital equipment which it cannot produce itself and may not easily purchase elsewhere through
normal trading channels. And, in the development of
large-scale farming, Soviet assistance has been useful.

In the military sphere, the tie with Moscow has provided China both with modern military equipment and
with the skills to utilize it. Russian military advisers have
assisted in reorganizing and training Communist China's
armed forces along modern, mechanized lines. And the
Soviet Union has provided a source of supply for jet aircraft and other heavy equipment which have greatly
expanded mainland China's military capabilities.

Beyond the material factors supporting the Moscow-
Peking axis, however, there are also elements of political
prestige which provide its driving force and lubricate its
action. In the short run, both Russia and China gain
significant psychological benefits from the coalition. Moscow, as well as Peking, derives luster from the achievements of China, now the first major Asian nation to
embark under Communist auspices upon a general program of revolutionary change aimed at eliminating the
backwardness of centuries and at attaining true political
independence and economic modernization. And Communist China's vigorous drive for dominance in Asia is but-
tressed, psychologically, through its bonds with the Soviet

Union, which offers an aggressive alternative to the Western, nontotalitarian path of industrialization.

At the time of Stalin's death in 1953, there was some speculation as to whether or not Mao Tse-tung might indeed emerge as the most important single figure in the Communist bloc. Actually, there has been no evidence that either Mao or any other Chinese Communist leader has significant direct political influence in Moscow or in Europe. It is probable, however, that Mao Tse-tung, in the eyes of some Asians and of many Asian Communists, may appear to be a revolutionary figure of more distinguished proportions than any Russian Communist now prominent in Moscow. Mao is not only the leader of a violent Communist revolution in Asia. He is also one symbol of a more general Asian revolt against three centuries of Western domination and condescension. It is because of this new, and increasingly important, role of Peking as a focus of anti-Western influence in Asia that the Russians, in the evolving course of Sino-Soviet relations, have listened with growing attention to the views of the Chinese Communist rulers, especially on Far Eastern questions.

In an age which often hopefully equates the fall of tyrants with the collapse of the movements they sparked, it may perhaps be well to place no undue emphasis upon Mao Tse-tung himself. He is both mortal and replaceable. The syndrome which has borne him to power is more lasting than the individual. Tradition and interest alike turn Communist China's primary focus of activity and influence toward Asia and center its ambitions upon preserving its position of strategic dominance there.

It appears probable that, by realistically estimating its potentialities, Communist China should be able, within the framework of its alliance with the Soviet Union, to pursue the national goals and the international objectives which it now holds. While in 1950 the Soviet Union was by far the predominant factor in the alliance, Communist China has now grown in stature and status to the point where it has a significant weight of its own in the balance between the two powerful Communist nations. But the

Chinese are still so dependent upon the Russians that there appears to be no real prospect that Communist China can, in the near future, move through the period of partnership with the Russians to the stage where it might become the paramount element in the coalition. Whatever Peking's weight in the balance of the Sino-Soviet alliance, the West would be foolhardy to ignore the fact that Communist China is now, and will continue to be, an increasingly important force in the Communist world, or to overlook the probability that the general community of belief and purpose underlying the alliance gives prospect of a reasonably durable union.

Whether the Chinese Communists feel that their own relations with the Soviet party may be affected by the changing relations between Moscow and its satellites in Europe remains very obscure, and there is no direct evidence of consultations between Peking and Belgrade on their relations with Moscow. Theoretically, Peking has a definite interest in encouraging the theme that there are several paths by which different nations may travel toward the ultimate goal of "socialism." In practice, however, it is unlikely that Peking would seriously attempt to challenge Moscow in areas, such as Eastern Europe, where China has no direct interests.

In the Asian context, there has certainly been no abandonment of major Chinese goals. Communist China, though intent upon modernizing its military establishment, does not necessarily have to resort to direct military action in areas of the Far East which do not menace its own national security. The threat in Asia may be more subtle. Peking may well limit its efforts to political warfare: to infiltration, subversion, pressure, sabotage, and clandestine aid to dissident groups. The emphasis in Peking's propaganda upon the "five principles," designed to undergird peaceful international relations in the Far East on terms favorable to its own aims, should not obscure the fact that the Chinese Communists continue to possess substantial and increasing capabilities for creating disruption in Asia without resorting to clumsy ventures which can clearly be labeled "aggression."

Mao Tse-tung's recent posture of political reserve may have little immediate importance in the Sino-Soviet struggle with the West. It may only reflect his confidence in the strength of his country and his people. In studying the brief record of Communist China under the rule of Mao Tse-tung, it is useful to ponder the sobering observation made by a perceptive missionary, Arthur H. Smith, over a half-century ago: "It is in his staying qualities that the Chinese excels the world." [3] These words, which can hardly inspire optimism on the part of the West today, are still as pertinent as when they were written.

[3] Arthur H. Smith, *Chinese Characteristics* (New York: Fleming H. Revell Company, 1894), p. 154.

CHAPTER TWO

MOSCOW-PEKING AXIS: THE ECONOMIC PATTERN *

by Alexander Eckstein

IN ADOPTING the Soviet pattern of response to the challenge posed by its economic backwardness, Communist China inevitably has placed itself in a position of unique dependence upon the Soviet Union in respect to the ideological and institutional wherewithal and rationale for the country's industrialization and economic development. Several questions immediately arise. What are the conditions which determine the degree of this dependence? To what extent are the Soviet and Chinese economies complementary, and what are the economic implications of that degree of interdependence? What strains does the Chinese obligation impose upon the Soviet economy? In general terms what light does this throw on the complexion of the Sino-Soviet alliance?

A rigorous analysis of these questions is greatly hampered by a very serious lack of data. While there are many gaps and statistical deficiencies in all of our information concerning the Soviet and Communist Chinese economies, this is doubly so in the case of their relations with each other.

* I wish to acknowledge the help of the Harvard Russian Research Center in making possible the completion of this study and to express my indebtedness to Mr. Y. C. Yin for his invaluable assistance in assembling data and preparing some of the tables.

It is against this background that the problem of Sino-Soviet economic relations must be examined. First, some of the salient features of China's economic backwardness will be sketched with particular emphasis upon a few of the impediments and propellents to economic growth in China as compared with the Soviet Union.[1] Next, an attempt will be made to investigate the changes in the structure of foreign trade under the impact of the Chinese Communist industrialization program, with particular attention to the conditions which affect the degree of China's economic dependence upon the Soviet Union. This will be followed by an analysis of the general character of Sino-Soviet economic relations and of its implications for United States policy.

THE INHERITED ECONOMY

Upon their conquest of the Chinese mainland, the Communists inherited what were essentially three different economies: the economy of traditional China still holding sway over most of the mainland; the more or less modernized, urbanized and commercialized economy of the Treaty Ports; and the comparatively advanced and rapidly industrializing economy of Manchuria.

The traditional economy. The traditional economy bears the earmarks of a stagnating and underdeveloped economy with all the typical features of backwardness. It is a largely rural economy caught in a vicious circle of poverty, in which both the capacity and the inducement to save and invest are lacking. The high population pressure upon arable land resources, compounded by prevailing inheritance practices and a lack of non-farm employment opportunities, has led to a continuous frag-

[1] This initial section is in part based upon the author's articles on "Conditions and Prospects for Economic Growth in Communist China," *World Politics*, v. 7, n. 1 (October 1954), pp. 1-37; n. 2 (February 1955), pp. 255-83; and n. 3 (April 1955), pp. 434-47. For more detail and documentation, readers are referred to these articles, as well as to *Prospects for Communist China* by W. W. Rostow in collaboration with Richard W. Hatch, Frank A. Kierman, Jr., Alexander Eckstein (Cambridge, Mass.: Technology Press of Mass. Institute of Technology, 1954).

mentation and pulverization of land holding. This situation was aggravated by inequalities in farm size, with 60 per cent of the farms averaging less than three acres in size.

A farm population of this high density could be maintained only with high intensity of land use, based on double-cropping of vast areas and on age-old soil conservation and irrigation practices. The crop yields obtained were quite high, actually exceeding somewhat the levels attained in Meiji Japan, but lagging appreciably behind those attained in Japan of today. This suggests that crop productivity in China has been pushed about as far as traditional practices and methods will permit, and that, as in Japan, large improvements in farm output can be attained only through the introduction of new technology and improved practices.

While yields per acre were relatively high, yields per man were quite low. Because of the high farm population density, limited alternatives for outside employment, and small size of farms, there was widespread underemployment in agriculture. All these factors combined have traditionally kept the Chinese peasant at the bare margin of subsistence. Because of this very closeness to the margin, most peasants were unable to save enough even to provide themselves with a cushion for meeting extraordinary expenditures necessitated either by natural disasters or by ceremonial obligations, such as weddings or burials. Such expenditures were for the most part covered by borrowing at very high interest rates. These rates in turn were justified by the high risks incurred by the lender, but they greatly aggravated the burden upon the peasantry and frequently led to land sales, or sales of surface rights in land, as a means of repaying the loan. Thus a vicious spiral was created within the circle; at one end the peasant resorted to credit for financing consumption rather than production, and the landlord, trader and native lender, at the other, accumulated capital but channeled it into consumption credit or land purchase and speculation. In effect, the process of capital accumulation, which rested on collection of land rent and interest, land speculation and trade, was made possible by squeezing the peasant's narrow margin. In turn, in order to keep the peasant alive, at least some of the funds had to be channeled back to him in the form of consumer credit and land purchase.[2] As a result, the net saving and investment of China's traditional farm economy was negligible.

This narrow, circular-flow pattern tended to hamper greatly the participation of the rural economy in the commercial sector and favored the persistence of a self-sufficient household way of life. Inadequate and costly transport has also been one of the key factors limiting the scope of the market. Because of the very scanty railroad network, a large share of trade is carried by primitive modes of transport that appear cheap per day, but are expensive per mile.[3] Yet the pattern of rural self-sufficiency was not nearly as complete as has frequently been supposed. Probably over one-quarter of the goods consumed by agricultural families were purchased. In turn, they sold about one-half of their output. But the bulk of the farm products marketed were exchanged within the same county and only an estimated 8 per cent was shipped to distant urban markets.

Consequently, China exhibited a highly cellular marketing pattern, with varying and fluctuating scarcity relationships and price tendencies in different areas. Frequent local famines were a reflection of this high degree of fragmentation. All these problems were greatly aggravated by civil strife and the lack of administrative unity.

The Treaty Ports sector. At the risk of oversimplification, the Treaty Ports can be viewed essentially as crea-

---

[2] In reality, this process, in most cases, was more complex than presented here. Also, it should be noted that these relationships were not equally applicable to all parts of China. Thus the picture sketched above was more representative of areas in which tenancy and population pressure were particularly high. Moreover, these particular aspects of rural stagnation are quite widespread not only in China but in many other underdeveloped areas as well.

[3] Mainland China (excluding Outer Mongolia and Tibet), with an area roughly the same as the United States, had a railroad network which was not much more than 1/20 of the latter's.

tures of, and vehicles for, the penetration of Western commerce into nineteenth-century China. In this sense they were but a symptom of the general expansion of the world economy into hitherto isolated areas. As was the case with so many other countries, foreign trade served as the highway over which many of the disequilibrating forces and tendencies were introduced into the stagnant and underdeveloped economy of traditional China. While the challenge thereby posed served as a stimulus to economic change and growth in several countries, with Japan perhaps as the outstanding example, in China it led only to an abortive "take-off" during the period of the "self-strengthening" movement. The dynamic response was long delayed and when it came it was clothed in the robes of Communist totalitarianism.

In the meantime, economic growth in the Treaty Ports sector itself was quite rapid. This growth, at first propelled by the expansion of foreign trade, spread to shipping, banking, warehousing, public and other services. It was followed by the development of modern industries, after the treaty of Shimonoseki (1895) had opened the way for building and operating foreign-owned factories in the Treaty Ports. During this period, cotton textile imports increased appreciably with the cheapening of overseas transport and the low-cost production of factory-made cotton yarn in India. This served to undermine the position of rural handicrafts, particularly the hand-spinning of yarn, and to create a market for manufactured textile products. The growth of this market, in turn, provided the impetus for the development of a cotton textile industry within China, an industry which, as in many other economies, took the lead in the process of industrialization. This was followed by the rise of other consumers' goods industries which developed as a by-product of foreign trade—flour mills, cigarette and match factories, and others. At the same time, power plants and light engineering works, as well as railroads, were developed to service these new industries.

This entire commercial and industrial complex remained largely confined to the periphery of the Chinese economy, being linked to the traditional sector through domestic trade. In effect, the links between these two economic sectors may not have been much firmer than those which are typical for two distinct economies engaged in foreign trade. As a result, the Treaty Ports sector was never fused or merged with, but rather was grafted on to, the traditional economy of "earthbound China."

The Manchurian economy. A favorable population-resource balance, combined with Japanese skill in organization and management, led, between 1931 and 1943, to rapid industrial growth and development of the Manchurian economy. Compared with China proper, Manchuria had many of the features of an undeveloped frontier, rather than an overcrowded and underdeveloped area. It was sparsely populated and, relative to China, richly endowed with forest, land and mineral resources. With this combination of favorable resources and institutional conditions, industry grew rapidly under the impact of Japanese capital imports, entrepreneurship, and comprehensive planning for economic development.

Between the early 1930's and 1943, pig iron production doubled, the output of coal rose two and a half times, power capacity quadrupled and cement production multiplied five-fold.[4] At the end of this period Manchuria, with only about one-tenth of the mainland area, had one-third of mainland railway mileage, 40 per cent of its coal production, close to 70 per cent of its power capacity, over 70 per cent of its cement, 85 per cent of its pig iron and over 90 per cent of its steel production. The pattern of Manchurian economic development presented a sharp contrast to the mold that had evolved in the Treaty Ports sector. Manchuria had emerged as a heavy industry base, modest in relation to the country's size and population, but of substantial proportions, nevertheless, while the Treaty

---

[4] E. B. Schumpeter and others, *The Industrialization of Japan and Manchukuo, 1930-1940* (New York: Macmillan, 1940), Table 103, p. 388; and this author's "Conditions and Prospects for Economic Growth in Communist China," *World Politics*, v. 7, n. 1 (October 1954), Table 1, p. 9.

Ports remained the center of the light, consumers' goods industries.

THE ECONOMY ON THE EVE OF THE
FIRST FIVE-YEAR PLAN

These three economies had developed more or less separately, linked principally through trade, but with definite political and institutional barriers between them which hampered economic integration and fusion. The task of breaking down these barriers devolved upon the Communists, who were determined to harness the resources of each part for the organization of what, in effect, became a new economic entity. This task was, of course, greatly facilitated by the termination of civil conflict and by the administrative unification of the country.

At the time of the Chinese Communist take-over in 1949, all three segments of the mainland economy were badly disrupted under the impact of prolonged civil war and Soviet dismantling of industrial plants in Manchuria. The most urgent problem facing the new regime was to restore agricultural production and to rehabilitate industrial plants and transport. At the same time, the institutional framework had to be restructured so as to bring the economy under the intimate control of the planning authorities. With these preparatory tasks out of the way, the regime apparently felt ready to launch its first Five-Year Plan.[5]

The Five-Year Plan, and the entire development program of which it is to be but the first phase, is largely patterned on the Soviet model. Thus, the Chinese Communists envisage a development focused on the rapid expansion of producers' goods and defense industries. This is to be accompanied by a more modest rate of growth in the manufacture of textiles needed for barter with the countryside. At the same time, agriculture is to be developed primarily through mobilization of underemployed

5 Officially, the Plan was launched in January 1953; however, it was fully elaborated only in the spring of 1955 and formally accepted by the People's Congress in July 1955.

farm labor for water conservation and other labor-intensive projects.[6]

In essence, the Plan intends to push the expansion of industry at the cost of agricultural development. Industrialization is accelerated at the outset; since agriculture is kept on a short investment ration, a larger share of investment resources can be concentrated in industry. This policy, in turn, sets up its own vicious circles. Just because agricultural development is sluggish, while the demand for farm products grows—owing to an increasing population, urbanization, and exports—the regime is forced to extract a rising proportion of farm output if this rising demand is to be met. This very process, however, further handicaps any incentive for agricultural development, so that the screw must be turned even tighter. Under these circumstances farm output is sacrificed for control and strong compulsions are set in force that drive the system toward collectivization.

Within the framework of this development policy, the state provides a guaranteed market for the goods and services produced. Any conceivable deficiency in effective demand is not one of the factors limiting growth, except possibly in a short-run sense. On the contrary, the more effectively consumption can be kept in check, the higher will be the rates of growth, other factors remaining constant. Under these conditions, government policy is dedicated to keeping consumption at the lowest levels compatible with political stability, i.e., maintenance of the regime in power, and with the requirements of raising non-farm labor productivity. As a general proposition, one may consider the Chinese Communist program as primarily power-oriented, i.e., designed to maximize the rate at which internal control is extended and consolidated, while the external war-making and political potential is being augmented as rapidly as possible.

The emphasis upon producers' goods is brought out

[6] See for instance Chou En-lai's *Report on Government Work* to the First Session of the First National People's Congress, NCNA Supplement n. 218 (London), October 14, 1954.

very clearly in the Five-Year Plan targets which were announced at the People's Congress of July 1955. The output in steel is to be trebled, power and cement doubled, and machine tools increased by three and a half times; cotton piece goods are to be expanded by less than 50 per cent, and grains by less than 20 per cent. According to Li Fu-ch'un the output of means of production is to be raised by 126.5 per cent and that of consumers' goods by 79.7 per cent.[7] In practice, this difference in emphasis is likely to be further accentuated; on the basis of past experience, plans for the heavy industry sector are much more likely to be fulfilled or overfulfilled than for the consumers' goods industries.

The image which the Chinese Communist planners seem to have in mind in formulating and launching their development plan is the Soviet Union of 1928, on the eve of its forced-draft industrialization effort. However, the 1952 economy of mainland China was probably much closer to that of Russia during its first major industrialization spurt in the 1880's and 1890's.

It is clear (Table I) that even as of 1900 Russia was much farther developed and the balance between resources and population was more favorable than China's on the eve of its first Five-Year Plan. The population pressure in rural areas was four times greater in China than in Russia. With the exception of coal and electric power, output of major industrial products in China lagged behind the Russian levels of 1900. Moreover, on a per capita basis Russia was also more advanced in these sectors. A similar picture emerges with respect to railroads. From the standpoint of mineral resource endowments, too, China of today is at a disadvantage as compared to Russia of 1900. China is particularly well endowed with coal and nonferrous metals, but is comparatively poor in iron ore and especially in petroleum. Yet, we must not forget that, at this stage, quantitative resource limitations are not likely to present a serious problem; much more immediate and

[7] *Report on the Five-Year Plan to the National People's Congress,* NCNA Daily Bulletin n. 1340 (London), July 6, 1955.

Table I

Indicators of Comparative Levels of Development in Russia and China

	RUSSIA		CHINA
	1900(a)	*1928(a)*	*1952*
POPULATION			
Aggregate size, in millions	94.2(b)	147.0	575.0(c)
Urban, as per cent of total	12.1	17.9	13.0
Rural, per acre of cultivated land	0.48	0.43	1.67
GNP per capita (in 1952 dollars)	—	240.0	50–60
INDUSTRIAL PRODUCTION			
Coal: total, in millions of metric tons	15.9	40.1	63.53
per capita, in kilograms	168.8	273.0	110.5
Pig iron: total, in million MT's	2.83	3.3	1.88
per capita, in kilograms	30.40	22.0	3.27
Steel: total, in million MT's	2.15	4.3	1.35
per capita, in kilograms	22.80	29.0	2.35
Electric power capacity:			
total, in million KW	—	1.9	2.85
per capita in KW	—	0.01	0.005
Cement: total in million MT's	—	1.9	2.86
per capita in kilograms	—	13.0	4.97
Cotton spindles:			
total, in millions	6.65	7.5	5.0
per capita	0.07	0.05	0.01
LENGTH OF RAILWAYS			
Total, in thousands of miles	36.5	75.7	15.0
Trackage per square mile	0.0044	0.0093	0.0033
RESOURCES (d)			
Coal reserves: in million MT's	1,200,000		265,000
Iron ore reserves: in million MT's	10,900		2,504

(a) Refers to year nearest to this for which data are available.
(b) Population of the Russian Empire in 1897, exclusive of Finland, Congress Poland, Bessarabia, and the Baltic countries.
(c) Based on Chinese Communist official census figure of 582 million for 1953; 1952 figure estimated by author on the assumption that rate of natural increase is 12/1000.
(d) Does not refer to any one year, but represents post-World War II estimates.

Sources: P. I. Liashchenko, *History of the National Economy of Russia to the 1917 Revolution*, transl. by L. M. Herman (New York: Macmillan, 1949).
Li Fu-ch'un, cited.
World Politics, cited, pp. 258 and 260.

pressing are the questions of accessibility and quality. Many of the deposits are not accessible to inland waterways or railroads. At the same time, while aggregate coal reserves are abundant, China is rather short of high-quality coking coal; similarly, most of the known iron ore deposits are low in iron content.

It may be rather misleading, however, to look at the resource position of a country like China from too static a point of view. Within its vast territory, there are large areas that are either geologically unexplored or very superficially surveyed. Under the active campaign of geological exploration which is being carried on by the Chinese Communists, it is more than probable that current estimates based on presently known reserves may have to be revised upward in the future.

Power and transport, rather than mineral resources, are the most critical bottlenecks in the industrial development of mainland China. While China's present generating capacity exceeds that of the Soviet Union in 1928, this capacity is being taxed to the limit. On the other hand, transport is a much more critical factor in China than it was in the Soviet Union of 1928. The density of the Russian rail network was almost twice as great as that of China today. This is of particular importance since the Chinese rural economy is much less commercialized and more fragmented than was Russia's in 1928, making it that much more difficult for the planners in Peking to harness the resources of the countryside to the goal of industrialization.

In attempting to draw up a comparative balance sheet of the obstacles to and prospects for industrialization in Russia and China, a few additional factors ought to be mentioned. The general social and cultural climate, including the state of literacy and education and the development of skills, all tend to emphasize Russia's advantages. The same applies to the defense burdens borne by the two countries on the eve of their first Five-Year Plans. In 1928, only about 10 per cent of Soviet budgetary expenditures was channeled into defense, while the corresponding percentage for Communist China was 26 for 1952. This is to some extent offset by the drastic disruption of the Soviet economy which resulted from the ruthless and violent collectivization campaign during the first Five-Year Plan. Similarly, certain advantages are derived by China from the fact that the Soviet Union provides a model to follow. The pioneering, experimentation and "social engineering" for Communist planning, with all its attendant costs, have already been borne by the Soviet Union, and the latecomers in totalitarian development can benefit by this.

This comparison makes it plain that China has a much longer road to travel along the path of industrialization than was true for the Soviet Union and the barriers and obstacles on this road are greater, so that the pace of progress may be expected to be slower. It would be erroneous and dangerous, however, to conclude from this that the prospects for economic growth in China are negligible. In this context, the Japanese experience may be highly relevant. Meiji Japan, starting from roughly the same stage of backwardness as mainland China of 1952, and with a resource base that was certainly no more favorable, raised its national product by approximately twelve times in about sixty years, between 1880 and 1940.

The actual rate at which the Chinese Communist economy will be able to grow will depend to a considerable extent upon the country's ability to supplement its own limited capital, technical, and entrepreneurial resources through imports from abroad, and particularly from the Soviet Union. This is the problem that must now be explored at some length.

CHANGING STRUCTURE OF CHINA'S FOREIGN ECONOMIC
RELATIONS

In aggregate terms, foreign trade has never been of major importance for the Chinese economy. In 1936, for example, per capita imports and exports (including Manchuria) were smaller than for any other country. Probably at no time have imports or exports represented more than 5 per cent of national product. Foreign trade, none the less, has played a major role in bringing the closed, traditional economy of China at least partially within the purview of the world economy, thereby providing the impetus for the rise of a small factory industry in the Treaty Ports and in Manchuria.

The Prewar Pattern of Trade

In general terms, the pattern of China's pre-World War II foreign trade was typical of underdeveloped and slowly growing economies. A permanently adverse balance of trade, offset by foreign loans, foreign investments, and remittances from overseas Chinese, was based on an exchange of livestock products (i.e., eggs and egg products, hog bristles, hides and skins), oilseeds and vegetable oils, and some industrial raw materials (coal, some iron ore, tungsten), for foodstuffs (rice, wheat flour, sugar), textile raw materials and manufactures, other manufactures, petroleum and its products, chemicals, and machinery. Each of the three main economic regions had its distinctive role in foreign trade. On the basis of 1934-36 data, foreign trade turnover was much greater for Manchuria than for China proper.[8] With approximately 10 per cent of the total mainland territory and 7 per cent of its population, Manchuria provided 40 per cent of aggregate exports and absorbed a somewhat smaller share of total imports. In effect, Manchuria's per capita foreign trade was eight to nine times above the average for China proper.[9] In a sense this was but another index of the more advanced stage of development attained by Manchuria.

[8] The choice of a prewar year or years for reference and comparative purposes presents a real problem. For years after 1937 the trading pattern for China proper becomes greatly distorted because of the Japanese occupation of seaports and the general shrinkage of the area under Chinese government control. On the other hand, there were marked changes in the trading pattern of Manchuria between 1937 and 1943 under the impact of the Japanese-sponsored drive for industrialization.

[9] Cf. U.S. Bureau of Foreign and Domestic Commerce, *Foreign Commerce Yearbook 1937,* (Washington: GPO, 1938), pp. 289-97.

In some respects, however, there were significant structural similarities in the foreign trade of Manchuria and China proper. Thus, the bulk of exports consisted of agricultural products—foodstuffs and raw materials of agricultural origin—while the principal categories of imports were textiles and other manufactures, industrial raw materials, and capital goods. Yet, within these broad categories there were marked differences. Manchuria's trade was much more concentrated, particularly on the export side. Close to two-thirds of Manchuria's exports consisted of oilseeds and their products, mostly soybeans, bean cake and oil. In contrast, the exports of China proper were spread out over a much wider range of commodities, including tung oil, silk and silk products, fibers, tea, nonferrous metals, miscellaneous handicraft products (embroideries, lace, wool carpets, hair nets, etc.), and a wide variety of other items.

On the import side of the ledger, differences were much less marked as late as 1934-36. However, after 1937, with the launching of a more ambitious industrialization drive in Manchuria, the structure of its imports changed, with capital goods assuming a greater weight. Also, during 1934-36, almost a quarter of Manchuria's imports were textiles; the corresponding proportion for China proper was only 6 per cent. By that time China proper had developed a cotton textile industry almost large enough to satisfy domestic demand and even to export some coarse-quality products, with imports confined mostly to high-quality textiles. This was not the case for Manchuria, which the Japanese treated as a raw material and heavy industry base and a market for their textile exports. In effect, Japan was able to make up partially for the shrinkage of its textile market in China proper through expanding its exports to Manchuria.

Similar differences were typical of the direction of trade. Manchuria's exports and imports were largely confined to a few trading partners. It sent 70 per cent of its exports to Japan and took 45 per cent of its imports from that source. In the case of China proper, Japan's share was only about 15 per cent and was exceeded by the United States with a share of 22 to 23 per cent. On the other hand, trade with the Soviet Union was only about 1 per cent of the total for both regions, and with Eastern Europe it was even less.

Clearly, Japan played an important role in the trade of both regions. For the mainland as a whole, over one-third of average 1934-36 imports were derived from Japan and about one-fourth of total exports were directed there. From Japan's point of view, trade with the Chinese mainland was of major importance, since it provided a market for about one-fourth of its exports and served as the source for one-seventh of its imports.[10] Of the goods imported into Japan, all the soybeans and bean cake, most of the coal, about one-half of the pig iron, and one-third of salt and iron ore were obtained from the mainland. In turn, Japan's leading exports to the mainland were cotton textiles, machinery and factory equipment of all types, and chemicals. Vis-à-vis the mainland, Japan was a capital exporter, a creditor and investor; this role was reflected in its sizable export surplus, particularly in its trade with Manchuria. At the same time, Japan's position in the China market was to some extent dependent upon its political position on the mainland. In China proper, Japan had large investments, particularly in the textile industries; Manchuria, on the other hand, was not only a Japanese puppet state, but was included in the Yen bloc, a factor which enabled Japan to seal this market off from international competition.

The Redirection of Trade Since 1949

With the advent of the Chinese Communist regime, this entire pattern of trade was changed. The combined impact of Mao's "lean-to-one-side" policy, the free-world trade controls, and the requirements of the mainland industrial-

[10] All of these data are based on the *Foreign Commerce Yearbook 1937*, cited. They refer to Japan's trade with China proper, Manchuria, Kwantung, and Hong Kong.

ization program has necessarily resulted in redirecting China's foreign trade and changing its commodity composition. Mainland trade with what is now the Soviet bloc, negligible before the war, has assumed overwhelming importance since 1949. Between 1952 and 1954 about 60 per cent of China's total trade was with the Soviet bloc, as compared to less than 1 per cent before the war.[11] While published data concerning the foreign trade of Communist China are exceedingly scanty, it is possible, on the basis of certain assumptions, to estimate the total value of its trade, its distribution between the Soviet bloc and the free world, and that portion of trade for which the Soviet bloc serves only as an intermediary between China and the free world.

Mainland China's foreign trade turnover may be estimated from Chinese sources as shown in Table II.[12]

The conversion of Chinese currency figures into terms of U.S. dollars is a most hazardous operation. In the absence of detailed trade statistics and information concerning unit values in commodity trade, the choice of an appropriate exchange rate becomes a very difficult problem. Yet, a trade figure derived from Chinese data and then converted into U.S. dollars is less ambiguous than one based on other methods available. On the basis of the figure given in Table II and using the official exchange

11 In this and all subsequent contents the term "China" refers to the mainland, i.e., China proper and Manchuria.

12 Estimates of mainland China's foreign trade are most frequently based on the value of free-world trade with China, converted into U.S. dollars, and its share in total China trade. Data on trade between free-world countries and China are regularly compiled by United States government agencies—cf. *Soviet Deterrents to Increased Foreign Trade*, Mutual Defense Assistance Control Act of 1951, Seventh Report to Congress, Washington, D.C., 1956. These calculations rest on percentages derived from trade returns expressed in Chinese currency values but applied to data based on dollar valuation. The margin of error thus incurred may be further compounded by virtue of the fact that figures for trade between China and non-bloc countries leave out of account that portion of trade for which the Soviet Union or the East European satellites act as intermediaries. As an alternative, the value of China's foreign trade may be estimated from data based exclusively on Chinese statistics, i.e., on the procedure followed in Table II.

Table II

DIRECTION OF COMMUNIST CHINA'S FOREIGN TRADE
in trillions of old JMP[a]

Year	Total Trade[b]	Soviet Bloc[c]		Free World[c]	
		a.	b.	a.	b.
1950	28.8	7.5	7.5	21.3	21.3
1952	38.3	23.4	27.6	14.9	10.7
1953	52.1	30.1	39.1	22.0	13.0
1954	59.9*	38.9	47.9*	21.0*	12.0

* preliminary

(a) Jen Min Pi (People's Currency)
(b) Based on Chinese Communist indices for total trade; for original data
and sources see Appendix A.
(c) Chinese Communist publications present data for direction of trade in
two ways. On the one hand, they give for each year the share of total
trade with capitalist countries, people's democracies and the Soviet
Union; series b is based on these percentages. On the other hand, they
have also published an index of trade with the Soviet bloc only; series
a is derived from this index.

rate,[13] China's 1954 trade may be estimated at U.S. $2.4
billion, which is the figure that we shall work with in the
rest of this paper.[14]

[13] The official exchange rate is 24,620 JMP to the U.S. dollar, the average 1954 Hong Kong free market rate was 39,500 and the rate which the
Chinese Communists seem to use for investment planning is 31,280; the
latter can be derived from the Five-Year Plan investment figures given
both in terms of JMP and gold. The official rate may be overvalued; on
the other hand, the Hong Kong rate is possibly undervalued; it is based
on a very thin market and mostly serves to finance local traffic between
Canton and Hong Kong.

[14] It should be noted that an estimate based on the other method
would yield a much higher figure, namely U.S. $3.3 billion. This latter
estimate, incidentally, coincides fairly closely with a Chinese Communist
1954 trade figure which was released in 1955; according to a report, delivered by the Minister of Foreign Trade, Yeh Chi-chuang, to the National
People's Congress on July 29, 1955, this amounted to 84.87 trillion JMP
(old) or U.S. $3.45 billion at the official rate of exchange. It is difficult to
explain the discrepancy between this figure and the one given in Table
II; this may be due to differences in exchange rates used, or the higher
figure may include military imports from the Soviet Union obtained on
a loan or grant basis. In any case, a U.S. $3.3 to 3.4 billion figure does not
seem reasonable since it would presuppose that the volume of China's
foreign trade has increased by about 70 per cent as compared to prewar.

As the data in Table II show, after 1949 foreign trade expanded rapidly under the impact of economic recovery. Precisely what this expansion means in terms of volume and how it compares with the prewar level of trade it is difficult to say because of the difficulties inherent in any attempt to express trade values in terms of comparable prices. If we allow for a two-and-one-half-fold rise in the prices of goods moving in foreign trade between 1934-36 and 1954, the volume of turnover may have increased by about one-quarter, from 800 to about 1,000 million prewar dollars.[15]

No matter which series in Table II one uses, it is quite clear that, while China's trade with the Soviet bloc was growing constantly, its commerce with the free world either remained approximately stationary or declined between 1950 and 1954. This decline, however, was much more marked in series *b* than *a*. While this factor cannot be documented, there is a strong possibility that the discrepancy between the two series represents that portion of China's trade with non-Soviet areas which has been transacted via the Soviet bloc. On the basis of this assumption, it would seem that China's indirect trade with non-Soviet-bloc countries has constituted one-ninth to one-sixth of

From the little we know about 1954 export quantities for individual commodities, an expansion of such magnitude does not seem to be indicated. On the contrary, Yeh Chi-chuang, in the above-mentioned report to the National People's Congress, indicated that in 1954 "some of the principal export goods have not yet reached the prewar level of exports." For instance, in 1954 the tea exported by China was only 65 per cent of that of the 1936 level, while raw silk was only 32 per cent of the 1931 level; also, many native products have not recovered their prewar export levels.

15 A Chinese Communist source states that in calculating the country's export values a doubling of the price level between 1936 and 1950-51 should be assumed. (cf. Sung Shao-wen, "Achievements by the Chinese People in Economic Reconstruction for the Past Two Years," *Hsin Hua Yüeh Pao* (New China Monthly Gazette) (Peking), October 1951, p. 1300. On the other hand, Soviet estimates of the total foreign trade of the Soviet Union in 1953 seem to be based on an implicit deflator of 274, with 1938 =100. (cf. L. Bol'shakov, "Voprosy razvitiia vneshnei torgovli Sovetskogo Soiuza," *Planovoe Khoziaistvo*, n. 4, 1954, pp. 79-89.) At the same time, according to the *United Nations Monthly Bulletin of Statistics* for November 1954, the average price increase in total trade of the free world was 124 per cent between 1938 and 1953 (1938=100; 1953=224).

its total trade. Of course, this also means that the actual level of trade between free-world countries and China is higher than has been indicated in Western trade returns or claimed by the Chinese Communists.[16] This would imply that in 1954 one-third, not one-fifth, of China's foreign trade was with the free world. Actually, the incentives for these indirect transactions are quite strong. Strategic trade controls on traffic with China are considerably more stringent than those applicable to the Soviet Union or Eastern Europe. As a result, such goods are purchased by European Soviet-bloc countries on behalf of China, yet are reported in Western trade statistics as exports to those countries rather than to China. Similarly, payment restrictions, transport considerations, and existing trade channels and connections may make it easier and more expedient to ship goods from China to the West through the Soviet Union. However, as long as the controls applied to China trade remain more stringent and more comprehensive than those applied to other members of the Soviet bloc, one may reasonably assume that, in this entrepôt trade, exports to China exceed imports.

According to Western statistical reports, between 1951 and 1954 the free world had an import surplus in its trade with China.[17] Unfortunately, it is not possible to check this against Chinese trade returns, since partial breakdowns such as those given in Table II can only be obtained for total trade and not for imports and exports separately. However, as was noted before, Western trade data do not take account of the middleman role played by the

16 It is interesting to note that the official *Communiqué on National Economic Development and Fulfillment of the State Plan in 1953,* issued by the State Statistical Bureau of the Central People's Government on September 12, 1954, claims that "in 1953 our trade with the capitalist world registered an increase of 52 per cent compared with 1952." According to series *a* in Table II, the increase in free-world trade between 1952 and 1953 was 48 per cent, which is quite close to the percentage just cited; on the other hand, series *b* indicates a percentage rise of only about 20 per cent. This would tend to support strongly my hypothesis that series *a* approximates much more closely the distribution between Soviet-bloc and free-world trade.

17 Mutual Defense Assistance Control Act of 1951, cited, pp. 87-8.

Soviet bloc. To the extent that our assumption concerning this Soviet entrepôt trade is valid, it is perfectly possible or perhaps even probable that the exports from the free world shipped to the Soviet bloc but actually destined for China exceed the reverse flow to an extent sufficient to wipe out what appears to be an export surplus in China's trade with the free world.

Changes in Commodity Composition

Foreign trade provides the highway over which technology, know-how and equipment for industrialization can be and are imported into an underdeveloped area such as China. Therefore, even though foreign trade may appear to be comparatively small in relation to a country's total flow of goods and services, it is not unimportant. On the contrary, in dynamic terms it inevitably plays a key role as illustrated by the fact that in 1954 the foreign trade component in fixed capital formation was about 15 to 20 per cent in mainland China.[18] In other words, foreign trade provided between 15 and 20 per cent of the total investment required for Peking's industrialization program. This is a high proportion when one considers that basic construction costs are covered by local materials and manpower. Therefore, given its industrialization objective and its limited current capabilities for manufacturing complex capital goods, one of the regime's principal tasks is to find ways and means of translating internal savings (largely in the form of agricultural output) into expanding its capital goods imports. The pace of industrialization and the rate of economic growth will in large measure depend upon the extent to which this transformation can be effected.

The economic objectives of the regime have necessarily been reflected in changes in the commodity composition of its foreign trade, particularly in its imports. Imports of consumer goods have been drastically curtailed, while capital goods and raw materials imports have been signifi-

18 For the basis of this estimate see Appendix B.

cantly stepped up. More specifically, imports of foods and textiles were largely displaced by mineral oils, chemicals, machinery and metals, and industrial raw materials, especially rubber and raw cotton. All these trends were already evident by 1950, the first full year of the new regime, and the only year for which we have detailed data. However, in some respects the picture which emerges for that year, as shown in Appendix B, is a misleading one. Raw cotton imports, for example, were particularly high that year, since domestic cotton production had not yet recovered, while the revival of the textile industry had a high priority. In effect, imports of raw cotton were traded for finished textile imports. However, as domestic raw cotton production recovered, imports of cotton declined, so that by 1953 and 1954 only comparatively small quantities of it were purchased abroad. The foreign exchange proceeds thus saved were diverted to imports of machinery and metals, which assumed a growing importance.

Changes in the structure of exports have been much less marked than in the case of imports. Mainland China has continued to base its export trade on foodstuffs, raw materials of agricultural origin, and mineral products. Most important among these are soybeans and products, which accounted for 25 to 30 per cent of total mainland exports. No wonder the Chinese Communist press is replete with exhortations to increase the production of oilseeds, which as of 1953 had not yet attained the prewar level.[19] Other major export products of continuing importance are tung oil, hog bristles and to some extent grains. The continuance of grain exports is not so surprising as it might appear at first glance, particularly if one considers their modest proportions. Before the war, China exported some coarse grains, mostly from Manchuria, and imported appreciably larger quantities of food grains. Those imports were largely destined for the Treaty Ports and were primarily a function of high costs of inland

[19] According to an editorial entitled "Strive for a Balanced Supply and Demand of Edible Oils," *Ta Kung Pao* (Official Gazette) (Tientsin), June 24, 1954, edible oil output had just reached over 80 per cent of the peak level.

transportation and inefficient domestic distribution. They constituted a very small proportion of total production and marketings, as do postwar exports.[20] Thus the margin between net grain imports and exports is quite narrow, and really depends upon the quality of the harvest in any one year and the efficiency of the system of distribution.

COMPLEMENTARITIES AND STRAINS IN SINO-SOVIET
ECONOMIC RELATIONS

Since China's trade has been so strongly channeled toward the Soviet Union and the rest of the Soviet bloc, what are the considerations that govern the level of trade between the Soviet Union and China? Are political or economic factors the primary determinants? Or, to put it in other words, what would be the level of trade if purely economic factors were the governing ones? How far does their trade deviate from the purely economic norm, and what strains, if any, does this impose upon Sino-Soviet relations? While these questions cannot be answered as precisely as we would like, an attempt will be made to analyze some of the variables bearing upon these issues.

The level of trade between China and the Soviet Union is determined basically by China's import needs and its ability to provide exports, and by Russia's capacity to absorb China's exports and to meet its needs for imports. Each of these factors must be considered briefly before we attempt to analyze the terms of trade and the extent of Soviet assistance to China's industrialization.

China's Import Requirements Under the Impact of Forced-Draft Industrialization

Chinese Communist commercial policy, as we have seen, aims to minimize imports of consumer goods, while maxi-

---

[20] According to Chinese Communist sources, average grain exports between 1950 and 1953 were about one and a half million tons; this is about 1 per cent of total cereals output and not more than 2 per cent of grain entering marketing channels. cf. Chen Yun's report on "Planned Supply and Planned Marketing of Commodities," at the September 23 Session of National People's Congress, NCNA (Peking), September 23, 1954.

mizing purchases of capital goods and essential raw materials for which domestic supplies are inadequate. This emphasis upon capital goods imports is best illustrated by the fact that the 156 projects or industrial units which are to be equipped by Soviet industry constitute the very core of the Five-Year Plan. The attainment of all major industrial targets depends on their completion. The share of capital goods in total imports can, however, be determined only approximately, since precise data on the commodity composition of China's trade are lacking for recent years.

On the basis of scattered and qualitative information, it may be estimated roughly that capital goods represented as much as two-thirds of total 1954 imports.[21] These capital imports in turn comprised between 15 and 20 per cent of the fixed capital invested during that year.[22] This is a high proportion, indeed, particularly if one considers that inevitably the costs for local labor and construction materials comprise a large share of total fixed investment. It is most unlikely that capital goods imports can be reduced in the near future. On the contrary, owing to the long gestation periods needed for capital projects amid rising levels of investment, the foreign trade component of capital formation may actually rise before it begins to decline. The same may be assumed to be true of industrial raw materials, which accounted for an estimated 20 per cent of China's imports in 1954. The latter consisted mostly of crude rubber, fertilizers, chemicals, petroleum and petroleum products, and some raw cotton. Consumer goods constituted the smallest share of 1954 imports, probably around 15 per cent. It may be assumed that this category of imports will be expanded slightly to keep pace with population growth and urbanization, but without allowing for an increase in per capita standards. Generally, in the face of strategic trade controls, it seems to be Chinese

21 See Appendix B; this undoubtedly included some military imports.
22 This percentage is based on actual capital expenditures as given in the officially published government budget data. This type of investment data was published for 1953 and 1954; at the same time planned investment figures were published for 1955 and for the Five-Year Plan period as a whole, i.e., 1953-57.

Communist policy to place primary reliance upon free-world countries for imports of consumer goods and of those raw materials and capital goods that are not embargoed.

A survey of the various categories of imports makes it clear that the preponderant share of China's purchases in the Soviet Union were products of industry. Therefore, in effect, it fell upon one sector of the Soviet economy to provide China with about U.S. $550 million worth of goods in 1954.

China's Export Capacity

In practice, China's import requirements are a function of its capacity to save, invest and grow. The higher the rate of saving and investment on the one hand and the rate of economic growth on the other, the greater, presumably, will be both the import requirements and the capacity to export. Viewed in this context, the capacity to export is a function of the over-all level and rate of saving. In the Chinese case, this specifically involves saving (not consuming) a portion of agricultural output so that it can be transformed into exports and thus into capital goods imports and finally into further domestic capital formation.

China's 1954 imports, as shown above, may be estimated at approximately U.S. $1.2 billion. Chinese Communist statements indicate that exports were largely made up of the same types of goods as in the past. Thus, some 60 to 70 per cent of 1954 exports were presumably of agricultural origin. In effect, agricultural products valued at around U.S. $780 million were shipped abroad, and these shipments may have to be stepped up in the near future as the process of industrial development gains momentum.

At the same time China's agriculture is called upon to meet other increasing commitments. It must feed a population that is growing at a rate of between 1 and 2 per cent a year, and it must meet the needs of a rapidly expanding urban population. These three demands combined are to be met during the Five-Year Plan period by increasing the output of food crops by 17.6 per cent, and of various fibers and other industrial crops by appreciably larger percentages.[23] And this is to be accomplished with a minimum investment in agriculture. Forestry, water conservation and agriculture have been allotted only 7.6 per cent of total Plan investment.

The policy which has set these agricultural targets clearly aims at maintaining China's self-sufficiency in foodstuffs and conserving foreign exchange by actually reducing the imports of sugar and raw cotton, while simultaneously expanding the exports of other industrial crops. The principal food staples of the population—rice and wheat—will continue to remain marginal items in China's exports, for the planned production rise, if realized, would barely serve to relieve current food shortages. These shortages are but symptoms of more fundamental strains which have characterized Chinese agriculture since 1952. In part they have been occasioned by a succession of poor harvests in 1953 and 1954. They have also been aggravated by rising commitments which have chronically tended to exceed the supplies actually available. As a result, the regime has been compelled to step up the pressure on the peasantry, to accelerate the drive for collectivization, and to introduce compulsory delivery programs for all the more important commercial crops. More recently, it has introduced food-rationing, both in cities and in food-deficit rural areas, as a means of curbing consumption.

In the face of these strains and the rising requirements of the Five-Year Plan, Peking's agricultural targets appear quite modest. Yet, given the small investments contemplated by the Plan and the lack of incentives for the peasant to work harder and produce more, these goals are most ambitious. As a matter of fact, in this as in so many other

23 cf. Li Fu-ch'un, *Report on the First Five-Year Plan for the Development of the National Economy*, submitted to the Second Meeting of the First National People's Congress, July 5 and 6, 1955. Li's *Report* gives the following targets for raising the output of industrial crops: cotton—25.4 per cent; jute and ambary hemp—19.7 per cent; cured tobacco—76.6 per cent; sugar cane—85.1 per cent; sugar beet—346.4 per cent; oil-bearing crops—37.8 per cent.

respects, the Chinese pattern duplicates that of other Communist economies: agricultural targets are low in relation to industrial goals but high in terms of the inputs contemplated; in turn, just because the planned inputs are low and incentives weak, agriculture is the sector in which, even with modest targets, the Plan usually remains underfulfilled.[24]

In the light of these problems, it is doubtful that Chinese agriculture will be able to go on playing the same central role in financing imports as it has in the past. Peking's policies may lead to a situation in which rising import requirements will have to be financed either by securing increased aid from outside or by expanding the export of nonagricultural goods. For this, perhaps the most promising possibilities are offered by coal and nonferrous metals, which accounted for about 10 per cent of prewar exports. If the Plan's very ambitious target for coal is met, there should be a greater export margin available for export, even allowing for the growing domestic requirements. Whether this margin will prove sufficient to make good a possible shortfall in agricultural exports is strictly in the realm of surmise.

In effect, this analysis points to increasing difficulties for China in meeting its export commitments during the next few years. However, given the character of the regime and its economic objectives, exports will inevitably have a very high priority. They offer the only means for assuring a continuous flow of capital equipment to industry, and particularly to the capital goods sector. Should the cloth fail to fit the suit, it is the consumer segment of the economy that is likely to be squeezed, while the regime may be expected to bend every effort toward meeting its export commitments. This policy may be expected to prevail regardless of whether China's trading partners are the free world or the Soviet bloc, unless Communist China should gain access to new sources of foreign assistance.

24 For a more detailed analysis of the factors that affect the demand for, and the supply of agricultural products in China, see Rostow and others, cited, pp. 265-74.

The Soviet Union as a Market for China's Produce

So far we have been examining the basis for Sino-Soviet trade from the perspective of the Chinese economy. We have explored China's import requirements for industrialization and its capacity to finance these imports from the proceeds of its exports. We have not yet addressed ourselves to the question whether, even if China can increase the supplies it has available for export, it will be able to dispose of them. Can China find ready markets for its products, particularly in the Soviet Union, which has become its principal supplier?

On purely economic grounds, the basis for trade between China and the Soviet Union appears a quite modest one. Viewed in broad terms, Chinese and Soviet resources are competitive rather than complementary. Like China, the Soviet Union is still largely an importer of capital goods and an exporter of farm products, minerals and industrial raw materials, so that the trade flows of the two countries parallel rather than complement one another. Yet, if we break down this broad picture somewhat further, we find that, while imports of machinery and metals loomed very large in prewar Soviet imports—accounting for about 55 to 70 per cent of the total in 1935-37—the Soviet Union also imported a variety of commodities that have been and are still among China's principal export products.

In Table III an attempt is made to measure the relative importance of the principal products which China has traditionally exported in comparison with prewar Soviet imports of these same products. Although China is currently exporting these types of goods to the Soviet Union, the absence of Soviet and Chinese trade statistics makes it impossible to provide a parallel table for recent years. In any case, for our needs the prewar comparisons may be more meaningful since in recent years the much higher level of Sino-Soviet trade reflects the noneconomic pressures which increasingly determine its volume and content. On the other hand, given the structural transformations

Table III

COMPARATIVE QUANTITIES OF CERTAIN TYPES OF PRODUCE
EXPORTED BY CHINA AND IMPORTED BY THE SOVIET UNION
BEFORE WORLD WAR II [a]

Commodity	Unit	China's Exports	Soviet Imports
Tea	ooo lb	90,000	41,000
Sausage casings	ooo lb	6,300	500
Hogs, live	number	350,000	100,000
Hides & skins	ooo U.S. $	5,233[b]	2,834[b]
Wool, new or washed	ooo lb	37,000	60,000
Tungsten	metric tons	4,933[c]	4,350[c]
Tin	metric tons	22,000[d]	8,000[d]

(a) In most cases data represent 1934-36 averages, with some items referring to 1935-36, 1934-38, and 1934-37. In addition to the commodities listed in the table, the following items are currently exported from China to the Soviet Union: rice, meat, oilseeds, vegetable oils, fruits, tobacco, hog bristles, silk—raw and tissues—and jute.

(b) These two are not strictly comparable, partly because the hides and skins may not be of the same type and partly because exports are f.o.b. while imports are c.i.f.

(c) Refers to 1946; 1934-36 exports from China were 6,300 MT, while Soviet imports were 3,450 MT in 1935 and 2,200 MT in 1937.

(d) Not strictly comparable since the export figure refers to ingots and slabs, while the import figure is for ore.

Source: U.S. Bureau of Foreign and Domestic Commerce, Foreign Commerce Yearbook, for 1937 and 1948, cited; D. B. Shimkin, Minerals, a Key to Soviet Power (Cambridge, Mass.: Harvard University Press, 1953), pp. 85-6 and p. 131.

which occurred in the Soviet economy between 1937 and 1954, it is quite possible and even probable that, in any case, Russia's import demand for the consumer goods and raw materials now supplied by China would have risen.

The Soviet Union of 1937 could have provided, in theory, a major outlet for most of the Chinese export products listed in Table III. Yet, the value of the actual Soviet imports in these categories, regardless of their source, constituted no more than 5 per cent, by value, of China's total exports.[25] Even if we allow for an underesti-

25 This may be something of an understatement since there was a variety of minor Soviet imports which are lumped together into a "miscellaneous" category and therefore cannot be taken into account.

mate of Soviet imports of 1937 and for an increase in Soviet import demand since then, it is doubtful that the Soviet Union would normally have provided a market for more than 15 to 20 per cent of total Chinese exports by 1952-54. Actually, during these recent years, the Soviet share of China's exports has been far higher, as a matter of fact, between two and three times higher.

In effect, about all this shows is that there is some physical basis for trade between China and the U.S.S.R. China exports some commodities for which there is a Soviet import demand. However, this does not yet tell us anything about the comparative cost conditions under which this trade is carried on. Can this trade be justified on economic as well as physical grounds? Or, to pose the question in another way, what are the comparative demand-supply relationships in the two countries for each other's exports and imports? To answer these questions in detail would be very difficult in the face of numerous statistical gaps and complexities. However, an attempt must be made to face up to these issues briefly in analytical if not in quantitative terms.

The bulk of Chinese exports, as we have seen, consists of consumer goods and raw materials for use in light consumer goods industries. These are, in large measure, commodities which stand low on the Soviet planners' scale of preferences, even though, potentially, they might enjoy a much higher priority in the eyes of the individual consumer. An entirely different situation confronts Chinese products in Western markets, where the actual, not only the potential, demand for them is quite high. Furthermore, apart from these considerations, the Soviet Union may be able to obtain many of these same goods, or close substitutes for them, from areas which are much closer at hand and from which transport costs are therefore lower.

Looking at the other side of the ledger for a moment, as of 1953 and 1954 the Soviet Union was still a net importer of capital equipment,[26] the very type of goods

26 cf. United Nations, Economic Commission for Europe, *Economic Survey of Europe in 1954* (Geneva, 1955), Table 67, p. 118.

which rate high on the Soviet planners' order of preferences. Thus, in a general way Soviet commitments to
export capital goods to China were directly competitive
with domestic demands in the Soviet Union and with the
demands of some of its East European satellites. This, of
course, does not exclude the possibility that the demand
intensity for specific types of equipment may vary between
China, the Soviet Union and the satellites. Yet this variation in needs probably alleviates the strain only to a
limited degree. While the Soviet Union exports certain
kinds of capital goods to Eastern Europe, it also obtains
many other types of machinery and metal products from
them. As a matter of fact, on balance the Soviet Union
imports more capital goods from its satellites in Eastern
Europe than it exports to them. Exactly the reverse situation applies to Soviet trade with China, for here capital
goods move only in one direction. Thus, from a Soviet
point of view these capital equipment exports may be assumed to be quite burdensome. This of course is not at all
the case from China's vantage point, and yet factors of
distance, transport and relative cost may operate in such
a way that China would be better off if it could import
capital goods from other sources.

It would appear from this analysis that a high level of
trade between China and the Soviet Union is disadvantageous for both trading partners. In the absence of free-
world trade controls, both partners could probably obtain
many of their imports from other sources at lower cost,
while they could find better markets for their exports.
Where the net disadvantage lies depends, of course, upon
the actual terms of trade between the two countries, a
problem that will be explored below. However, on the
basis of the considerations sketched above, a high level of
trade between these two countries seems to be much more
artificial from a Soviet than from a Chinese point of view.
One possible reflection of this situation is found in the
frequent reports of Soviet sales of Chinese produce in
West European markets at prices appreciably below Hong
Kong quotations. Regardless of who ultimately bears the

costs of this "dumping," the fact alone would tend to point to a glut of Chinese products in Soviet markets.

Soviet Export Capacity

According to United Nations estimates, about one-fifth of total Soviet trade was with Communist China, so that the latter has become Russia's most important trading partner.[27] What is the impact of this comparatively high level of trade upon the Soviet economy, and more particularly upon Soviet industry? More specifically, to what extent is Soviet industry capable of satisfying China's import requirements, at levels which the Chinese are able to finance, without jeopardizing the domestic commitments and plans of the Soviet Union itself?

According to the estimates presented above,[28] Communist China's 1954 imports from the Soviet Union may be valued at about U.S. $550 million, and the bulk of them —about U.S. $410 million—were capital goods. Assuming that the burden of these capital goods exports fell exclusively upon the Soviet engineering and metals industries, shipments to China may have absorbed about 1.5 to 2.5 per cent of total Soviet output and a slightly lower percentage of total supplies (i.e., domestic output plus net imports).[29] While there are no data on Soviet military aid to China, it is probable that military aid shipments are not included in the estimated capital goods figure; if these are included, the Chinese share in Soviet output may be more appropriately estimated at from 2 to 4 per cent. At the same time, Soviet capital goods exports to China may be considered as possibly equivalent to about 2 per cent of total annual Soviet investments at home.

In relation to either heavy industry output or total in-

27 cf. *Economic Survey of Europe in 1954*, cited, Table 64, p. 113, and data in Appendix B converted into U.S. dollars at the official rate of exchange.

28 See above, pp. 75-7.

29 Based on rough estimate of gross output for metals and engineering industries of U.S. $16-28 billion at 1953 prices. For derivation of these estimates see Appendix D.

vestment, Soviet capital goods exports to China do not seem to represent a critical drain upon Soviet resources or commitments. On the other hand, neither can these shipments be considered a negligible factor, either in over-all resource or structural terms. Actually, the figure of 2 per cent of the investment total may represent a considerable burden for the Soviet Union, particularly if one considers that the Soviet range of choice in allocating investments to sectors other than heavy industry is a rather narrow one. Moreover, in the absence of more detailed statistics, we cannot exclude the possibility that the pressure and strains engendered by Soviet exports to China may be concentrated upon specific and critical bottleneck items which are in great demand in all areas of the bloc.[30]

Although capital goods exports to China may account only for a relatively small proportion of Soviet output, we must not assume that, other things being equal, these are the types of goods the Soviet Union would actually choose to export. From the Soviet planners' point of view, an exchange of Soviet capital goods for foodstuffs and other consumer goods results in bartering high-priority items against commodities which have a far lower priority in their eyes. In economic terms, this could be justified in either or both of two ways. Russia could charge higher than world prices for its exports and pay lower than world prices for its imports from China. Or, if imports from China released Soviet resources that otherwise would have been channeled into food and consumer goods production, Russia could then use these resources to expand its capital goods and other industries in which it has an advantage over China. In reality, Sino-Soviet trade relations are, of course, not governed exclusively or perhaps even primarily by economic considerations. Even if its expanded trade with China should prove to be disadvantageous to the Soviet Union, Moscow may conclude that the political

<hr />

30 In this analysis, foreign trade between China and Eastern Europe, with its possible effects upon the satellite economies, has been left out of account.

gains to be reaped outweigh the economic losses which must be absorbed in the process.

The Terms of Trade

On the basis of our explorations thus far, it is apparent that China's demand for Soviet exports is likely to be much more inelastic than the Soviet demand for Chinese products. China's imports from the Soviet Union are highly strategic to the fulfillment of its industrialization program, whereas Soviet imports of Chinese products are more or less peripheral for the economy of the U.S.S.R. Furthermore, because of the effects of free-world trade controls, China is almost completely dependent upon the Soviet bloc for its imports of capital goods and of certain industrial raw materials. The Soviet Union, on the other hand, can obtain livestock products, tea, oilseeds, and so forth from other countries in exchange for gold or for those raw materials that are in surplus in the Soviet Union. In other words, Russia can obtain elsewhere as much of these products as it needs without exporting capital goods which are required for Soviet-bloc development. In the face of this situation, on purely economic grounds and leaving aside any political bargaining or exploitation, we would expect the terms of trade to be highly unfavorable to China.

There are, of course, no published statistics for Sino-Soviet trade, nor any detailed data concerning the prices or other terms on which that trade is carried on. Chinese Communist authorities have released only a few barter ratios affecting a limited range of commodities, and, unfortunately, much of this information is vague; many of the commodity items mentioned, such as hides, are far from homogeneous and vary widely in quality. Were it not for these factors of uncertainty, it ought to be possible, on the basis of these sample ratios, at least to approximate the terms of trade, by ranging them against comparable ratios as calculated for the trade of Hong Kong. Theoretically, if trade between China and the Soviet Union is carried on at world prices, the published ratios should more or less correspond to those that emerge from a comparison of unit values of Hong Kong imports from China with those of goods imported into Hong Kong for resale to mainland China. Yet, because of the lack of homogeneity, a comparison can be calculated with a satisfactory degree of confidence only for the three ratios presented in Table IV.

Table IV

1953 BARTER TERMS OF TRADE OF SELECTED COMMODITIES, HONG KONG COMPARED WITH COMMUNIST CHINA

	Barter Terms of Trade	
Commodities	China	Hong Kong[c]
Cottonseed Oil—Fertilizer	1:5[a]	1:4.1
Raw Silk—Fertilizer	1:160[b]	1:134
Raw Silk—Steel	1:94[b]	1:80

(a) cf. "Chia-ch'iang fu-shih-p'in sheng-ch'an ho kung-ying kung-tso" (Strengthen the Work of Producing and Supplying Subsidiary Foodstuffs), editorial in *Jen Min Jih Pao* (People's Daily) (Peking), April 18, 1954.

(b) *Ching-chi Tao Pao* (Economic Bulletin) (Hong Kong), n. 19 (May 23, 1955), p. 18.

(c) For the basis of the Hong Kong computations see Appendix C.

The data available for constructing Table IV are so limited in scope that it is obviously difficult to draw any far-reaching conclusions from them. However, it is interesting to note that in all three cases the Hong Kong ratios were somewhat lower than the ratios applied in Sino-Soviet exchanges, the difference ranging from 10 to 20 per cent. This corresponds to our expectations based on a more general analysis of the factors involved, and tends to indicate that the terms under which Sino-Soviet trade is carried on are less favorable for China than those it could command in trade with the free world. If mainland China's trade with the Soviet Union were conducted in Hong Kong at world prices, Peking could perhaps have acquired 5 to 10 per cent more imports in exchange for the same amount of exports.

On the other hand, the divergence between the two sets

of ratios is so modest that, in and by itself, it provides no indication that the Soviet Union is "exploiting" China.[31] The same impression is gained by studying various other types of scattered evidence, too numerous and detailed to present here. In effect, then, if the terms of trade are actually adverse from China's point of view, this is more likely to reflect relative scarcity relationships in the two countries, rather than the deliberate use of superior Soviet bargaining power to gain an economic advantage.[32]

SOVIET AID TO CHINA

Our information is particularly incomplete and confusing with respect to this aspect of Sino-Soviet relations. The basis for Soviet economic aid and, in general, for the new and intimate economic ties that have subsequently developed, was laid down by the treaties and agreements signed on February 14, 1950. In larger terms, economic relations between the U.S.S.R. and Communist China were to be cemented in four ways: trade, aid, technical assistance, and the organization of joint-stock companies. Sino-Soviet trade has been analyzed in preceding sections. Apart from trade, what have been the level and character of Soviet aid to China?

Soviet aid. The 1950 agreements provided for a five-year Soviet loan to China of U.S. $300 million, at a 1 per cent nominal rate of interest, to be repaid in ten annual installments in the form of raw materials, tea, gold and American dollars. The first payment was to be made not later than December 31, 1954. It can thus be assumed that for three years, from 1950 to the end of 1952, Soviet aid to China was being advanced on the basis of this loan, at a level of $60 million a year. In the course of 1952, as preparations were being made for China's first Five-Year Plan, a high-level Chinese delegation spent about eight months in the

31 In the sense that it reaps unusually high, i.e., monopoly profits, by selling very "dear" and/or buying very "cheap."
32 This is not meant to suggest that Soviet bargaining power may not actually be superior, but merely that, if it is, the Soviets choose not to exercise it in this field.

Soviet Union, apparently for the purpose of negotiating, bargaining and securing additional aid.[33] The upshot was a new Protocol to the 1950 loan agreement and a series of dramatic announcements concerning new Soviet aid. Moscow promised its assistance for the construction or renovation of 91 new enterprises and 50 enterprises already in the process of building or rehabilitation. Apparently, the 50 enterprises fell within the purview of the original 1950 agreement, while the 91 enterprises represented a new obligation. However, it was rather obscure as to how these new Soviet commitments were to be financed. It is not clear whether they involved an upward revision of the annual loan of $60 million, or only an expansion of Sino-Soviet trade, with increased equipment deliveries to be financed by rising exports from China.

A new series of accords, presumably designed to replace the 1950 loan agreement which was about to expire, was announced on October 11, 1954.[34] These provide for a new long-term credit of 520 million rubles, or U.S. $130 million at the official rate of exchange. Unlike the original agreement of 1950, the information released concerning these new arrangements is extremely vague. There is no indication as to what "long-term" means in this context; whether it refers to the period over which the loan is to be used or to the period of repayment. Therefore, we do not know what the annual credits under this new loan actually amount to.

However, since the new loan was tied to the financing of additional equipment for the 141 enterprises referred to above—i.e., additional in the sense that it was to be over-and-above that envisaged in the 1953 announcement

33 Li Fu-ch'un, then Vice Chairman of the CPG Committee on Economics and Finance and now Chairman of the Planning Commission, went to Moscow with Chou En-lai on August 17, 1952, and stayed there until May 1953; Yeh Chi-chuang, heading a Chinese trade delegation, stayed in Moscow from November 1952 until June 1953. cf. H. L. Boorman, "Chronology of Sino-Soviet Relations," U.S. Information Agency, *Problems of Communism*, v. 3, n. 3 (Washington: GPO, 1954), pp. 14-21.
34 Text of the Soviet-Chinese Communist Communiqué on Seven Accords, *New York Times*, October 12, 1954.

—and to providing equipment for another 15 enterprises, and since the construction of these enterprises was to be completed by 1959, it may be surmised that the new loan also extends up to that year, thus covering a period of five years. If we accept this hypothesis, the loan of 1954 would involve an annual obligation of only U.S. $26 million. In this connection, it is worth noting that the new line of credit was announced at a time when the last installment of the 1950 loan (U.S. $60 million), and the first repayment of U.S. $30 million, were due. Therefore, on the face of it, the credits granted with so much fanfare in 1954 do not quite cover the installments due on the old loan, much less provide for the financing of future Chinese trade deficits. This view is reinforced by repeated Soviet and Chinese Communist claims that their trade is "basically in balance."

On the other side of the ledger, Peking's 1954 accounts for government expenditures show a Soviet aid item for that year equivalent to U.S. $500 million.[35] This was an unanticipated item, inasmuch as it did not appear in the original budget plan for 1954. Similarly, the 1955 budget refers to Soviet credits, but without giving their magnitude. According to the report on the budget, this item represented the proceeds of a loan incurred by the Chinese in payment for military material which was turned over to them upon the Soviet withdrawal from the Port Arthur naval base in May 1955. These two bits of information, combined with the evidence adduced above, tend to suggest that in recent years Soviet loans or grants-in-aid to China have been largely confined to financing military deliveries, while capital goods imports are largely financed on a barter basis.

Joint-stock companies. In effect there have been five joint-stock companies operating in Communist China.

[35] This information is not provided directly. However, the Minister of Finance, Li Hsien-nien, in his 1955 budget report to the July 6 session of the National People's Congress cited figures from which the Soviet credit for that year can be easily computed. Apparently it totaled about 1.22 billion new yuan which, converted at the official rate of exchange, amounted to about U.S. $500 million.

Two of these—the Chinese Changchun railway and the Dairen shipyards—were going enterprises prior to the Communist take-over, while three others—for air transport between China and the Soviet Union, for extraction of petroleum and for mining of nonferrous and rare metals in Sinkiang—were organized in consequence of the agreements of February 14, 1950. In the case of the first two companies, the Soviet Union's contribution was represented by Japanese shares and holdings which had been expropriated by its occupation authorities in Manchuria. This arrangement paralleled closely the pattern established in the East European satellites, where the Soviet share in the joint-stock companies was based on expropriated German assets. The situation was different with respect to the other three companies. They were much more based on a genuine partnership, with the Soviet government providing the capital goods, such as planes and oil-drilling and mining equipment, and the Chinese furnishing labor and materials for local construction.

These differences were also reflected in the manner in which the enterprises were liquidated. In accord with the 1950 agreements, the Chinese Changchun railway was returned free of compensation to Chinese management on January 1, 1953. In contrast, the other companies were turned over only two years later, with the Chinese assuming an obligation for the Soviet investment share, this obligation to be paid off over a number of years. Neither the total amount of compensation nor the size of the annual payments has been announced.

While the Sino-Soviet joint-stock companies bore a strong family resemblance to those imposed on Eastern Europe, there were also some important differences. In the Chinese case, there was the fact of real, tangible Soviet investments as compared to preponderantly fictitious paper contributions in the case of the satellites.[36] Except for the Chinese Changchun railway, which represented, historically, a very special case, these companies were of

36 An important exception to this is represented by the substantial Soviet investments in the Rumanian oil industry.

marginal and peripheral importance for the Chinese economy. In some of the satellites, on the other hand, particularly Rumania and Hungary, they served as prime instruments for Soviet economic penetration and subjugation.

Technical assistance. Given the acute scarcity of trained technical, managerial and even ideological skills, technical assistance has been of first-rate importance in the Sino-Soviet economic relationship. It constitutes one of the essential prerequisites for the successful implementation of the Chinese Communist industrialization program in general, and, in particular, of the first Five-Year Plan. This is true not only in the narrow technical sense, as exemplified by assistance in plant design, construction, and operation, but also in the broader field, the philosophy and policy of economic development.

Broadly speaking, the Chinese Communists have taken over the Soviet industrialization blueprint with some local adaptations, particularly in the field of agrarian policy. However, not only have the goals and objectives been imported, but in many cases the means of execution as well. This is particularly true, for example, of methods of accounting at all levels—enterprise, industry, and national banking policy and control, monetary management, budgeting, and also, increasingly, in taxation policy.

Importation of Soviet techniques of management both in the economy and in individual plants necessarily led to importing Soviet advisers—military experts, engineers, and administrators. The available evidence indicates that, unlike the case of the satellites, these advisers do not exercise any management or control functions. This does not mean that Soviet advisers cannot and do not exert considerable influence, but it is a more subtle and indirect one than that which has been exerted by their counterparts in Eastern Europe.

STRATEGIC TRADE CONTROLS

Even in the absence of free-world trade controls, the direction and structure of Soviet-bloc trade would differ radically from the prewar pattern. Both political considerations and bloc industrialization programs work in this same direction. These changes are particularly evident in the case of the East European satellites, where the character of planning and the pattern of investment allocation have led to agricultural stagnation, marked by the failure to attain, much less exceed, prewar levels of farm output. In turn, these structural transformations have tended to undermine the traditional basis of trade between Eastern and Western Europe.

Structural changes have been fostered and reinforced partly by the reorientation of postwar trade, but this shift has been in part a result of the new industrialization programs. However, the greatly increased postwar trade between the Soviet Union and Eastern Europe has also been governed by other considerations. Foreign trade has served as one of the instruments for Soviet penetration of the satellites; it has been partly designed to render Eastern Europe economically dependent upon the Soviet Union. It is no wonder that, whereas Eastern Europe's trade with the Soviet Union was negligible before the war, by 1948, at a time when there were as yet no trade controls, almost one-quarter of total satellite exports were being channeled to the U.S.S.R.[37]

Somewhat similar patterns may be observed in the evolution of China's foreign trade. Here too, the new economic programs, with their marked emphasis upon industrialization, are inevitably reflected in the changing structure of foreign trade. As noted earlier, this great shift has thus far been much more marked on the import than the export side of the ledger. Even this more limited transformation has far-reaching implications for the direction of China's trade, and particularly for the future of its trade with Japan. At the same time, political considerations, such as

[37] *Economic Survey of Europe in 1954,* cited, Table 63, p. iii.

China's "lean-to-one-side policy" and probably a Soviet determination to assure at least some degree of economic dependence by China, have made for a comparatively high level of trade between the two new allies. Thus, as early as 1950, when strategic trade controls were not yet being enforced on any significant scale, one-quarter of China's trade was being carried on with the Soviet Union.

It would of course be very difficult to assign any precise quantitative weight to the impact of controls upon the direction of China's trade. However, on the basis of the evidence adduced thus far, it may be stated almost categorically that a lifting of trade controls would lead to a relative reduction in Sino-Soviet or Sino-bloc trade and to a corresponding increase in China's trade with non-Communist countries.[38] Even under these circumstances, Sino-Soviet trade is not likely to return to the very low prewar level. Probably it would not fall below the 25 per cent of total China trade which it had attained in 1950, prior to the enforcement of trade controls. This would naturally tend to limit, at least to some extent, the possible scope of exchanges between China and the non-Communist world.

The special problem of Japan. The future outlook for Sino-Japanese trade is of crucial significance. Before the war, trade between the two countries was of major importance for both.[39] In recent years it has dwindled to negligible proportions. In 1954 only about 1 per cent[40] of Japan's total trade was carried on with China, as compared to a prewar share of approximately 20 per cent. Postwar balance-of-payments problems combined with strong

[38] This may become less and less true in the long run as structural transformations within the mainland economy lead to marked changes in the commodity composition of China's exports.

[39] cf. above, p. 68.

[40] cf. United Nations, Economic Commission for Asia and the Far East, *Economic Survey of Asia and the Far East, 1954* (Bangkok, 1955), pp. 136 and 205. Based on figures in *Japanese Economic Statistics* of January 1956 of the Economic Planning Board of the Japanese government, about 2½ per cent of Japan's trade was with China in 1955. Generally, Japan's trade with China seems to have reached its low point in 1952, and has been slowly expanding since then.

emotional and political considerations have generated in Japan potent pressures for increasing trade with China, and the whole question has taken on an importance far beyond its economic significance. To the Japanese it seems to represent a symbol of their lack of full sovereignty in an area of decision-making which they consider critical. In discussing this problem with Japanese government officials, economists and businessmen, one almost gains the impression that to them the future of their China trade constitutes an act of religious faith. They seem to believe that somehow it will provide the key to solve Japan's postwar trading difficulties, opening a vast export market and providing a cheap source of raw material, so that the costs of industrial production can be reduced and Japan's exports rendered competitive in world markets.

In Japan there seems to be comparatively slight recognition of the fact that Japan's prewar trade with China was based on a unique convergence of economic and political power factors. The Japanese had large investments in China proper and Manchuria. Manchuria was completely under their political and economic control, and the mainland as a whole was a major market for Japanese exports, particularly textiles, and an important supplier of foodstuffs and some industrial raw materials. Actually, if Manchuria had not been included in the Yen bloc and had not been in a position of political dependence, its trade with Japan would have been at an appreciably lower level.

Of even greater importance perhaps are the economic consequences of the Communist conquest of China. The whole Chinese Communist development program is focused upon maximizing the rate of industrial growth, with primary accent upon rapid expansion of the producer goods branches of manufacture, combined with a drive for autarky in the consumer goods sector. With this in view, Chinese Communist planners have assigned a high priority to a marked increase in raw cotton and cotton textile production.[41] This expansion of domestic textile production

41 Raw cotton output is to be raised by 25.4 per cent and cotton textile

coupled with a high rate of forced saving and a policy of keeping consumption in check has already led to a virtual cessation of cotton textile imports. The textile industry is, however, the one that has borne the brunt of Japan's postwar trading difficulties. In 1953, textile exports were less than one-third of the 1934-36 level, while shipments of machinery and transport equipment had practically attained the prewar volume.[42] Of course, since over one-half of Japan's prewar exports were in textiles and only about 15 per cent in machinery and metals, the drastic curtailment of textile exports accounts for a large share of the postwar shrinkage in total exports.

The year 1955 may have marked a turning point in the postwar recovery of the Japanese economy. It was a year during which the textile industry continued to stagnate, but this was more than counterbalanced by a marked expansion of the metals, engineering and chemicals industries. Even more striking was the rise in the exports of these industries, a factor which contributed very appreciably to narrowing the trade gap.[43] These developments suggest that the Japanese economy has finally begun to respond to the need for a far-reaching restructuring imposed by the shifts in postwar trading patterns. It is exactly the type of economic transformation that is conducive to a broadening of the base for Sino-Japanese trade.[44] While it is doubtful that Japan can count on the Chinese mainland as an outlet for its depressed textile industry, the situation is quite different in respect to metal products, machinery and transport equipment. Thus, there is no question but that, with an expansion of its capital goods industries and a redirection of its trade in capital goods,

production by 50 per cent between 1952 and 1957. cf. Li Fu-ch'un, *Report on the First Five-Year Plan for the Development of National Economy*, cited.

[42] *Economic Survey of Asia and the Far East, 1954*, cited, Table 9, p. 215.

[43] Japan had a trade deficit of about U.S. $800 million in 1954, which was cut by about 40 per cent in 1955.

[44] That is a broadening in relation to the recent past and not as compared to prewar trade; also based on an assumed removal of trade controls.

Japan could satisfy a part of China's capital goods require-ments. On the other hand, to the extent that Japan can continue to expand its capital goods exports, it may have less need for the Chinese market.

One of the economic dilemmas facing Japan is that one of the preconditions for maintaining high rates of invest-ment and of expansion of domestic production is a high rate of imports. From this point of view, the problem of securing access to low-cost raw material imports assumes particular urgency and prompts Japanese businessmen to turn covetous glances in China's direction. Before the war, the Chinese mainland was a major supplier of soybeans and bean products, coal, pig iron, iron ore, and salt to the Japanese market. Since the war most of these products have had to be obtained from more distant sources at a somewhat higher cost.

One of the first questions that needs to be posed is whether mainland China would be able to provide Japan with these raw materials at prewar levels, in view of the restructuring of internal demand in China. In this con-nection perhaps a distinction ought to be made between soybeans and salt, on the one hand, and the raw materials for industry, on the other hand. Soybeans, for instance, have continued to be exported in appreciable quantities in recent years, mostly to the Soviet Union. Yet, it is questionable whether Communist China, even with a con-siderable redirection of trade following a relaxation of controls, would be able to ship prewar quantities to Japan. According to official Chinese Communist statements, oil-seed production in 1954 was still below prewar. At the same time, with a rapidly growing population and a greater emphasis placed upon the need to increase soil fer-tility, domestic bean and bean cake requirements may be expected to rise.

These considerations apply with even greater force to industrial raw materials and semimanufactures. In the early 1940's about one-half of the pig iron produced in Manchuria was exported to Japan. While there have been some shipments to the Soviet Union even in recent years, one may safely surmise that the great bulk of pig iron now produced in China will actually be consumed by the local steel industry. The same may hold true for iron ore, unless important new deposits are discovered and brought into use. At the same time, if Communist China comes anywhere near meeting the Five-Year production targets for coal, it may possibly have a substantial surplus for export.

A weighing of all the factors involved tends to indicate that the basis of trade between China and Japan has been greatly narrowed, as compared to the situation that prevailed prior to 1945. It is not intended to suggest that trade between the two countries could not or would not expand in the absence of controls. It is merely designed to show that such increases may be expected to fall considerably short of Japanese hopes. While a reactivation of Sino-Japanese trade may help to alleviate Japan's trading and balance-of-payments difficulties, it is not likely to be the magic key to a solution of Japan's economic problems.

What about the position of China in this relationship? Are there in China parallel pressures for trade with Japan? In recent years China's trade has been carried on preponderantly with the Soviet bloc, and this has been a high-cost type of trade, from the standpoint of both partners. In a sense, this is a cost imposed upon the bloc by free-world trade controls. On purely economic grounds, removal of trade barriers should lead to a marked reorientation of China's trade, with new markets being sought in Japan. However, this need not lead to a similar expansion of imports from that country, not only because of the limited capacity of Japan to provide China with capital goods, but even more perhaps because Japan is also a high-cost producer of such goods.

In analyzing the outlook for Sino-Japanese trade, it would be misleading to ignore political considerations which may affect markedly the terms under which trade is carried on between the two countries. The Chinese, in particular, may be prepared to sacrifice economic for political advantages. Viewed in these terms, increased trade with Japan may serve a double purpose: it could be used as an instrument for making Japan increasingly dependent upon China—first, economically and, later, also politically —and at the same time it might make China less dependent upon the Soviet Union—likewise, at first economically and then politically.

Relative gains or losses in the maintenance of trade controls. The maintenance of strategic and related trade controls entails some economic loss for all concerned: the United States, the free world as a whole, the Soviet Union and its satellites, and China. A quantitative assessment of these losses would involve great conceptual and statistical difficulties and, in any case, lies outside the scope of this study. Nevertheless, some tentative and qualitative conclusions can be drawn.

In over-all resource terms, the net loss resulting from a reduction in trade through the enforcement of controls may be considered as quite small for both sides, though it is possibly greater for the Soviet bloc than for the free world as a whole. However, the Soviet bloc, with its relatively greater capital scarcities, may be considered as a greater loser because free-world controls make it somewhat more difficult than would otherwise be the case to acquire some types of capital equipment freely or promptly. Yet there is a real question as to how much effect all this may have on the military capabilities of the Soviet Union or the bloc as a whole.[45]

Granting that strategic trade controls may have a more adverse economic effect upon the Soviet bloc than upon the free world does not of course mean that all countries or areas within the two camps are affected equally. Their effect upon the United States may be negligible, while upon Japan, Hong Kong, Burma and Ceylon it may be

[45] The problem involved can perhaps best be illustrated with the aid of a hypothetical example. Let us suppose that trade controls deprive the Soviet bloc of certain capital goods and raw materials so that as a result the military output of the bloc will be reduced by 1 per cent, while the loss in trade for the free world is so minimal and involves such commodity categories that it has no measurable effect on military capabilities. Thus the difference in the degree of loss involved is very great but the level of loss is so small in either case that it does not make much difference.

quite appreciable. These very differences in their economic impact give rise to one of the chief complications which beset the whole field of trade controls. In the United States these measures are mostly considered as an inexpensive yet fairly effective foreign policy instrument. Among our allies, and even more in the uncommitted areas, they enjoy varying degrees of unpopularity. While trade controls may appear to be cheap in economic terms, they may be quite costly, politically, to the United States.

Similarly, trade controls are bound to have a greater effect upon China than upon the Soviet Union. Under the pressure of trade controls, China has to depend largely upon the Soviet Union for its supplies of capital goods and military material. This economic dependence inevitably narrows China's capacity to pursue an independent policy. At the same time this may also involve economic losses for China, arising from the adverse terms of trade. For example, on the basis of the tentative data in Table IV, it may be estimated that China's 1953 and 1954 exports could have purchased perhaps 5 to 10 per cent more imports if it had been free to trade with all countries.

The commitment to satisfy China's capital goods requirements imposes something of a drain upon Soviet industrial and investment resources. However, the burden thus incurred seems to be of rather modest dimensions. Moreover, the diversion of capital goods to China may involve no more than some sacrifice of domestic capacity and agricultural production, food processing and light industry, and replacement of this potential output by imports from China. From a Soviet point of view, even if this process of substitution were to involve some loss in economic terms, this may be more than compensated by possible political gains which Moscow can reap from China's economic dependence upon the Soviet Union.

SOME IMPLICATIONS FOR UNITED STATES POLICY

In recent years, trade between China and the Soviet Union has been at a much higher level than would seem to be rational or justified from a purely economic point of view. This high level of trade may be considered a consequence of the Sino-Soviet alliance, on the one hand, and of free-world trade controls, on the other. Trade at present levels appears to be economically disadvantageous to both partners, possibly more so to the Soviet Union than to China.

The differences in the degree of the resulting disadvantage for each may be equalized by the terms of trade, which appear to be adverse from China's point of view. This adversity, however, may be an expression of the differing demand-supply relationships in the two countries, rather than a result of superior Soviet bargaining power or Soviet "exploitation" of China. While the latter possibility cannot be ruled out, the degree of adversity shown by the very scanty data could be explained on economic grounds alone. In order to demonstrate that there is actual "exploitation," the terms of trade would have to be much more unfavorable than those which have become known to us.

At the same time, the level and rate of capital formation and the fulfillment of China's entire investment program depend to a large extent upon Soviet deliveries of capital goods and upon Soviet technical assistance. In spite of this, there is no evidence to indicate that the economic plans of the two countries are being purposefully integrated or closely coordinated, except for whatever degree of integration may be attained through foreign trade. While these deliveries of capital goods to China may be said to compete with domestic and other Soviet-bloc commitments, the burden thus imposed upon Soviet industry would appear to be of rather modest proportions.

In the light of this analysis, it may be assumed that a removal of trade barriers and controls would lead to a reduction in Sino-Soviet trade and a corresponding expansion in China's trade with non-Communist countries. The structure of trade emerging from a postembargo situation would depend upon both economic and political considerations, as may be illustrated in the case of

Japan. In economic terms, the basis of trade between Japan and China has been greatly narrowed, as compared with the prewar situation. At the same time, however, there is room for a considerable expansion beyond current levels. While such expansion can be expected to contribute to a solution of Japan's postwar trading and balance-of-payments difficulties, this contribution is likely to be much more modest than is generally envisaged in Japan.

What are the policy implications that emerge from these findings? Assuming that one of our foreign policy objectives is to introduce and foster possible strains in the Sino-Soviet alliance, can this best be accomplished through a policy of "pushing them together" or "pulling them apart?" What contribution can economic measures make toward the pursuit of one or another of these foreign policy paths?

This problem can be examined from three different but closely related points of view. What are likely to be the effects of economic measures upon the economic and political strains within the Soviet bloc? Upon the capability of the Communist powers for aggression? And upon the general state of world tension?

In reality trade controls have been primarily designed to limit or restrain Soviet-bloc capabilities for aggression. There is, however, another school of thought that sees in trade controls a means of aggravating the economic and, consequently, the political strains within the Soviet bloc in general and within the Sino-Soviet alliance, in particular. Accordingly, the embargoes are viewed as a means of implementing the policy of "pushing them together." It is believed that, with China pursuing an ambitious and far-reaching industrialization program, one which requires large capital goods imports, the Soviet leaders will inevitably be faced with an increasingly critical problem of allocating their producers' goods and military output among Soviet, satellite and Chinese Communist needs. With the Chinese pressing ever harder, such a policy may be expected to reduce bloc capabilities, while at the same time straining Sino-Soviet relations, possibly even to the breaking point.

On the other hand, some view the growing economic interdependence between China and the Soviet Union as adverse to American interests. In this view, such interdependence serves to emphasize the mutuality of Sino-Soviet interests and goals and therefore tends to strengthen the alliance between these two Communist partners. Adherents of this school would like to pursue a policy of "pulling them apart," and they advocate the lifting of trade embargoes as a means of accomplishing this objective. In this latter conception there lurks an implicit assumption that it is to the interest of the United States to encourage mainland China to pursue a policy that is or may become more or less independent of that of the Soviet Union.

We need to examine carefully and more explicitly whether Communist China, left to its own devices, may not be actually more aggressive and a greater threat to world peace than one allied with the Soviet Union. There is a real question whether irrational, xenophobic, and nationalist ingredients are not much more potent in the Chinese Communist revolution than in the Soviet leadership of today. The Chinese Communist regime bears many earmarks of aggressive youth. Chinese Communism operates within a different cultural and social context, and also in an economy and a political milieu that is at a much earlier stage of development than the relatively much more highly industrialized Soviet Union. Under such circumstances, situations could conceivably arise in which the Soviet Union would have much more to lose in an armed conflict than would China. Marx's slogan, "Proletarians of the world arise, you have nothing to lose but your chains," may still apply to Communist China but not to the Soviet Union. It can be argued that the Soviet Union may be potentially the more responsible of the two partners, the one which might serve to curb aggressive moves by Communist China for fear that such moves might involve the Soviet Union itself in an all-out armed conflict.

However this may be, both schools of thought—those who advocate "pushing them together" and those who favor trying to "pull them apart"—proceed from the implicit or explicit assumption that trade embargoes do, in fact, tend appreciably to reduce Soviet, Chinese and bloc resource availabilities. On the other hand, the preceding analysis points to the conclusion that trade controls, embargoes and similar economic measures represent rather ineffective and insensitive instruments for implementing these objectives. In and of themselves, these measures can hardly be expected either to induce a collapse of the Chinese Communist regime, to impose critical strains upon Soviet industry and the Soviet economy, or to result in a rupture of the Sino-Soviet alliance.

At the same time, even from the little we know, it is clear that the Chinese Communists would have liked to receive more economic assistance from the Soviet Union than Moscow has been or is ready to extend. The Chinese are presumably more impatient about the pace of their industrialization program than are their Soviet partners. Also, from China's point of view, the maintenance of trade controls is disadvantageous in both political and economic terms. On the other hand, the Soviet Union may derive certain political advantages from this policy, even though it imposes upon it an economic burden, however slight.

From a Soviet point of view, the ideal situation theoretically, might be one in which all controls and barriers upon Soviet foreign trade were removed, while a total blockade continues to be maintained by the free world against China. This, of course, would mean maximum dependence for China with minimum strain for the U.S.S.R. However, in evaluating the possible weight which can be assigned to this source of actual or potential friction, it is necessary to consider the alternatives that face Communist Russia and China, linked not only by economic, but also by ideological and power bonds, in seeking to achieve their broadest political goals. In this wider context, the divergence of their economic interests may pale into insignificance.

APPENDIX A

DERIVATION OF TABLE II

(a) *Total Trade*

The total trade figures are based on a calculation of the 1950 trade total in terms of Chinese currency, to which were then applied the annual indices of total trade based on 1950. 1950 trade value could be derived from the following sources:

Hsin Hua Yüeh Pao (New China Monthly Gazette) (Peking), April 1951.
Jen Min Shou Ts'e (People's Handbook) (Shanghai, 1952), p. 293.
Yang Po, "Hsin Chung-kuo ti hai-kuan cheng-ts'e yu tui-wai mao-i cheng-ts'e" (New China's Customs Policy and Foreign Trade Policy) in *Chung-kuo ching-chi lun-wen hsüan,* 1950 (Selected Chinese Economic Essays in 1950), v. 6 (Peking, 1951), pp. 140-46.

These sources gave the monthly indices (with January 1950 = 100) for total trade, imports and exports. At the same time, they gave the monthly percentage of trade surplus or deficit as related to monthly exports or imports as the case may be, as well as the ratio of imports to exports for the year as a whole. Most important, however, one can find a value for total trade for the first six months of 1950; applying to this figure the various percentages and indices, 1950 trade values could be computed with a considerable degree of reliability.

For subsequent years, there are no data available in similar detail. However, the following total trade indices were published (1950 = 100):

Year	Index
1952	133
1953	181
1954	208

Sources: "Communiqué of the State Statistical Bureau on Results of the 1953 State Plans," *Hsin Hua Yüeh Pao* (New China Monthly Gazette) (Peking), n. 10 (1954), p. 226.
Li Che-jen: "Our Foreign Trade in the Past Five Years," *Ta Kung Pao* (Official Gazette) (Tientsien), October 6, 1954.
Ching Chi Tao Pao (Economic Bulletin) (Hong Kong), January 10, 1955, p. 7.

(b) *Direction of Trade*

Table A

DIRECTION OF CHINA'S TOTAL TRADE [1]

in percentages

Year	Soviet Union	People's Democracies	Total Soviet Bloc	Free World	Total
1950	23.3	3.9	26	74	100
1951	38.8	14.6	61	39	100
1952	53.4	18.6	72	28	100
1953	56.0	19.0	75	25	100
1954	n.a.	n.a.	80	20	100

[1] These are all based on officially published data: series *b* in Table II is derived from these percentages.

Sources: Yeh Chi-chuang, "Three Years of China's Foreign Trade," *New China's Economic Achievements* (Peking, 1952), p. 238.

People's China (Peking), n. 12 (1953), p. 15; n. 19 (1953), p. 15; n. 6 (1955), p. 43.

"Communiqué of State Statistical Bureau on Results of 1953 State Plans," *Hsin Hua Yüeh Pao* (New China Monthly Gazette) (Peking), n. 10 (1954), p. 226.

NCNA, February 11, 1955.

Ta Kung Pao (Official Gazette) (Tientsin), November 8, 1954.

M. I. Sladkovskii, *Ocherki razvitiia vneshne-ekonomicheskikh otnoshenii Kitaia* (Moscow, 1953), pp. 279-80.

On the other hand Li Che-jen, in an article on "Fraternal Economic Cooperation" in *China Reconstructs* (Shanghai), v. 4, n. 8 (August 1955), pp. 6-9, gives the following indices for China's trade with the Soviet bloc (1950=100):

Year	Index
1951	255
1952	312
1953	409
1954	519

APPENDIX B

ESTIMATED COMMODITY COMPOSITION OF CHINA'S FOREIGN TRADE

Table B

COMMODITY COMPOSITION OF MAINLAND CHINA'S
FOREIGN TRADE [a]

in percentages [b]

Exports

	1936	*1937*	*1950*
Products of Agriculture	*56.4*	*57.2*	*67.3*
Livestock products	12.2	12.9	17.9
Grains	3.1	2.2	3.5
Oilseeds and products	26.1	26.8	26.1
Tung oil	6.4	6.7	7.0
Other crop products (tea, tobacco, fruits and vegetables)	3.4	3.1	4.6
Raw fibers, incl. wool and silk	5.2	5.5	8.2
Minerals and Metals	*8.0*	*10.7*	*5.3*
Coal	3.2	3.0	1.2
Iron, steel and products	1.7	1.7	1.5
Other metals	3.1	6.0	2.6
Other Products	*35.6*	*32.1*	*27.4*

Imports

	1936	*1937*	*1950*
Foodstuffs	*12.7*	*11.8*	*3.0*
Grain and products	4.1	3.7	1.0
Sugar	3.2	2.5	2.0
Other food, drink and tobacco	5.4	5.6	negl.
Raw materials	*6.4*	*5.0*	*29.5*
Cotton, raw	3.3	2.5	18.0

(a) For 1936 and 1937 the trade between China and Manchuria and China and Kwantung leased territory is included in the data; this, of course, involves a certain amount of double counting.

(b) For 1950 the official customs returns give the value of imports and exports only in percentages with items accounting for less than 1 per cent omitted.

Source: "Economic Development in Mainland China, 1949-53," United Nations, ECAFE, *Economic Bulletin for Asia and the Far East,* v. 4, n. 3 (November 1953), pp. 17-31.

(Table B continued)

Imports

	1936	*1937*	*1950*
Rubber, crude	0.6	0.5	11.5
Timber	2.5	2.0	negl.
Mineral oils	*5.9*	*6.5*	*8.4*
Chemicals	*5.3*	*5.6*	*10.3*
Machinery and Metals	*25.9*	*27.9*	*29.1*
Machinery	5.6	6.5	8.3
Vehicles, vessels and parts	6.6	5.8	6.2
Metals	8.8	11.0	13.1
Misc. metal manufactures	4.9	4.6	1.5
Manufactured Consumer Goods	*20.1*	*20.8*	*2.5*
Textiles	14.4	14.5	negl.
Other	5.7	6.3	2.5
Other Products	*23.7*	*22.4*	*17.2*

ESTIMATED COMMODITY COMPOSITION OF CHINA'S IMPORTS
IN 1954

These estimates are based on the following data and assumptions:

(a) As brought out in the text of the paper, all indications point to the absence of appreciable Soviet economic assistance. On the basis of this, reinforced by repeated Soviet and Chinese Communist claims that mainland China's trade is in balance, we have in fact assumed that there was no trade deficit in 1954, if military assistance is excluded.

(b) We have assumed throughout the paper that the trade figures do not include military imports financed on a grant-in-aid or loan basis.

(c) According to Chinese Communist press statements in 1953 and 1954, 13 per cent of total imports were consumers' goods (Li Che-jen: "Our Foreign Trade in the Past Five Years," *Ta Kung Pao,* Tientsin, October 6, 1954; *Economic Bulletin,* Hong Kong, February 14, 1955, p. 10). Moreover, 3 per cent of China's imports from the Soviet Union and 12.3 per cent of the imports from the People's Democracies were consumers' goods.

(d) Chinese Communist sources also state that of total P.D.

(People's Democracies) imports into China, 74.6 per cent were capital goods and 13.14 per cent were raw materials (*Jen Min Jih Pao,* Peking, August 13, 1953). It was assumed that this import composition remained unchanged between 1953 and 1954. It was also assumed that Soviet imports of capital goods constituted the same proportion of total Soviet imports as those for the P.D. With a 3 per cent figure given for Soviet imports of consumers' goods, raw materials were estimated as a residual proportion of 22 per cent. In reality, capital goods imports are probably less than these percentages would indicate since they undoubtedly include those military items that are financed from Chinese foreign exchange proceeds.

(e) Free-world imports were derived on the basis of (1) the percentage shares as calculated from Western exports to China and (2) the assumption that imports obtained via the Soviet-bloc entrepôt route were all capital goods.

On the basis of these data and assumptions the following table was constructed:

Table C

ESTIMATED COMMODITY COMPOSITION OF CHINA'S IMPORTS
IN 1954

in trillions of old JMP and in per cent

	Capital Goods		Raw Materials		Consumer Goods		Total	
	Amt.	Prct.	Amt.	Prct.	Amt.	Prct.	Amt.	Prct.
Soviet Union	10.21	75	3.00	22	0.41	3	13.62	100
People's Democracies	4.37	75	0.76	13	0.70	12	5.83	100
Free World	5.00	48	2.35	22	3.15	30	10.50	100
Total	19.58	65	6.11	20	4.26	15	29.95	100

According to official Chinese Communist releases, 1954 investment in fixed capital was 86.86 trillion old JMP (Li Hsien-nien's Report to the July 6 session of the 1st National People's Congress on *1954 Final Accounts and the 1955 Budget*). Assuming that the capital goods category as computed in Table C consisted actually of investment goods only, this would constitute 22.5 per cent of the fixed capital formation figure. However this must be viewed as an upper limit since, more than probably, capital goods imports included some military items.

APPENDIX C

DERIVATION OF TERMS OF TRADE IN TABLE IV

As was indicated in the text and in the footnotes to the Table, the China ratios were given as such in published sources, while the Hong Kong ratios were calculated on the basis of Hong Kong unit import values. These calculations were based on data given in (a) the *Far Eastern Economic Review* (Hong Kong); more specifically in the Trade Supplement to that journal, v. 18, n. 1 (January 27, 1955), (b) in the United Nations *Commodity Trade Statistics,* Series D, v. 4, n. 3 (January–December 1953), and (c) in *Ching-chi Nien Pao* (Economic Yearbook), 1954 (Hong Kong, 1954), p. 137. However, in some cases it was not possible to obtain unit import values. Thus, the calculations for raw silk are based on the average 1953 wholesale price of Canton 20/22 silk in Hong Kong. A 15 per cent deduction was made from this price on the assumption that this represented the trade mark-up.

For steel the average European export price for steel bars was used (cf. United Nations, *Economic Bulletin for Europe,* v. 6, n. 2, First Quarter 1954, p. 98), and to this was added an estimate for transport, freight and unloading costs based on an ECE study of *European Steel Exports and Steel Demand in Non-European Countries,* Geneva, 1951, p. 51.

APPENDIX D

DERIVATION OF ESTIMATED METALS AND ENGINEERING OUTPUT IN THE SOVIET UNION IN 1954

The point of departure for these estimates was provided by Professor Alexander Gerschenkron's calculations of a dollar index for Soviet heavy industry: cf. *Review of Economics and Statistics*, v. 37, n. 2 (May 1955), pp. 120-30. Proceeding from the 1937 output estimates for machinery and for iron and steel expressed in terms of gross 1939 values adjusted for incomplete coverage of machinery output (Table 5), it was assumed that: (a) output in the two industries continued to grow at the average 1928/29-1937 rate up to 1940, (b) by 1948 output had recovered to the 1940 level, and (c) between 1948 and 1954 the prewar rate of growth had been resumed. The 1954 output figures were then converted into 1954 dollars by use of the producers goods component of the U.S. wholesale price index. On this basis, the 1954 output of the iron and steel industry would be 8,740 million U.S. dollars and of the machinery industry 18,960 million, yielding a total of 27,700 million.

At the same time, an alternative calculation was made based on the rate of growth in the physical output of steel on the one hand and machine tools on the other. (cf. Economic Commission for Europe, *Economic Survey of Europe for 1954*, Geneva, 1955, Appendix Table 54, pp. 262-63.) These data show for steel a rate of increase of 2.5 times and for machine tools of 2.9 times between 1937 and 1954, as compared to approximately 4.5 times according to calculations based on the Gerschenkron rates. Thus, estimates based on physical rates of growth yield a 1954 output value for the two industries combined of 16,410 million U.S. dollars.

CHAPTER THREE

IDEOLOGY AND THE SINO-SOVIET ALLIANCE

by Benjamin Schwartz

FEW WILL QUARREL with the notion that economic and power factors play an important role in Sino-Soviet relations. Many observers, however, tend to deprecate the role of ideology in shaping these relations. The assertion that ideology has played and will continue to play a leading role in this partnership is, of course, part of a larger assumption that ideology has played a significant role in the history of Communism in general. Since this proposition is rejected by many, any attempt to deal with the role of ideology in Sino-Soviet relations should be preceded by an expression of views on the larger question.

THE ROLE OF IDEOLOGY: THREE VIEWS

In the prolonged and complex discussion of this subject over the past decade, the outlines of three overriding points of view can be discerned, at the risk of some oversimplification: the monistic ideological approach, the sociological approach, and the power approach. Perhaps no one view fits neatly into any of these three categories, and within the confines of each of these approaches there have arisen contending schools of thought. Nevertheless, the use of these categories is convenient for purposes of analysis.

The advocates of the monistic ideological approach tend to see in the history of Communism simply the implementation in practice of the ideas of Marx and Lenin. Lenin, Stalin and Mao have simply carried into practice the blueprints of Karl Marx. Like the Communists themselves, those who uphold this approach are inclined to accept the view that Lenin, Stalin (at least until his recent denigration) and Mao have simply "extended and applied" Marx's teachings. For them, there is no problem of the relation of doctrine to practice. They may, to be sure, see in Lenin and Stalin the admixture of certain elements of Russian thought. In any case, however, the development of the Communist world is to be explained in terms of a monolithic Communist religion which directs and informs the actions of its leaders.

In their interpretation of Sino-Soviet relations, supporters of this approach simply point to the Communist religion, shared by the Chinese Communist and Soviet rulers. The common bonds of faith are sufficient to explain the present nature of the alliance and to insure its endurance in the future. Tensions of power, nationalism, differences in historic background, are all outweighed and will continue to be outweighed by the ideological bond. The façade of complete harmony which we find in official writings is to be taken at face value.

The advocates of the sociological approach may differ among themselves in their accounts of the origins of Communist totalitarianism. Some of them may concede that ideology played some role in the beginning. Some of them may insist that the modern Russian social system (as well as the Chinese) is simply the projection into the present of the "oriental" society of the past, while some may explain Communism as the result of the confrontation of economically backward societies with the highly industrialized societies of the West. Whatever their differences on the question of genesis, they all tend to agree that Communist totalitarian society as "a going concern" is held together by iron relations of sociological interdependence and that the vicissitudes of ideology have little to do with the development of the system.

In explaining the evolution of Sino-Soviet relations, the advocates of the sociological approach tend to emphasize the growing basic similarities of social structure in the Soviet Union and in Communist China. They point to the role of the Communist party in both societies, to the emergence of a ruling class of *apparatchiki* in both societies. They point to the totalitarian controls established in both societies and to the present appropriation by the Chinese Communists of the basic Stalinist model of economic development. Indeed at the present time the Chinese Communists seem more genuinely committed to the Stalinist pattern of economic development than even the more stalwart of the Eastern European satellites (although some hesitations and vacillations on this score were manifested at the Chinese Communist Party Congress in September 1956). In general, the sociological approach would insist that, to the extent that the social structures of China and the Soviet Union can be considered identical in all essential respects, the two states can be expected to work together for their common goals in world politics.

Advocates of the power approach emphasize the power interests of ruling groups as the determining factor in both internal and external affairs. The totalitarian social system did not develop spontaneously or inevitably. Over the course of its history the Soviet leadership has confronted numerous situations to which it might have responded by courses of action different from those which it chose. However, the decisions of the ruling groups have been largely motivated by the desire to maximize and make secure their own power within the Communist world and in the world as a whole. All the decisions of the leaders can be explained in terms of the priority of power, and totalitarianism is the consequence of their highly successful efforts. Again, according to this view, the vicissitudes of ideology, as such, play no dynamic role in shaping the course of events.

In dealing with Sino-Soviet relations some of the advocates of this approach are inclined to explain Sino-Soviet relations in terms of direct organizational control of the Chinese Communist government by the Kremlin. Those who reject this explanation and doubt the existence of direct control tend, of course, to stress the shared power interests of Communist China and the Soviet Union. It is not difficult to itemize a list of such common interests. Communist China and the Soviet Union probably share an interest in ejecting American influence from Asia in general, and from Japan in particular. They probably both desire to see Vietnam and Korea drawn completely into the Communist orbit. On the side of factors which tend to bind Peking to Moscow, it has been urged by some that a relatively weak China cannot afford to be hostile to a powerful Soviet Union with which it shares an exposed border several thousand miles long. Finally, since Mao's promulgation of the policy of "leaning to one side," China has become increasingly dependent on the Soviet Union for economic and military support. All these power factors taken together are, from this point of view, sufficient to explain and predict the nature of the Sino-Soviet alliance.

While the ideological approach in its monistic form seems oversimplified, the evolution of ideology has, in fact, played a crucial role in shaping events within the Communist world. It is possible to assert both that the general tendency has been toward the disintegration of Marxist-Leninist ideology and that ideology has continued to be of basic importance even in its process of disintegration. One may accept without reservation the contention that, ever since Lenin began to use Marxism as a "guide to action," whenever actual circumstances have contradicted some basic point of doctrine, the doctrine has either been discarded as being unessential or has passed over from the category of an operational concept to the status of an empty verbal formula while some new "theoretical analysis" has been spun to rationalize the situation. With Lenin, the notion that the inexorable forces of the mode of production would themselves lead the workers to emancipate themselves; that the economic situation of the workers would directly create in them a proper Socialist mentality; that capitalism would collapse at its highest point of development; that the bourgeois revolution would be led by the bourgeoisie—all these commonly accepted Marxist notions were simply discarded when they ran athwart the exigencies of current political demands. Lenin was, of course, extremely resourceful in devising new "theoretical analyses" to account for these and other shifts. Later, when the notion that a Socialist revolution in backward Russia must be accompanied by a proletarian revolution in the West had ceased to have operational consequences, the theory of "socialism in one country" was devised to plaster over this decay in doctrine.

In spite of this steady decay, elements of ideology have continued to shape the Communist world in complex and subtle ways, and on many levels. If it is, indeed, a fact that the ideology has been disintegrating, this is in itself a fact of enormous consequences. The image which leaps to mind is that of a retreating glacier flowing into the sea. Huge chunks of the glacier fall off. The glacier, however, continues to flow and to shape the terrain over which it flows. The fact that the ideology is disintegrating does not preclude the possibility that residual elements of ideology continue to shape the world image of Communist ruling groups. It does not mean that these groups are indifferent to the process of decay or can ever afford to be indifferent even from the point of view of the power which they exercise or claim.

One of the difficulties is that the term "an ideology" suggests an organic, synthetic whole. Before it underwent its Leninist transformation, Marxism did, indeed, constitute a grandiose, albeit unstable, synthesis of nineteenth-century strands of thought. As Professor Gerschenkron states the dilemma, "it is tempting to suggest that in a very real sense the advent of the Bolsheviks to power spelled the end of Marxist ideology." [1] If he simply means that

[1] Ernest J. Simmons, ed., *Continuity and Change in Russian and Soviet Thought* (Cambridge, Mass.: Harvard University Press, 1955), p. 106.

Marxism as an architectonic structure was destroyed, one might be inclined to agree. If he means that elements and combinations of elements drawn from the Marxist-Leninist complex of ideas have not continued to shape the Communist world, this would seem to be serious over-simplification. After all, in the course of his own manipulations of doctrine, Lenin himself developed a derivative or secondary body of doctrine of his own, which subsequently came to form a part of the orthodoxy under the name of Leninism. Thus, in considering the role of ideology in the Communist world, it is by no means sufficient to compare the texts of Marx with Soviet or Chinese realities. The mediating doctrines of Lenin must also be considered.

Even today elements of the Marxist-Leninist complex may still form part of the genuine belief-world of both the Soviet and Chinese Communist ruling groups. It is entirely conceivable that they still believe that in some fashion "History" is inevitably on their side; that in some fashion they ultimately embody the interests of the masses of mankind, because their power is based on a "socialized" economy; that "capitalism" [2] is doomed to destruction; and so forth. There is, of course, nothing in such beliefs which would contradict the power interest of these groups. On the contrary, such beliefs would add energy and *élan* to their power aspirations.

Leaving aside, however, the treacherous question concerning the subjective beliefs of the leaders, there still remains the question of the role of ideology within the power complex itself.

Thus, in studying the Communist party as a political organism, it is possible to conceive of the party in the abstract as a sort of power machine which can operate independently of the state of mind of those who participate in it. Once one begins to study the party in the concrete, however, one speedily discovers that ideas concerning the

2 Until recently, the entire non-Communist world was subsumed under this heading. Now, with efforts to woo non-Communist neutrals, these states are no longer shoved under the category of "world capitalism."

cosmic role of the party, the relations of the party member to his party, and the "ideal" Communist party member are the warp and woof of the party's very existence. If these ideas begin to fade, the leaders have every reason to be concerned.

The pursuit of power takes place continuously within the framework of the ideological tradition. Even if Stalin had not conceived of himself as a great Marxist-Leninist philosopher, the mere circumstance that he came to occupy Lenin's throne forced him to play the role of philosopher-king. The same holds true of Mao Tse-tung. Since Stalin's death, there has, to be sure, been a striking diminution in the attention devoted to ideological statements, but his successors have nevertheless been forced to place themselves on record concerning fundamental ideological issues. The very tendency of Khrushchev and his colleagues to treat ideological matters in a somewhat cavalier spirit is a factor which has had far-reaching consequences.

One enormously important aspect of ideology lies in the appeal which its symbols and moral claims exert on many elements in the non-Communist world, particularly in Asia. The Leninist theory of imperialism, the notion that the Communist party represents the interests of the masses of mankind, the simplified Marxist-Leninist account of the progress of mankind, have had an immense appeal throughout the non-Western world, and the Soviet leadership has been able to exploit the widespread receptivity to these ideas in order to advance their own cause. Here, the ideological factor is simultaneously an immense factor of power.

Finally, it is by dint of its unique ideology that the Communist leadership has till now been able to claim that an unbridgeable abyss separates the "camp of socialism" from the unredeemed world. At least until the Twentieth Congress of the Communist Party of the Soviet Union, this notion of monolithic Communist solidarity involved much more than a mere commitment to something called "socialism." It involved the assertion that Marxism-Leninism as interpreted in Moscow provided the only authentic guide along the "path to socialism" and that the Soviet Union provided the only authentic model of socialism. Since the Twentieth Congress, to which we shall return later, some striking new breaches have appeared. Here it was openly proclaimed that there are "many paths to socialism," even though the important reservation was made that socialism can be achieved only where Communist parties ("the working class and its vanguard" in Khrushchev's terms) hold the leading positions. The full extent to which this retreat in doctrine may have weakened the usefulness of ideology as an instrument for dividing off the world of darkness from the world of light is only gradually becoming apparent.

With Lenin and Stalin, ideology demanded not simply a commitment by all Communists to the "general truths of Marxism-Leninism" but also the unquestioning acceptance of Moscow's party line at any time and on any matter whatsoever. This strict commitment was, of course, based on the idea that the party, as the concentrated embodiment of the proletariat, had an unfailing grasp of the historic truth at any point in time. While, undoubtedly, one of Stalin's main obsessions was organizational control —the placing of his "own men" in all key positions of power—one unfailing criterion for measuring the loyalty of "his" men was their eager willingness to accept his ideological authority on all matters at all times and without question.

Stalin's image of a "Socialist world" was one in which both organizational and ideological control would be centered in Moscow. In his mind, the two elements probably constituted two facets of a single whole. Any crack in one facet was bound to be reflected in a crack in the other. Thus, while Moscow's rupture with Tito may have arisen out of an issue of power, we need not assume any lack of serious intent when the Kremlin immediately began to seek out all sorts of defects in the Yugoslav Communist approach to ideology and to apply a more rigid ideological control to its satellites. The events of late 1956 in Poland

and Hungary, as well as the reaction of the ruling group in Moscow to these events, suggest that Stalin's successors have tended to believe that they could maintain organizational control even while partially relaxing ideological control. To Stalin, on the other hand, absolute ideological control was itself an essential component of power.

In sum, despite the general drift toward disintegration, ideology has continued to play a role as a part both of the genuine belief-world of the Communist leaders and of the power system itself. Its decay cannot but affect the strength of the power system.

Ideology has played and continues to play a crucial role in Sino-Soviet relations. The monistic ideological approach correctly stresses the importance of ideology, but it errs in its failure to perceive the stresses and strains which shape the evolution of the ideology. It completely overlooks the problem of the disintegration of ideology and the ways in which ideology is bent and strained when it encounters new and recalcitrant situations or when it becomes enmeshed with power interests. The monistic ideological approach would never have conceived of the possibility of anything like the Kremlin-Tito conflict.

On the other hand, the sociological approach to the problem of Sino-Soviet relations assumes that the mere existence in different states of identities in social structure will inevitably lead to indestructible alliances between them. The whole of human history argues against any such supposition; even within the bounds of Communist history, the Tito conflict is a case in point. Before 1948, Yugoslavia was creating a Soviet type of social structure at a faster pace and with more *élan* than any other state within the Communist orbit. When a conflict arose in the power sphere, however, the growing similarity of social structure proved to be of no consequence.

It is, furthermore, by no means easy to distinguish sociological from ideological facts. The role of the Communist party in the Chinese system, the appropriation by the Chinese of the Stalinist model of economic development, have their ideological roots. The Communist party as a political organization cannot be divorced from the whole ideological context within which the party operates. Of course, the Stalinist model of economic development might, conceivably, be adopted in some country without accepting the whole Marxist-Leninist ideology, as simply one model of economic development. In the case of China, however, the unquestioning acceptance of the Stalinist economic model was preceded by the prior acceptance of Marxism-Leninism. Most of the first-line leaders of the Chinese Communist Party had become Communists in the early 1920's even before the Stalinist model had been fully crystallized in the Soviet Union. The "social basis" of their power, to be sure, is now very similar to that of the Soviet *apparatchik* class. This social fact, however, rests upon a prior commitment to a common ideology.

In considering the power approach to Sino-Soviet relations, it seems to me that we can reject at the outset the notion that Communist China is organizationally controlled from Moscow. The balance of evidence available indicates strongly that the alliance between Moscow and Peking is an alliance between two autonomous centers of power.

If we proceed to explain the alliance wholly in terms of common power interests, the results are inconclusive. We have listed above certain items which would argue for a meeting of interests. One can also enumerate possible points of friction. The question of the control of border areas—Turkestan, Outer Mongolia, Manchuria—offers one possible area of friction. The question of the relative role of the Soviet Union and China in non-Communist Asia is another. The trip of Khrushchev and Bulganin to South and Southeast Asia in 1955 was clearly designed to "sell" the Soviet Union in this area and hardly attests to any eagerness to see these areas pass completely into the Chinese orbit. It has been suggested by Dr. Eckstein that the economic alliance between the Soviet Union and Communist China is by no means a "natural" economic relationship, based on an inherent complementarity between the two economic systems.

The fact that a relatively weak China shares a common border with a strong Soviet Union would perhaps discourage any policy of open hostility, but there is a long distance between a policy of nonhostility and the close alliance which has existed since 1950 between these two powers. Under ordinary circumstances, a state in this situation might be expected to maintain a posture of correct relations with its neighbor while striving to checkmate its power by seeking strong allies elsewhere. In China's situation, this would correspond to the hoary tradition of using "the far-off barbarians to control the barbarians close at hand."

Of course, Communist China is now dependent on the Soviet Union for military, economic and technical aid, but this one-sided dependence has resulted from a prior decision to "lean to one side." If Communist China were determined to break out of this form of dependence, it could probably do so, and, as a matter of fact, there is considerable evidence that at the present time the Chinese would be only too happy to reduce their peculiar dependence on the Soviet Union.

Neither sociological nor power factors can account fully for the peculiar alliance between the Soviet Union and Communist China. The factor of shared ideology, a shared core of belief, remains crucial. There are aspects of the alliance which can be explained only in terms of the overriding importance of this factor. The strenuous effort on the part of the Chinese Communists to make every detail of Soviet ideology available to the Chinese public is perhaps without parallel in the history of relations between states. The Chinese Communist leadership probably shares implicitly with the Soviet leaders the belief that "History" is on their side, that "capitalism" is doomed, that the Soviet model of industrial development represents "socialism," that Communist parties (although not necessarily the Soviet party alone) are the infallible instruments of history. There can be no doubt that they share the Soviet leaders' solicitude for strengthening ideology as an element of power.

The ideological aspect of Sino-Soviet relations has been a crucial, but also a highly problematic aspect, one which has been subject to numerous stresses and strains. Ideology has played a dynamic role, and yet has been constantly corroded by new historic circumstances and new power considerations.

IDEOLOGICAL ISSUES IN SINO-SOVIET RELATIONS

Before 1927, the ideological development of Chinese Communism was inextricably enmeshed in the ideological conflicts, which were then raging in the Kremlin.[3] The Chinese situation created problems which, in turn, provided grist for the mills of the various factions in Moscow, but in these conflicts the Chinese Communists themselves played a relatively passive role.

Between 1927 and 1935, it gradually became apparent that the Maoist strategy provided the only possible path for the growth of Chinese Communism. Although "Maoism" represented, in the first instance, a development in the area of strategy rather than ideology and, at that time, the Chinese Communists did not adopt any explicit party line differing from the formulas then dominant in Moscow, this new strategy had certain immediate implications for ideology. The isolation of the Chinese Communist Party from the industrial proletariat and its complete dependence on peasant support for its survival struck directly at the notion that a Communist party must have some visible tie to the urban proletariat which it claims to represent. In all of Lenin's writings, as well as in Stalin's *Problems of Leninism,* the necessity for the link with the proletariat was taken for granted. It is, of course, quite true that Lenin's concept of a self-directed party and Stalin's actions in practice had opened the door to the divorce of the party from the proletariat, but nothing in their own experience had forced them to discard this element of Marxist orthodoxy.

3 For a fuller account of ideological issues in Sino-Soviet relations during the period before 1937, see my *Chinese Communism and the Rise of Mao* (Cambridge, Mass.: Harvard University Press, 1951).

Until the early 1930's, the notion that a Communist party must secure for itself an industrial proletarian base still had operational consequences, as is clear from the Kremlin's nagging directives of that time to the Chinese party. Again, this does not mean that Stalin was concerned only with maintaining the purity of an ideology. As always, he was obsessed with the problem of placing his own trusted men in key positions of power. It is no accident, however, that those whom he regarded as his men (first, Li Li-san, later, Wang Ming and others) shared his views on the necessity of urban proletarian support. While political considerations may in the end always override considerations of ideological purity, it is wrong to assume that Stalin ever abandoned ideological positions in a spirit of cavalier nonchalance. Every abandonment of an ideological position weakened to some extent the fabric of the ideology as a whole, and ideology itself was a crucial element in the whole power complex.

With the clear emergence of the Maoist strategy as the only viable path in China, the notion of the necessity of an actual urban proletarian base ceased to have operational consequences. This element of orthodoxy had become a dead letter. The Chinese Communists have, as a matter of fact, even boasted of this peculiar development of Chinese Communism as one of Mao Tse-tung's unique contributions to the storehouse of Marxism-Leninism. Mao has demonstrated, as it were, that a party guided by a correct Marxist-Leninist philosophy can convert intellectuals and peasants into spiritual proletarians. The party's proletarian essence is no longer guaranteed by maintaining ties to its supposed class base but wholly by its possession of the correct proletarian doctrine. The Chinese example shows how the corrosion of doctrine can take place not only in Moscow, but also in other sectors of the Communist world.

Another gap in the ideological relations of the Chinese and Soviet parties was not to become apparent until after the Chinese Communists had assumed power in 1949. This divergence arose over the problem of "people's democracy."

CHINA AND THE CONCEPT OF "PEOPLE'S DEMOCRACY"

The rise of the Chinese Communists to power followed hard on the heels of the crisis which had been touched off by the break with Tito. Mao's assumption of power in China may well have coincided with a certain disturbance in Stalin's image of a "socialist camp." As Professor Ulam has pointed out in *Tito and the Cominform*,[4] previous experience had probably led Stalin to believe that a mere assertion of his displeasure, a mere verbal chastisement by the Kremlin, would be sufficient to undermine Tito's power. Subsequent events demonstrated that a Communist party which had created its own power base within a given nation, a party led by its own dynamic leader fully familiar with Communist techniques of control, could not easily be captured from within once it had achieved state power. In the so-called people's democracies of Eastern Europe, which were already under effective Kremlin domination by 1948, this realization led to a tightening of both organizational and ideological control. In the case of China, where the party's history had been not unlike that of Yugoslavia, it led the Kremlin to display a new circumspection.

If Stalin's ultimate image of the "Socialist camp" continued to be that of a world tightly controlled from the Kremlin, one may surmise that after 1949 he postponed, rather than renounced, his hope of ultimately gaining control of the Chinese Communist Party. Up to his death, he seems to have accepted, however reluctantly, the necessity in practice of treating the Chinese Communist regime as an autonomous center of power.

While not much could be done toward instituting organizational control over China, every effort was made to reassert the Kremlin's ideological supremacy. Every Soviet account written before Stalin's death of Chinese Communist history stressed again and again that all the theoretical foundations of the Chinese Communist victory had been laid by Stalin. Moscow made no concessions to Chinese

4 Cambridge, Mass.: Harvard University Press, 1952.

claims that Mao had made original theoretical contributions to the storehouse of Marxism-Leninism. In all Soviet accounts, Mao figured, at most, as the talented executor of Stalin's theoretical teachings.

At the same time, every effort was made by Moscow to fit Communist China into the category of the "people's democracies" as that concept was interpreted after 1948.[5] This very effort disclosed an ideological gap between the two leaderships.

The concept of "people's democracy" was first elaborated as a theoretical framework to explain the nature of the Soviet-imposed regimes of Eastern Europe. According to the theory as it was developed before 1948, these regimes were presumably coalition governments made up of bourgeois, petty-bourgeois, peasant and proletarian elements under the "hegemony of the proletariat." While the notion of united fronts under "proletarian hegemony" was not new to Communist strategy, the peculiar feature of the new situation lay in the fact that united fronts now governed several states, and a new theory was required to account for the difference between this new form of government and the "Soviet" form. It was also necessary to explain why non-Communist parties were included in these governments. Another peculiar feature of these regimes was that they still had many "bourgeois-democratic" tasks to perform before reaching the stage of "Socialist" development.

Before 1948 not much attention was devoted in the writings of theorists such as Varga and Trainin to the question of the future development of these states. This prudent reticence probably arose from a desire to stress the "united front" aspects of the satellite regimes during their period of initial consolidation. There were, however, spokesmen, many spokesmen like Gomulka in Poland, who took advantage of this diffidence to hint that their own nations might pursue "a path to socialism" differing somewhat

5 For a fuller discussion of this question, see my article on "China and the Soviet Theory of People's Democracy," U.S. Information Agency, *Problems of Communism*, v. 3, n. 5 (Washington: GPO, 1954), pp. 8-15.

from that which had been followed by the Soviet Union. After the break with Tito, Moscow announced clearly and abruptly that there was only one road to socialism, the Soviet road, and that all the "people's democracies" would have to tread that path. The Soviet Union had been able to make the transition from the quasi-capitalist stage of the New Economic Policy to the Socialist stage only because its state was based on the "dictatorship of the proletariat." According to Lenin's dictum, while different countries might display certain variations in their forms of government during the period of transition to socialism, in essence all governments of this type would have to be dictatorships of the proletariat. After 1948 Moscow constantly reiterated that the regimes of Eastern Europe were, in their essence, dictatorships of the proletariat on the road to socialism and that they should behave accordingly. Again, in Stalin's mind, effective organizational control involved firm ideological control, and firm ideological control involved a total acceptance of the Soviet model of development. The whole Soviet development had, after all, been merely the "historic actualization" of the truths of Marxism-Leninism-Stalinism.

At this point, it will be useful to consider the theoretical difference between the "hegemony of the proletariat" and the "dictatorship of the proletariat" as expounded in the most recent edition of the Soviet *Encyclopaedia*. The definitions which it presents reflect the crystallized orthodoxy of the Stalin era, but they are also solidly based on pronouncements by Lenin. Basic to the difference between the two concepts is the entire notion of the two-stage development of noncapitalist countries, or of countries in which capitalism has been developed but feebly. On their path to socialism all these countries must pass through a "bourgeois-democratic" stage. During Russia's 1905 revolution, Lenin clung to the view that Russia was not yet ready for socialism and still had to traverse a period of "bourgeois-democratic" development. However, in Russia the bourgeois-democratic revolution would be carried out not by the weak and perfidious Russian bourgeoisie, but by the peasantry in alliance with the proletariat. The peasantry would represent the "bourgeois" element in this alliance, since its demands for land and political freedom were essentially bourgeois demands.

During the bourgeois-democratic stage, the proletariat would, of course, not be strong enough to establish its own exclusive class dictatorship, but would have to ally itself with other classes, notably the peasantry, which were interested in the overthrow of feudalism. It would have to circumscribe its program to conform to the "bourgeois" demands of its class-allies—demands for land distribution, civil rights, an effective parliament, and so forth. However, within this alliance, by dint of its historic destiny, the proletariat would gradually be able to achieve a position of "hegemony." The concept of the "hegemony of the proletariat" is defined in the *Encyclopaedia* as "the leadership of the toiling masses of city and countryside by the proletariat in the revolutionary struggle to carry to an end the bourgeois-democratic revolution, to establish a dictatorship of the proletariat, and to bring a Communist society into being." [6]

The concept of "dictatorship of the proletariat" becomes relevant only when the stage of transition to "socialism" is close at hand. In the words of the *Encyclopaedia*, "The dictatorship of the proletariat is the state power of the proletariat in the transitional period from capitalism to Communism, established as a result of the revolutionary overthrow of the power of the bourgeoisie and the smashing of the bourgeois state apparatus." [7] In defining the concept of dictatorship, Lenin states that "the scientific concept of dictatorship means nothing more nor less than unrestricted power absolutely unhampered by laws and regulations and resting directly on force." [8] Within a dictatorship of the proletariat, power is exercised exclusively by the proletariat and by its vanguard, the Communist party, against all "exploiting classes," for the

6 *Bol'shaia Sovetskaia Entsiklopediia* (2d. ed.; 1952), v. 10, p. 311.
7 Same, v. 14, p. 344.
8 Same, v. 14, p. 342.

proletariat and the proletariat alone can achieve socialism. Both Lenin and Stalin stressed, of course, that the dictatorship of the proletariat represents not only the proletariat but the "numerous non-proletarian toilers, notably the 'rural proletariat.' " [9] It represents thus a "special form of alliance" in which only one of the allies possesses actual political power.

The *Encyclopaedia* emphasizes that the problem of the "dictatorship of the proletariat" constitutes "the main problem of Marxism-Leninism, for it is this concept which divides Lenin irrevocably from all social democrats."

Having decreed that the "people's democracies" were, in essence, "dictatorships of the proletariat," the Kremlin was not slow to extend this concept to the new developments in Asia. There were, to be sure, differences between North Korea, China and Eastern Europe. Because of their backwardness, the Asian states of the "Socialist camp" still had many "bourgeois-democratic" tasks to complete. However, once these states approached the period of the transition to socialism, they would necessarily become dictatorships of the proletariat.

It was precisely on this issue that a marked gap continued to exist between Chinese Communist and Soviet theory throughout the period from 1949 to the Twentieth Congress of the Communist Party of the Soviet Union in February 1956. While the Chinese were willing to accept the term of "people's democracy" as equivalent to their own "new democracy," they did not accept the post-1948 interpretation of this concept. In the interests of ideological harmony, the gap was not advertised. Nevertheless, it persisted and was even enshrined in the preamble to the Chinese Constitution of 1954.

As early as 1952, the Chinese Communists proclaimed the beginning of the period of transition to socialism, but they failed to acknowledge the necessity for a dictatorship of the proletariat in China. On the contrary, in China the party of the proletariat would proceed all the way to social-

9 Same, v. 14, p. 345.

ism in alliance with the peasantry, the petty bourgeoisie, and the national bourgeoisie under the "hegemony of the proletariat." The "bourgeois" sectors of the economy and even the minds of the bourgeoisie would be peacefully transformed, step by step, until they merged into socialism. During the last months of 1956, the Chinese Communists speeded up this "peaceful transformation." Private industry was converted into "state capitalist enterprises" at a greatly accelerated rate and the bulk of the "national bourgeoisie" were pictured as joyfully welcoming the new order, thanks to the intense "education" which they had undergone. The novel notion here is that an "exploiting class" may be "educated" into accepting socialism. It is interesting to note that not only has the façade of coalition government been maintained, but in recent months there has been a new propaganda emphasis on the participation of non-Communist "democratic groups" in this government, thus emphasizing the compatibility of such groups with "socialism."

This does not mean that the rich peasants and the "national bourgeoisie" have ceased to be exploiting classes in the Chinese interpretation of Communist ideology. So long as the bourgeoisie continues to exist as a class, it is an "exploiting" class and will go on exuding its noxious bourgeois ideology. However, the "hegemony of the proletariat" over the state makes it possible to contain the effects of this noxious influence. Meanwhile, an immense effort to "educate" these exploiting classes to the acceptance of socialism (the "3-anti" and "5-anti" movement of 1952 is interpreted as part of this educative process) has been under way. Some elements of these classes will prove uneducable, but the class as a whole will be peacefully transformed, and its members may even expect to hold honorable managerial positions in the new economy.

The authoritative *New China Monthly Gazette (Hsin Hua Yüeh Pao)* of October 1955 extolled this "different" Chinese path as constituting a new contribution to Marxist-Leninist theory.

One of Mao Tse-tung's brilliant contributions to the store-house of Marxism is the principle that under certain socio-historic conditions, in a state in which the proletariat has gained power, it can carry out a basic transformation of the capitalist elements in accordance with Socialist principles. None of the previous classics of Marxism-Leninism contain this type of theory, and no other state in the world has ever had this experience. In the Soviet Union and the people's de-mocracies of Southern and Eastern Europe, capitalism is being eradicated by violent and forceful means. However, because of the concrete conditions of our country, we are able to arrive at the same goal—the eradication of capitalism—by peaceful methods of Socialist transformation.[10]

The *New China Monthly Gazette* developed the notion that the Soviet Union had required a dictatorship of the proletariat because the Russian bourgeoisie had proved for-midable and hostile in the revolution of 1917. The same was true of Eastern Europe. In China, however, the national bourgeoisie had been weak and tended to cooperate with the proletariat; hence, the possibility of a "peaceful transfor-mation" of the bourgeois class. The concept of the "dicta-torship of the proletariat" is here reduced from the status of a universal truth to that of a local Russian response to a parochial Russian situation.[11] It implies that in China the whole "people," and not the industrial proletariat alone, is "building socialism." There is a kind of straining to-ward the notion that the Communist party is not merely the class party of the proletariat (although this is always mentioned), but somehow an embodiment of the "general will" of the Chinese nation as a whole, with the exception of those labeled as "counterrevolutionaries."

What, if any, have been the practical consequences of this ideological divergence? It may be reflected in certain features of the Chinese scene. The extraordinary emphasis on "ideological remolding" and on "persuasion" (in the Chinese sense), the genuine desire to make maximum use

10 Shu Wei-k'ung, "The Gradual Tempo of China's Transitional Period."
11 It is interesting that Khrushchev took up this same idea at the Twentieth Party Congress of the C.P.S.U.

of the talents of the so-called "national bourgeoisie," the sedulous maintenance of the outward trappings of coalition government, the recent courting of the so-called democratic groups and parties, are all reflections of it.

On the other hand, whether the Chinese Communist Party calls its rule "hegemony of the proletariat" or "dictatorship of the proletariat," its effective control of China is not one whit less absolute than that of the Communist Party in the Soviet Union. While a façade of coalition government is maintained,[12] the so-called democratic parties echo the Communist party line with parrot-like monotony. Furthermore, the Chinese seem to be implementing the Soviet model of economic development far more vigorously than any of the avowedly "proletarian dictatorships" of Eastern Europe.

The persistence with which the Chinese have clung to their "difference" may well have a significance above and beyond its implications for domestic policy. It has maintained and magnified the image of Mao Tse-tung as a great theoretical innovator in his own right. By the same token, it has reaffirmed the ideological autonomy of the Chinese Communists within the "Socialist camp." Further, by stressing the "peculiarity" of China's path to socialism —the ability of the Chinese Communists to march to socialism at the head of the "whole people"—Peking tacitly indicates to non-Communist Asia that China offers its peoples a uniquely relevant message, distinct from that of Russian Communism.

THE CLOSING OF THE GAP

What has been the effect of Stalin's death on the ideological relations between Moscow and Peking?

Immediately after his death, there began, within Russia, a relatively cautious diminution of the Stalin image. With this, it became possible to drop the previous insistence on

[12] The so-called democratic groups and parties, such as the Democratic League, the Revolutionary Kuomintang Committee, etc., are all represented in the governmental structure.

Stalin's decisive role as the theoretical engineer of the Chinese Communist victory. It immediately became possible to make some concessions to the claims made in China for Mao as a theoretical leader in his own right. Both before and after Stalin's death, Mao's writings were being translated into Russian and were reviewed extensively. While the reviewers conceded that Mao had "creatively" applied Marxism-Leninism to Chinese conditions, they did not go so far as to specify his concrete contributions to the "storehouse of Marxism-Leninism."

Considerable credit was now being given to Mao as the architect of the Chinese Communist victory, but the gap still remained between the Soviet concept of "people's democracy" and the Chinese interpretation. Although the years 1952-55 were marked by a sharp diminution in Soviet discussions of ideology, whenever the issue was discussed, as in the 1954 party textbook on *Political Economy*, Moscow reaffirmed emphatically the standard dogma of the universal necessity for the dictatorship of the proletariat during the period of transition to socialism.

Strangely enough, during the last few months of 1955, on the very eve of the epoch-making Twentieth Party Congress, there was actually a revival of emphasis on this dogma. An article by Dubina, published in *Kommunist* (October 1955), on "The Leninist Theory of Socialist Revolution," restated the Soviet position with renewed vehemence. "The experience of building socialism in the countries of the people's democracy," he wrote, "has clearly demonstrated the utter groundlessness of the chatter on the part of nationalist, opportunist elements who assert that their countries are proceeding to socialism by some special path, new in principle as it were and excluding class war, by the path of a peaceful growing over of capitalism into socialism." The universal necessity of the "dictatorship of the proletariat" was again stressed as the be-all-and-end-all of Communist orthodoxy.

Even more significantly, the same theme was developed by Kaganovich in his speech of November 6, 1955, celebrating the thirty-eighth anniversary of the October Revolution. At the very beginning of his speech Kaganovich proclaimed:

Only he is a Marxist, Lenin wrote, who extends the acceptance of the class struggle to the acceptance of the dictatorship of the proletariat. This is where the profound difference lies between a Marxist and an ordinary petty (and even big) bourgeois. This is the main thing in Marxism-Leninism and the fundamental thing in the October Revolution.

It is also interesting to note a rather peculiar use of Communist terminology in the slogans which *Pravda* published for the same anniversary of the revolution. One slogan conveyed Soviet greetings to the people's democracies, including such backward countries as Albania and Outer Mongolia, which are "constructing socialism." Another conveyed greetings to the Chinese People's Republic which is constructing "the foundations of socialism." Since the attacks of February 1955 on Molotov's much advertised error, there can be no misunderstanding of the profound difference in Soviet usage between "socialism" and "the foundations of socialism." Clearly, the distinction thus drawn between Albania and China did not lie in Albania's more advanced state of economic development but in the fact that China had not yet proclaimed itself a dictatorship of the proletariat.

The fact that these reassertions of orthodoxy were being pressed on the very eve of the Twentieth Party Congress, which was so soon to move in precisely the opposite direction, lends much weight to the hypothesis that deep differences of opinion on these ideological issues were being fought out in the highest policy-making circles. If Khrushchev and those close to him were then pressing for the adoption of the more elastic formulas which finally prevailed at the Twentieth Congress, it is conceivable that the more orthodox views expressed just prior to it reflected the vehement feelings of the opposition group, headed perhaps by Kaganovich. The sober and unenthusiastic tone of Kaganovich's speech at the Twentieth Congress would tend to reinforce this hypothesis.

An article in *Problems of Philosophy* (January 1956), entitled "How Do We Explain the Diversity of State Forms of Dictatorship of the Proletariat?", foreshadowed a new and more flexible approach. After describing the peculiarities of Chinese Communist development, including the notion of the peaceful transformation of the bourgeoisie, the author then proceeded to accept this variant "path to socialism" as a legitimate subvariety of the "dictatorship of the proletariat."

The real turning point was the Twentieth Congress of the C.P.S.U. Not only were the Chinese and Yugoslav paths to socialism declared fully legitimate, but Khrushchev himself went far beyond the Chinese in asserting "the possibility of employing the parliamentary form for the transition to socialism." This formulation, it is true, was by no means unambiguous. The notion that parliaments and united fronts might properly be utilized by Communist parties in their march to power is by no means an original one. What Khrushchev seemed to be suggesting, however, was that Communist parties operating in countries of "bourgeois democracy" could now legitimately claim that the achievement of socialism did not necessarily require "the smashing of the old state apparatus." The Soviet path to socialism, Khrushchev now states, was simply a Russian response to Russian conditions, to the intransigence of the Russian bourgeoisie at the time of the revolution.

The verbal formula, "dictatorship of the proletariat," has not been dropped. It has simply been emptied of all semantic content. It is now proclaimed that Communist parties may use the "bourgeois" state apparatus to achieve socialism, that in some countries, as in China, socialism can be achieved by a multiclass coalition under "proletarian hegemony," and that, under some circumstances, the bourgeoisie may give up power without an armed struggle. To the extent that the term "dictatorship of the proletariat" had any meaning, it denied each of these possibilities. It is not strange that the Soviet leaders have been reluctant to drop the verbal formula. It was a concept which has played a central role in Marxist-Leninist ideology. As Kaganovich remarked, ". . . it had been the main thing in Marxism-Leninism."

Despite their assertion of the possibility of a variety of roads to socialism, Khrushchev and Co. have not left their ideological position entirely unprotected. While the paths to socialism may now vary, "the political leadership of the working class and its advance detachment is the indispensable and decisive factor for all forms of transition to socialism." In other words, socialism cannot be achieved except through the leadership of the Communist parties. What Khrushchev has been saying to those Communist parties which are not in power is, in effect, that the Soviet Union is as interested as ever in having them attain power, but is no longer interested in the theoretical formulas and strategies which they may use to attain it. So far as both China and Yugoslavia are concerned, the new line, nevertheless, constitutes a striking admission of their claim to enjoy ideological autonomy, if not outright ideological independence.

In speculating on the pressures which lie behind these new revisions of doctrine, it would, of course, be one-sided to attribute them entirely to Moscow's need for closing the ideological gap with Communist China. The notion of the legitimacy of the parliamentary road to socialism was undoubtedly designed to improve the fortunes and freedom of maneuver of the French and Italian parties. The desire to win back Tito's allegiance to the "Socialist camp" was undoubtedly another factor of immense importance in the doctrinal pronouncements of the Congress.

Events subsequent to the Twentieth Congress demonstrated that Moscow's hopes were premature, for important gaps still persisted between the ideological positions of the two parties. The Yugoslavs have, in fact, furnished a vivid example of how far the revision of ideology can be carried when Moscow no longer exercises any semblance of ideological control. The Yugoslavs have not only denied the necessity for instituting a dictatorship of the proletariat, but have even asserted that in some countries Social

Democratic parties may become vehicles for the achievement of socialism, that many classes may participate in the building of socialism, and that even the forms of socialism may vary from country to country.[13] In this there is hardly a tenet of Marxism-Leninism which retains any absolute value. The role of ideology as an instrument for drawing a firm qualitative distinction between the "camp of socialism" and the outside world is obliterated completely.

The Twentieth Congress by no means went the full way toward accepting these Titoist innovations. Evidently, Moscow's hope was that, if it went some way in meeting the Yugoslav's ideological demands, the latter would reciprocate by retracting their more drastic tamperings with the remaining fabric of the ideology. Its hopes have not been realized, and the Yugoslav Communists have not refrained from pressing their own views on the Soviet satellites in Eastern Europe. Whether the events of late 1956 in Poland and Hungary will make the Belgrade leadership more cautious or still more forthright in pressing for the recognition of not only "national" but independent paths to socialism remains to be seen.

Whatever Khrushchev's calculations as to the effects elsewhere of his revisions of dogma, the Kremlin's desire to close the ideological gap with Communist China was certainly of primary importance. Peking's assertion of China's unique path to socialism, in one sense, presented Moscow with a more pressing problem than did the case of Yugoslavia, precisely because China was in the "Socialist camp," whereas Yugoslavia, by its own declaration, was not. At the Twentieth Congress, the Chinese case was mentioned repeatedly as an illustration of the "creative application of Marxism-Leninism." Shepilov, who became Foreign Minister three months later, dwelt in some detail on the

---

[13] For an exposition of these views, see, for instance, Jovan Dordević, "A Contribution to the Discussion of Social Classes and Political Parties," *Review of International Affairs* (Belgrade), v. 6, n. 124 (June 1955), pp. 8-10; also R. Lowenthal, "New Phases in Moscow-Belgrade Relations," U.S. Information Agency, *Problems of Communism*, cited (1955), v. 4, n. 6, pp. 1-10.

peculiar features of the Chinese path and added, significantly, that "from the viewpoint of scholastics of Marxism, such an approach to the problem of transforming exploiting ownership into Socialist ownership is tantamount to trampling underfoot the principles of Marxism-Leninism; in actual fact this is creative Marxism-Leninism in action." [14] In discussing the question of "paths to socialism," the Resolutions of the Twentieth Congress singled out China as the test case par excellence:

The Chinese People's Republic has introduced many special features into its form of Socialist construction. Before the victory of the revolution, the economy was extremely backward and was semi-feudal and semi-colonial in character. On the basis of its ability to capture the decisive commanding heights, the People's Democratic Government is now bringing about a peaceful transformation of private industry and commerce and their step-by-step conversion into component parts of socialism.

The Soviet leadership has conceded China's right to follow its own path to socialism, and it has thus closed the ideological gap, even though the verbal formula, "dictatorship of the proletariat," has not been dropped. An indication that the Chinese Communists interpret the Congress' action in this light is furnished by the Chinese Politbureau statement of April 4, 1956, entitled "On the Historic Experience Concerning the Dictatorship of the Proletariat." While the main significance of this document is that it clarifies China's attitude toward the current denigration of Stalin, from the point of view of this paper, its main significance lies in the fact that for the first time in Chinese Communist history this document classifies China as a "dictatorship of the proletariat." It specifically equates China's "people's democratic dictatorship" with the dictatorship of the proletariat. Since the Soviets have now redefined this term in such a way as to remove all its meaning content, the Chinese are able to reciprocate by accepting

14 The reference to the "scholastics of Marxism" suggests that the viewpoint attacked here actually had support in high party circles.

the term, for in accepting it, they have conceded nothing of their own views concerning China's "peculiar path." The gap has been closed, not by bringing the Chinese ideological formula into line with Moscow's orthodoxy, but by adjusting Soviet ideology to accommodate the Chinese innovations. Ideological solidarity has, thereby, been reaffirmed.

The price, however, has been the reaffirmation of China's ideological autonomy and a further tampering with what remains of Marxist-Leninist ideology. In the short run, ideological solidarity can, presumably, be maintained only through ideological concessions; in the long run, the weakening of the ideology as a coherent whole cannot but exercise a weakening effect. If the ideological link has been a crucial one in Sino-Soviet relations, the constant wearing away of the core of shared ideological beliefs must inevitably weaken that core, and the alliance must come to rest more and more on the shifting sands of power interest.

THE IDEOLOGICAL LINK: WILL IT BIND?

A larger question emerges: What is the Kremlin's present conception of a Communist world? Have the Soviet leaders reconciled themselves to the vision of a Communist camp in which all Communist parties will enjoy both organizational and ideological autonomy, united only by a minimum core of shared beliefs?

The initial reaction of the Khrushchev leadership to the events of October and November 1956 in Poland and Hungary tended to indicate a confidence on their part that the ideological concessions which they had made to China and Yugoslavia were entirely compatible with maintaining their organizational control over the East European satellites.

The ruthless suppression of the uprising by the direct intervention of massive Soviet forces showed Moscow's determination to reassert its domination over Hungary, once events and popular feelings had swept over the heads of the "national" Communists. In any case, the recent course of Khrushchev and Co. suggests an extremely nonchalant attitude toward the possible repercussions of their own ideological pronouncements.

If the Soviet leadership is finally driven, no matter how reluctantly, to grant organizational and ideological autonomy to all Soviet satellites, the only remaining force binding them to Moscow will be a common core of shared beliefs. Some observers argue that a federation of Communist states which had rid itself of the great bulk of Marxist-Leninist dogma and had reduced its Communist orthodoxy to a streamlined core of doctrine might turn out to be a more formidable force than Stalin's tightly controlled empire. The question remains: What is this enduring hard core of doctrine? Over the last thirty years much has fallen by the wayside that was once considered essential doctrine. Is there at present any core on which China, Yugoslavia and Gomulka's Poland will be able to agree? In the decisive days of November 1956 Gomulka announced that not only would Poland's path to socialism differ, but Polish socialism would be radically different from the Russian variety.

The risk, newly emphasized by the popular uprising in Hungary, that "national Communism" represents an unstable compromise, may lead the leaders of Communist China, Poland and Yugoslavia to bethink themselves. It may lead them to stress the need for preserving a normative common core of doctrine, uniform for all Communist regimes. Whether such a core can be found is now open to question. Whether, even if found, it can be maintained in a world of autonomous Communist states is even more questionable.

In spite of the gradual disintegration of shared Communist orthodoxy, the immediate prospects for the relations between Moscow and Peking do not necessarily point to any "break." Over recent years, Soviet policy has moved steadily toward an increasing recognition, first, of China's organizational and, then, of its ideological autonomy. The potential pressure toward "Titoism" has thus been released in time. Furthermore, in the present state of the world, the Chinese Communist leaders are probably as anxious as the Kremlin itself to preserve a common core of Communist doctrine, in spite of their own manipulations of the ideology. At the same time, the drastic disintegration of the ideology—a disintegration to which the Chinese party has contributed substantially—has greatly weakened ideology as a binding fabric, not only between Moscow and Peking, but among all the states of the Communist world.

CHAPTER FOUR

THE BORDERLANDS AND THE SINO-SOVIET ALLIANCE *

by Howard L. Boorman

TO THE NORTH and west of the eighteen provinces of China proper, the historic homeland of Sinic civilization, lies a broad belt of territories stretching from the borders of Korea and Siberia through the remote reaches of Chinese Central Asia to the lofty tableland of Tibet and the Himalayas.[1] In modern times these areas have been an arena of seesaw conflict between China and Russia. Has that contest for power ended today or is it continuing in a new Communist guise?

By drawing an imaginary straight line across the map from Aigun in Heilungkiang province, close to Siberia, to Tengchung (Tengyueh) in Yunnan province, which borders on Burma, a geographer may divide the land mass of China into two regions of striking contrasts. The area to the northwest of such a line includes roughly two-thirds of China's total area but only about 5 to 10 per cent of its population; the portion southeast of the line contains about one-third of the area and 90 to 95 per cent of the people. To the northwest lie the major mountain ranges,

---

* I am glad to acknowledge with gratitude the assistance of the School of International Affairs of Columbia University in the preparation of this paper, and of Mr. Albert Lu of the Columbia research project on Men and Politics in Modern China in the assembling of materials.

[1] The problem of Tibet has been omitted from this paper since that area is more directly involved in Sino-Indian than Sino-Soviet relations.

the high plateaus, the loesslands, the deserts, the thinly populated regions of the interior. To the southeast lie the great river valleys and plains of agricultural China, with enormous concentrations of population in the broad plains of the Yellow and Hwai Rivers, the rich middle and lower reaches of the Yangtze, the fertile landlocked Szechwan basin, and the teeming Canton delta in the south.

Although connected in many ways with the complex history of the Chinese people, the vast, sparsely populated regions of China's hinterland were not truly integrated into the national life of China until the Chinese Communist military and political conquest of the country in the mid-twentieth century. The neat political boundaries drawn by cartographers have more frequently than not been misleading, for in these deserts and steppes local chieftains and local loyalties have been far more important than national leaders and national loyalties.

The borderlands are important in any study of Chinese Communist policy toward the non-Chinese peoples who form a substantial portion—in many areas of Inner Asia the overwhelming majority—of the population. These areas are also important as a focus of potential conflict or cooperation between Peking and Moscow. Will Russian and Chinese power, often at loggerheads in the past, find a new equilibrium along the Sino-Mongolian-Soviet border, a border comparable in length only to that between the United States and Canada?

MANCHURIA: TOUCHSTONE OF ALLIANCE

Manchuria—or the Northeast, as it is now called by the Communist rulers in Peking—is the richest and most strategic of China's borderlands. Connected with China proper by a narrow coastal plain which touches the Great Wall at Shanhaikwan, modern Manchuria is unquestionably a part of China. Its population is overwhelmingly Chinese and its economy has been linked to the cities and seas to the south, but its history has been strikingly different from that of China within the Wall. Homeland of the Manchus, rulers of China from the mid-seventeenth century, the area remained largely a Manchu preserve until the late nineteenth century. Since the 1890's it has been a focus of friction for the rival power of China, Russia, and Japan and has been involved, directly or indirectly, in every modern war fought in Eastern Asia. Both Communist China and the Soviet Union have compelling strategic interests in Manchuria, while its natural resources, its well-developed rail network, and its heavy industries have made it the principal base for Peking's ambitious program of national industrial development.[2]

Nearly as large as France and Germany combined and almost as populous as Italy, Manchuria is a land of long, bitter winters and hot, humid summers; of rich farmlands in the south; of forested mountains in the north and east; and of great rivers, the Sungari, the Nonni, and the Liao. To the west, its open plains blend into the steppelands of Mongolia. To the east, it looks across the Yalu and the Tumen rivers to northern Korea and across the Ussuri and the Amur to the Soviet Union.

This is a region inhabited by tall, sturdy Chinese peasant farmers, many of them refugees from poor harvests in Shantung and Hopei. The impact of modern imperialism and revolutions has brought other peoples. There have been fur-hatted Russians, émigrés striving to make their way in a new and hostile land. There have been the Japanese, architects and administrators of conquest: Japanese generals and sergeants of the Kwantung Army; Japanese builders of the complex economic-political subempire which was the South Manchurian Railway Company; Japanese engineers developing the industrial and electric power resources of the area; Japanese bureaucrats in Hsinking, the "New Capital" of the ill-fated and short-lived puppet, Manchukuo. Since the beginning of this century, there has been a significant minority of Koreans, refugees

[2] A convenient summary of developments is given in the two articles by Chao Kuo-chun, "The Government and Economy of Manchuria," *Far Eastern Survey*, v. 22, n. 13 (December 1953), pp. 169-75, and v. 23, n. 1 (January 1954), pp. 9-14.

from political and economic oppression in their own country.

If it was still essentially a frontier region, the Manchuria which came under Chinese Communist domination was not virgin territory politically. Regional separatism and militarism were the dominant notes of its history in the two decades after the fall of the Manchu dynasty in 1911. As the central power of Peking faded, the Three Eastern Provinces came under the rule of Chang Tso-lin and then of Chang Hsueh-liang, his son. The career of Chang Tso-lin, the "Old Marshal," was the very stuff of which legends have traditionally been made in China. Born of an illiterate and poverty-stricken peasant family, he rose to be the dominant political and military figure in the richest area of China. First achieving prominence as the leader of a band of outlaws, Chang Tso-lin and his followers became irregular allies of the Japanese during the war of 1904-05, harassing the Russians in minor skirmishes. He emerged from the conflict with considerably enhanced prestige and, more important, with the strongest armed forces in southern Manchuria. Favored by Japan, whose influence was already well established, Chang Tso-lin succeeded in consolidating his control during the Chinese revolution of 1911-12.

The isolation of Manchuria from the rest of China, already well advanced by the end of the dynasty, grew stronger after 1911. During the Old Marshal's final decade, 1918-28, Manchuria was, for all practical purposes, autonomous. Despite his unsuccessful adventures in north China during the 1920's, Chang Tso-lin, with the support of the Japanese, was at all times the ruler of his own domain northeast of the Great Wall. While the Old Marshal could be, and was, accused of many things, he had at least sufficient capacity for independent leadership and shrewd intrigue to preserve a relatively high degree of stability and security in Manchuria at a time when virtually all the rest of China was torn by disunity and chaos. The Japanese, pursuing their own major ambitions, tended to favor the preservation of this sort of local and autocratic autonomy in Manchuria as a barrier against a revival of Russian imperialism to the north and the rising tide of Chinese nationalism to the south.

It was only when Chang Tso-lin, increasingly intractable with advancing years, threatened seriously to undermine Japanese plans for Manchuria that major frictions developed. In June 1928, the Old Marshal was killed by an explosion—for which the Japanese were immediately and generally given credit—which wrecked his train near Mukden. With the death of this redoubtable bandit turned warlord, a brief but colorful chapter in the history of modern Manchuria came to a close.

Actually, Chang's family dynasty outlasted him by about three years. After the Old Marshal's death, one of his sons, Chang Hsueh-liang, consolidated power in Mukden. Defying strong warnings by the Japanese, as well as pressure from particularist Chinese factions in Manchuria, Chang Hsueh-liang voluntarily declared his allegiance to the Kuomintang and to the new National Government of China, which had established itself at Nanking in 1928. The National Government in turn confirmed the Young Marshal's position as the senior political and military figure in Manchuria. While this Mukden-Nanking *rapprochement* was significant symbolically, it did not mean that the Kuomintang was, in practice, able to insert its own effective authority—its armies—into Manchuria. The area remained a borderland with a strong sense of localism compounded of the facts of its recent history, its geography, and the feelings of the people who lived there. The overwhelming majority of its inhabitants were either indigenous to the area or new settlers from north China, and neither group had any natural affection for the Kuomintang, a political party patently dominated by Chinese from south of the Yellow River.

The Young Marshal's control in Mukden, like his father's regime at Peking in 1927-28, was doomed to a short life by the pressure of outside events. Antagonized initially by Mukden's formal alliance with Nationalist China in December 1928, and increasingly angered by the anti-

Japanese manifestations of the new Kuomintang nationalism during the following months, the Japanese Army expansionists finally decided to take matters into their own hands. Thus began their active military aggression on the mainland, in September 1931, the first step in their rapid and comparatively bloodless conquest of Manchuria. By the beginning of 1932 the Japanese had driven Chang Hsueh-liang from his home provinces and were busily engaged in erecting the puppet state of Manchukuo. The Japanese occupation effectively tore the region apart from national developments in China for nearly fifteen years. For practical purposes, the Japanese controlled Manchuria from 1931 to 1945, and the influence of the National Government, only nominal during the 1928-31 interlude, was thereafter nonexistent. Indigenous Manchurian political leadership was driven into exile or underground, or was neutralized by absorption into the Japanese-controlled apparatus of Manchukuo. Chang Hsueh-liang, following the kidnapping of Chiang Kai-shek at Sian in 1936, was held by the Kuomintang as a prisoner of state.[3]

It was only in mid-1945, when Japan finally faced total military defeat, that Manchuria again came into contact with the mainstreams of Chinese political life, and once more the area was caught in the maelstrom of power politics. The defeat of Japan left a political and military vacuum in Manchuria, and this time the Soviet Union was ready and eager to fill it. The Sino-Soviet Treaty of August 1945, whose groundwork had been laid at Yalta five months before, confirmed Russia's recovery of most of the positions which it had held in Manchuria prior to the Russo-Japanese War: rights in the naval base at Port Arthur and the port of Dairen, and a partnership in the Chinese Eastern and South Manchurian railways (now united into a single system called the Chinese Changchun railway). By Japan's defeat, general political authority passed temporarily to the Soviet Red Army, which swept vigorously in to occupy Manchuria in August 1945. Re-

[3] The Young Marshal has remained in protective custody, recently in Taiwan, for twenty years.

maining for only a few months through late 1945 and early 1946, the Russian forces were responsible for widespread looting, rape, and devastation which aroused great fear and hatred on the part of the local populace. In addition, before they withdrew, the Soviet forces proceeded to remove a very large amount of the Japanese-created industrial equipment.

The demise of Japanese power and the relatively brief but very destructive Russian invasion and occupation set the stage in Manchuria for the decisive conflict between the Kuomintang and the Chinese Communist Party. In August 1945, both contenders were keenly aware of the critical importance of Manchuria in the struggle for power in China. Neither had significant general influence, much less control, over it.

At the time of the Japanese surrender, the Chinese Communist Party leadership in Yenan—"in preparation for the liberation of the whole nation"—ordered one-third of its Central Committee and about 20,000 of its cadres to proceed at once to Manchuria.[4] Among others, Lin Piao, Ch'en Yun, P'eng Chen, Kao Kang, and Li Fu-ch'un hastened overland, across Inner Mongolia and Jehol, to the Northeast. Others came by boat from Communist-controlled areas of Shantung, across the Yellow Sea.

In restrospect it is simple to define the Chinese Communist aim in Manchuria: total control. It is much more difficult to follow the exact relations between the Chinese and Soviet Communist Parties during the period from 1945 to 1949.[5] In any case, collaboration between the Soviet forces and the Chinese Communists greatly facilitated the spread of Communist power, especially in northern and central Manchuria. In general, the Russians, while maintaining an outward policy of strict correctness toward the National Government, strove to frustrate Na-

4 *Jen Min Jih Pao* (People's Daily) (Peking), November 22, 1953.

5 The role of Li Li-san, who returned to the Far East with the Soviet Red Army in 1945 after fifteen years of exile in Moscow, has probably been exaggerated. There is no evidence that Li has exercised major political influence in the Chinese Communist Party since his return from the Soviet Union.

tionalist plans to establish full control over Manchuria. Specifically, the Russians provided substantial material assistance, in the form of surrendered Japanese equipment and weapons, to strengthen the Chinese Communist forces. Yet the ruthless removal of essential industrial equipment from an area so soon to come under complete Communist domination leaves unanswered the question of whether the Russians really expected an early victory of the Chinese Communists and, if so, whether they viewed their Chinese comrades with complete trust. With or without Moscow's approval, the Chinese Communist cadres proceeded to concentrate their energies on organizing the rural areas, transferring to the countryside of Manchuria the experience in peasant agitation and mobilization gained during their years in the "old liberated areas" in north China. Conscious of the strong localism of the Manchurians, the Chinese Communists had brought with them from Yenan a number of Manchurian Chinese who had formerly been close political and military associates of the Young Marshal in Mukden.

In the face of this strong Chinese Communist challenge, the Kuomintang approach to Manchuria—an area of which, like the Communists, it had little first-hand experience—was primarily urban-centered. Nationalist divisions transported there were well trained and well equipped, but they inevitably required more logistical support than the more mobile Communist forces. To handle the complex economic and financial problems of the area, the Kuomintang sent an elaborate and expensive bureaucracy composed for the most part of officials who, by background and experience, were ill-equipped to deal with the basic issues involved. A corrosive problem was that of political alienation: the Kuomintang officials, predominantly southern Chinese, failed to establish significant rapport with the political ambitions of the Manchurian Chinese.

Unfortunately for the National Government, the critical area in the conflict was the countryside. Following some initial defeats due to the superior equipment and firepower of the Nationalist divisions, the Communist forces sat it out in the north, across the Sungari River, until they could weld a new army out of their raw recruits and outfit it with their new Japanese gear and weapons. Gradually they extended their political hold over the rural areas and mobilized the local peasants with cleverly slanted propaganda. Wherever possible, they employed Manchurians who would work with them. Whenever possible, they disrupted rail and other lines of communication in order to isolate the Nationalist troops and officials in the larger cities.

Throughout 1947 and 1948 the military balance in Manchuria was clearly being tipped more and more in favor of the Chinese Communists. By the end of 1948 they had occupied Mukden, the last Nationalist stronghold in southern Manchuria. In the slightly more than three years since 1945, the Chinese Communists had gained complete control of the agricultural and industrial resources of China's richest region. Their military drive came to a halt only a year later, on the shores of the South China Sea.

As the Communist offensive moved south of the Great Wall at the end of 1948, many of the senior military and political figures moved on to north China. However, Kao Kang, at the time a rapidly rising figure in the upper ranks of the Communist hierarchy, remained behind in Mukden as the senior party, government, and military official in the Northeast. In July 1949, Kao made his first recorded trip to Moscow as head of an industrial and commercial mission which negotiated a one-year trade agreement between Manchuria and the Soviet Union. In August 1949, he became head of the new Northeast People's Government, the first, and only, full-scale regional government established by the Chinese Communists during their early period in power. No explanation has been given as to why it was considered necessary for Manchuria to press on with these separate economic and political developments during the summer and early autumn of 1949 when the party was, within a very few weeks, to establish a nation-wide government in Peking. With the formal establishment of the Central People's Government on October 1, 1949, Kao Kang was chosen as one of its six vice-chairmen. The initial definition of the new Sino-Soviet relationship in Manchuria was worked out during Mao Tse-tung's sojourn in Moscow at the beginning of 1950. In addition to a Treaty of Friendship, Alliance, and Mutual Assistance and arrangements for Soviet financial assistance, the two governments negotiated an understanding concerning their rights in Manchuria. The new agreement was strikingly similar to that which had been concluded between the Soviet Union and the National Government of China in August 1945. The principal railroad network, the Chinese Changchun railway, was to continue under joint Sino-Soviet administration.[6] The major naval base, Port Arthur, was likewise to be "jointly used," with Soviet troops garrisoned there as they had been since 1945. Both these arrangements were to be terminated upon conclusion of a peace treaty with Japan or at the end of 1952, whichever came earlier. At that time the Russians were, without compensation, to transfer to the Chinese Communists all rights in the rail network and all property belonging to it, and to withdraw Soviet troops from Port Arthur and hand over all installations there. Finally, the civil administration of Dairen, the principal port at the southern terminus of the railway, was to be solely in the hands of Communist China.

Two further agreements, concluded somewhat later, also affected Manchuria. One of the three airlines to be operated by the Sino-Soviet Civil Aviation Company, established in 1950, ran through Manchuria, connecting Peking and Chita by way of Mukden, Harbin, and Tsitsihar. And in 1951 a joint Sino-Soviet company was created to handle the building and repair of ships at Dairen.

[6] The new (Communist) Chinese Changchun Railway Company, a joint Sino-Soviet enterprise, was formally established in April 1950. It exercised control over the principal T-shaped rail system running diagonally across Manchuria from Manchouli to Suifenho and from Harbin to Port Arthur-Dairen, thus comprising the former Chinese Eastern and South Manchurian railways.

The Manchurian wing of the Sino-Soviet alliance structure was thus completed before the outbreak of the Korean war in June 1950. After the Chinese Communist intervention in October, Peking was in the position of attempting to push through its initial programs of political unification and economic rehabilitation within China, while waging a major war in Korea. The Northeast was of crucial importance to Peking in meeting both its internal and its external commitments. In domestic policy, Manchuria, politically and economically the most "advanced" region within the People's Republic, served as a laboratory for initiating major political campaigns, a testing area for new industrial and agricultural techniques, and a proving ground for economic planning and development programs. Campaigns introduced into the Northeast usually spread very shortly to the rest of mainland China.

And from the standpoint of the Korean war, Manchuria also provided Peking with its principal staging area for combat troops going into the line and its principal channel for handling the substantial flow of Russian military equipment. It furnished airfields, communications lines, hospitals, munitions dumps. Its industrial and agricultural production was essential both for military supply and for supporting an increasingly mobilized war economy.

When Moscow and Peking undertook new high-level discussions late in 1952, Manchurian issues were among the most pressing matters. In the absence of a peace treaty with Japan, the future of Port Arthur and the Chinese Changchun railway had to be decided by the end of 1952, according to the earlier agreement. In mid-September an official communiqué from Moscow announced that the Soviet government would transfer all its rights in the railway to China without compensation; this followed the terms of the 1950 agreement. The transfer of the railroad proceeded on schedule and there is evidence that it was genuine. In the matter of Port Arthur, on the contrary, the communiqué announced that the Chinese had asked the Russians to postpone their departure. The arrangements about Port Arthur undoubtedly reflected the strategic situation at the time, notably, the situation in Korea and the weakness of the Chinese Communist Navy. While the notes exchanged took care to emphasize that the proposal for the Russians to remain had originated with the Chinese, the net result was that the Russians continued to maintain their own military and naval establishment at a major base in Manchuria.

Stalin's death in March 1953 and the cessation of the fighting in Korea later that year opened a new phase in the Sino-Soviet alliance. The post-Stalin leaders in Moscow appear to have been increasingly interested in the consolidation of firm relations with their principal Communist ally in the Far East. Manchuria has been closely involved in the negotiations and agreements between the two allies during the past three years.

The Khrushchev-Bulganin visit to Peking in the autumn of 1954 marked a substantial improvement in the Chinese position in Manchuria. The Russians agreed to withdraw Soviet forces completely from Port Arthur and to restore the naval base to full Chinese Communist control by the end of May 1955. In addition, the Sino-Soviet companies, established in 1950 and 1951, were to be transferred to exclusively Chinese control.

In 1955, the Russian shares in the joint shipbuilding and repair company at Dairen were sold to Communist China, which agreed to pay for them by exports to the Soviet Union. During May 1955, the Russian troops completed their withdrawal from Port Arthur and on May 24, the Chinese and Russian members of the Joint Sino-Soviet Military Commission in Port Arthur signed the final protocol of transfer.[7] On May 26, the senior officers of the

[7] The communiqué stated:
In pursuance of the Sino-Soviet Agreement on Port Arthur of February 14, 1950, and the Sino-Soviet joint communiqué dated October 12, 1954, on the withdrawal of Soviet armed forces from the jointly used Chinese naval base of Port Arthur and placing this base completely at the disposal of the People's Republic of China, the Government of the U.S.S.R. has withdrawn its armed forces from the jointly used Chinese naval base of Port Arthur and has transferred without compensation the installations in this area to the Government of the People's Republic of China. The

High Command of the Soviet Armed Forces departed from the Port Arthur area, and three days later they left from Suifenho, on the Manchurian-Soviet border, for Vladivostok. After nearly ten years the Russians had completed their withdrawal.

We cannot know precisely what assumptions motivated Stalin's policy toward Manchuria at the time of the Japanese surrender a decade before. Presumably, however, Soviet estimates had been drastically altered by the rapid Chinese Communist conquest not only of all Manchuria but also of the entire mainland of China between 1947 and 1950. Within Manchuria, the basic trend, gradual during the period of rehabilitation of 1950-52, and then much more rapid, has been to integrate the entire area steadily and systematically into the national patrimony of the People's Republic. The available evidence does not indicate that Manchuria has become progressively detached from China proper, due to Russian pressure, or that it has been a truly critical issue in the relationships between the two major Communist powers.

Both in theory and, on the whole, in practice, the Russians appear to have accepted the underlying premise of Chinese Communist political supremacy in Manchuria. The original negotiations between Mao Tse-tung and Stalin, in February 1950, recognized Peking's sovereignty. The civil administration of Manchuria (with some qualifications for the Dairen-Port Arthur area) has remained throughout in Chinese hands, and the apparatus of the regional and local party and government structure has

---

Government of the People's Republic of China has completely taken over the naval base of Port Arthur and the installations in this area.

On May 24, 1955, the Joint Sino-Soviet Military Commission in Port Arthur created under the February 14, 1950, agreement signed a final protocol on matters relating to withdrawal of the Soviet armed forces from the jointly used Chinese naval base of Port Arthur and the transfer of the installations in this area to the People's Republic of China.

The measures regarding the withdrawal of the Soviet armed forces from the naval base of Port Arthur and the transfer of the installations in this area to the Government of the People's Republic of China have been carried out by the Joint Sino-Soviet Military Commission in a spirit of thorough mutual understanding and friendly cooperation.

been controlled from Mukden and Peking. In the spring of 1951, the previously independent banking and currency system of the Northeast was unified with that of China proper. And political and economic policies in Manchuria have consistently conformed, both in timing and in nature, to those in the rest of Communist China, or have actually preceded them.

Russia has long had a basic strategic interest in Manchuria and this is no less true today. The environment in which Russia's Manchurian policy operates has been greatly changed, however, since the area is now an integral part of a Communist China closely allied with the Soviet Union. Russian influence in Manchuria, especially during the Korean war, 1950-53, was doubtless greater than in China south of the Great Wall. But this influence appears to have been felt primarily in the spheres of military support and training and of economic and technical assistance. It appears probable that Russian activity in these sectors in Manchuria will continue, although the trend since 1953 has been toward consolidating Chinese control and contracting direct Russian influence and activity.

Since 1949, the respective spheres of Chinese and Russian authority in Manchuria have been altered significantly. The reasons behind the shift may better be sought in the general purposes and functioning of the Sino-Soviet alliance and in its policy toward the non-Communist world than in specific developments within Manchuria. The transfer of the principal Manchurian rail network to full Chinese control at the end of 1952 was an event unusual in the Communist bloc; it marked one of the few cases since 1945 when the Russians, having once acquired rights in an important strategic area, voluntarily surrendered them. The termination of joint Sino-Soviet occupation of Port Arthur and the replacement of Russian troops by Chinese Communist units in mid-1955 was an even more noteworthy development. In part, the Russian withdrawal was doubtless facilitated by the armistice in Korea, concluded in 1953, and by the Geneva agreement of 1954 on Indochina. In a broader sense, however, these concessions attested to the steady increase in Communist China's military potential, to the rapid growth in its political and strategic power in Asia, and—not least—to Moscow's apparent confidence in Communist China's ability to pursue its objectives in close cooperation with Soviet purposes.

MONGOLIA: OLD TRADITIONS AND NEW FORCES

In the year 1227, while pursuing a campaign against the rebellious Tangut kingdom, a Mongol general died in what is now the province of Kansu in northwest China. Genghis Khan, one of the greatest conquerors in all of world history, had led the Mongol nomads of Inner Asia out of obscurity and had instilled them with a unified consciousness as a people, making of them, for a fleeting moment, an exceedingly explosive force in human affairs. At the time of Genghis Khan's death, the great Eurasian land mass, from Peking to the Caspian, trembled before his hard-riding Mongol cavalry columns, disciplined and ruthless. Whatever the long-term results of the Mongol impact, it is clear that it was sparked by a military and political genius of unique proportions, one not to be easily forgotten by his own people.

To them there must be nothing singular in the fact that the bones of this extraordinary, illiterate Mongol conqueror have today, seven centuries later, found their way into the politics of modern Mongolia. In 1939, the purported remains of Genghis Khan were moved by the Chinese National Government to Kansu province. A decade later, in 1949, they were moved still farther west to an important lama temple in Tsinghai, where they were captured by advancing Chinese Communist divisions. In April 1954, the Chinese Communists moved the bier with its purported remains back to its "original burial place" in what is now Inner Mongolia. There, at Ezen Horoo, late in 1955, the Communists completed the construction of an impressive new Genghis Khan mausoleum. The erection of this mausoleum, reportedly built in "traditional

Mongol style" with blue and yellow tiled roofs, is an incongruous appendage to the general program of "Socialist construction" now being pressed forward in Communist China. Yet it is a gesture which cannot be dismissed lightly. It suggests that the Chinese Communist leaders in Peking are aware of the long-range political implications of the fact that they now have in their possession historic relics of great significance to all Mongols.

In the twentieth century the Mongol-inhabited areas of Inner Asia, a broad belt of grasslands and steppes, over five hundred miles wide, between China's Great Wall and Siberia, have been split, more especially as a result of the Chinese revolution of 1911 and the Russian revolution of 1917. Mongol nomads dominate the plains of western Manchuria and range without a break as far as Sinkiang, almost two thousand miles to the west. Today, however, Inner Mongolia, the Mongol territory nearest to the traditional Chinese realm, is included within the borders of Communist China, while Outer Mongolia, the portion farthest from China, is a political satellite of the Soviet Union, having broken completely away from China over three decades ago. We must therefore consider both the new position of the Inner Mongolia Autonomous Region and Communist China's relations with Outer Mongolia, the Mongolian People's Republic.

Peking's general policy has been to view the question of Inner Mongolia as a domestic problem and that of Outer Mongolia as an external issue, thereby seeking to avoid the suggestion that Communist China's internal Mongol problem is in any way connected with the status of the Mongolian People's Republic. In Ulan Bator, the capital of Outer Mongolia, the line appears to be that, while the Communist victory in China has opened a new stage in Sino-Mongol relations, Outer Mongolia continues to look principally to Moscow as the center of the world Communist camp. There has been no hint of any Communist planning which might look toward the political unification of Inner and Outer Mongolia, and it would appear that both the Soviet Union and Communist China would be chary of encouraging or tolerating any pan-Mongolist tendencies.

Peking and the Reshaping of Inner Mongolia

The Inner Mongolia Autonomous Region is the oldest of the "autonomous areas" devised by the Chinese Communists for the administration and control of non-Chinese minorities within the national framework of the People's Republic. Its record illustrates the policies followed by Peking in dealing with a strategic borderland area, one in which there have long been substantial political tensions between the pastoral Mongol nomads and the agricultural or commercial Chinese. It is also significant that the policies applied have been conceived and implemented by Chinese Communists, not by Mongol Communists imported from Outer Mongolia.

Possibly the most important political fact about Inner Mongolia of today is that since 1911 it has never developed into a distinct entity as did Outer Mongolia, despite the fact that, for nearly four decades after the Chinese revolution, there was no national political authority in China capable of bringing the Mongols of Inner Mongolia under truly effective and uniform control.[8] Local Chinese warlords, with limited regional interests, dealt with the local Mongols in accordance with their varying political and military energies and ambitions. The establishment of the National Government in China in 1928 led to the development of a Mongol policy which was, relatively, more unified and more consistent than had been possible during the warlord period. Nanking created new provinces in Inner Mongolia—Chahar, Suiyuan and Ninghsia—to assist in maintaining its control. In reaction to Chinese political encroachment and economic exploitation, Inner Mongolian nationalism, under indigenous Inner Mongol leadership, developed gradually. The most important leader of this rising Mongol consciousness was Prince Demchukdon-

8 See Owen Lattimore, *Nationalism and Revolution in Mongolia* (New York: Oxford University Press, 1955), pp. 22-9, for a discussion of Inner Mongolia during this period.

grub, known to the Chinese as Te Wang, who, by about 1930, had had considerable success in organizing anti-Chinese sentiments among the Mongols in the entire area from western Manchuria to the Ordos desert in Suiyuan.

Japan's aggressive actions on the mainland, begun in 1931, spread to Jehol in 1934 and to western Inner Mongolia about 1936-37. The Japanese, intent upon winning the cooperation of the anti-Chinese Mongols in their war against the Chinese, employed the tactic of promising political autonomy without violent revolution. In this they had some success, although it is significant that the Japanese, after 1937, actually kept the Mongols separated into the two areas: eastern Mongolia, which they organized as the Hsingan provinces in western Manchuria, and western Inner Mongolia, established as a distinct administrative entity, *Meng-chiang*, under the nominal but influential leadership of Te Wang.

From about 1944 to 1946, just before and after the close of the Japanese war, there was great political activity in Inner Mongolia. The Kuomintang, the Chinese Communists, the Mongols of Inner Mongolia, and the Mongols of Outer Mongolia were jockeying for power within the vastly changed framework of Sino-Soviet-Mongol relations. During the post-1945 period various Mongol "autonomy movements" appeared in eastern Mongolia and Inner Mongolia proper. The new and decisive factor, however, was that the Chinese Communists, partly through their own program of political agitation, partly because of the political ineptness of some Kuomintang leaders, were successful in gaining military control of all Inner Mongolia, from the steppes of western Manchuria to Ninghsia. Peking now claims that the "regional autonomy movements" of eastern and western Inner Mongolia were "united," under Chinese Communist auspices, at a meeting held at Chengteh in Jehol province as early as 1946. In May 1947, the "People's Government of the Inner Mongolia Autonomous Region" was established at Ulanhot (Wang-yeh-miao) under the control of Mongols who were either members or supporters of the Chinese Communist Party.

The significance of the new regime at Ulanhot ("Red City" in Mongol) was not at once apparent in the turmoil of the civil war which was sweeping over China. Inner Mongolian cavalry units, later incorporated formally into the Chinese Communist forces, did fight beside regular Chinese Communist units in Manchuria during 1947-48. Representatives from the Inner Mongolia Autonomous Region attended a meeting at Mukden, in August 1949, at which the regional Northeast People's Government was established, although they took no active part in the discussions. In September of the same year, the People's Political Consultative Conference met in Peking. There, Inner Mongolia was represented by a separate delegation, and it became clear that the Inner Mongolia Autonomous Region was to be a distinct administrative entity within the People's Republic.

The story of the Inner Mongolia Autonomous Region from its birth at Ulanhot in the spring of 1947 has been marked by two important trends: a steady growth in the size of the geographic area embraced by the Region, and the increasing consolidation of total Chinese Communist power over it. For some years after the original establishment of the Chinese Communist regime there in 1947, and even after 1949, there was much confusion regarding even such elementary facts as the size and approximate population of the Autonomous Region. Maps and atlases printed in Communist China were often contradictory. In retrospect, it appears that the confusion arose partly from the fact that the Region was being expanded in geographic extent as the Communists proceeded to consolidate their effective control of the areas involved. Symptomatic of this process is the fact that the capital of the Region was moved from Ulanhot to Kalgan early in 1950, and thence to Huhehot in 1952.[9]

The most important Mongol areas not included in the Inner Mongolia Autonomous Region in 1949 lay in

[9] The Chinese Communists officially changed the name of Kweisui, former capital of Suiyuan, to Huhehot—"Blue City" in Mongol—in the spring of 1954.

Suiyuan province, at the great bend of the Yellow River. Suiyuan had been governed for many years by General Fu Tso-yi, who began his career as a subordinate of Yen Hsi-shan, long-time warlord governor of Shansi province to the south of Suiyuan. From the standpoint of the Chinese Communists, the distinctive political and military background of Suiyuan province apparently suggested the advisability of dealing with the local situation there at a somewhat slower pace than in other parts of north China. Fu Tso-yi, politically alienated from the central hierarchy of the Kuomintang and militarily overwhelmed by the Chinese Communist forces as they swept down from Manchuria, surrendered Peking to the Communists without a fight at the beginning of 1949. However, two of his subordinate generals, Tung Ch'i-wu and Sun Lan-feng, still retained command of a portion of Fu's troops in Suiyuan itself. Because of this situation, the Communists permitted Tung Ch'i-wu to remain as governor after the province surrendered to them.

These arrangements were not dissolved until nearly three years later. In mid-1952, Peking initiated a series of new moves which resulted in consolidating its direct control over the area. On July 1, 1952, the principal organs of the government of the Inner Mongolia Autonomous Region, together with the Inner Mongolia regional apparatus of the Chinese Communist Party, moved from Kalgan (in Chahar province) to Huhehot (in Suiyuan). On July 21, Peking announced that Ulanfu, long the dominant Chinese Communist political figure in Inner Mongolia and head of the Autonomous Region government, had been named concurrently governor of Suiyuan, replacing Tung Ch'i-wu. On August 1, Red Army Day in Communist China, Peking and Huhehot announced the merging of the Suiyuan and Inner Mongolia military districts into a unified *(Sui-Meng)* military district. These changes made Suiyuan, in all but name, virtually an integral part of the Inner Mongolia Autonomous Region.

The full merger of Suiyuan with the Inner Mongolia Autonomous Region was finally approved by the national authorities in Peking in January 1954, and the two areas were amalgamated in March. The Autonomous Region now includes seven principal Mongol leagues, four in western Inner Mongolia (Ikechao, Ulanchap, Chahar, and Silingol) and three in eastern Mongolia (Jaoda, Jerim, and Hulunbuir), comprising almost exactly the same area as the Hsingan province which the Japanese had set up during their occupation.

The Suiyuan-Inner Mongolia merger, when it finally took place, was significant for two reasons: the action was initiated by the Chinese Communist Party in Peking, a clear indication of the source of final political authority; and the development had the anomalous result of making the Mongols of Inner Mongolia a definite minority group within the "Autonomous Region" which had ostensibly been created to foster their own national life. With the addition of Suiyuan, the population of the Inner Mongolia Autonomous Region totals about 6.1 million, of whom only about one million are Mongols. It is possible that Peking, in initiating the move, intended to dilute whatever pan-Mongolist tendencies or ambitions might still exist in Inner Mongolia. In the spring of 1956, by a further administrative shift, the territory inhabited by the Alashan and Edsingol Mongols in northwest China (the former province of Ninghsia) was likewise incorporated into the Inner Mongolia Autonomous Region.

Since 1949, the Chinese Communists have consistently indicated that they view Inner Mongolia as an integral part of a unified country. Their principal political representative in the area has been Ulanfu, a Sinicized Mongol born into the Tumet Banner in Suiyuan. He has been a member of the Chinese Communist Party for over twenty years. During the Japanese war, Ulanfu was active both at Yenan and among the Mongols in Suiyuan, and in 1945, at the Seventh Congress, he was elected an alternate member of the Central Committee of the Communist party. In the period after the Japanese surrendered, Ulanfu was the most active Chinese-oriented Mongol Communist in Inner Mongolia and, since 1947, he has dominated the party, governmental and military hierarchies in Inner Mongolia. He has also been a leading spokesman for Peking on policy toward minority nationalities and is now a Vice-Premier in the Central People's Government in Peking.

Today the Chinese Communists are able to control Inner Mongolia through Ulanfu and the regional apparatus of the party. Administratively, the area is controlled by a regional government, directly subordinate to Peking. In the military sphere, Inner Mongolia is subordinate to the top military command in Peking, and the Inner Mongolian cavalry units are a part of the national forces of Communist China. The many organizations through which the Chinese Communists control, mobilize, and indoctrinate the population—the New Democratic Youth League, the Democratic Women's Federation, and the others—all have regional branches in Inner Mongolia. Industrial and commercial programs for Inner Mongolia are carefully integrated with national economic development plans, and the former local currency was unified with the national currency system in the spring of 1951. Through the official newspaper in the area, the *Inner Mongolia Daily,* as well as through its close control over radio, books, magazines, and other communications media, Peking ensures its domination over whatever intellectual life there may be in Inner Mongolia.

Much of the tedious Communist prose which now emanates from Peking and Huhehot tells only of great achievements in the realm of "economic and cultural construction," of the growth in the number of pastoral mutual-aid teams and agricultural producers' cooperatives, of the continuing campaign to curb venereal diseases, and of the rapid growth in the number of livestock and the value of industrial production in the area. Certain facts of political importance do, however, stand out. The projection of Chinese Communist controls into the agricultural sections of Inner Mongolia actually involves only an extension of the general apparatus of political and economic controls utilized in China proper. But the techniques of total control, when exercised over nomadic herdsmen beyond the Great Wall, necessarily undergo some adaptation.

Thus far, the Chinese Communists have apparently been able either to forestall or overcome widespread Mongol resistance. It is equally certain that the deep-seated political, social, economic, and—not least important—linguistic frictions between Chinese and Mongols in Inner Mongolia have not been completely dissipated by the impatient blasts of Marxist-Leninist theory. Peking is aware of the deep mutual contempt with which Chinese and Mongols have normally regarded each other and of the political tensions which have frequently been engendered by these antipathies. In this area, as in many others, Peking looks to the future as well as to the present. It lays great stress upon the careful training and the indoctrination of tame young Mongol cadres who will be both willing and able to carry the party's political burdens and to implement its programs, as Inner Mongolian Communists, under the guidance of Peking. Over 15,000 young Mongol Communists have been trained by the party during the past six years.

As Inner Mongolia has been integrated within the Communist mold, there is doubtless more activity there today than at any time in the past half century. Huhehot, capital of the Autonomous Region, has grown into a bustling regional center. Chinese Communist planners are intent that Paotow, deep in the interior, be developed gradually into an important center of heavy industry and that Hailar, on the Chinese Changchun railway, grow to be an important meat-packing and tanning center. The Tsining-Ulan Bator railway, linking Inner and Outer Mongolia, has been opened for through traffic, and construction is going forward on a projected line from Paotow, the present terminus of the rail line from Peking, over 600 miles west through Inner Mongolia and southward along the Yellow River to Lanchow, in the northwest.

Unfortunately, official news releases tell nothing of the political tendencies among the Mongols of Inner Mongolia. A decade ago, Russian and Outer Mongolian Communist forces raced down into Manchuria and Inner Mongolia as far as the Great Wall, remaining for several months before they withdrew, and, following the Japanese surrender, there was some contact between Inner Mongolian political groups and Ulan Bator. Since 1949, however, the question of the relation between Inner Mongolia and Outer Mongolia or the Soviet Union has scarcely been mentioned. It is impossible to estimate the persistence of Mongol nationalism as a political factor in Inner Mongolia today, or even to learn whether Te Wang has ever been captured or executed by Peking.

The single development of decisive long-range importance may be cultural rather than political. Beginning in 1949, Communist Inner Mongolia has introduced the study of the Mongolian written language now used in Outer Mongolia. In August 1955, Peking announced that a new phonetic version of the Mongol written language, written horizontally and based on the Cyrillic alphabet, is to be introduced into Inner Mongolia. With its customarily methodical approach, Peking has allotted four years to carry out this basic linguistic reform. An initial period is to be used to train teachers, cadres, and printers; to expand printing equipment; to prepare materials for books and other publications; to carry on propaganda in preparation for the introduction of the new written language; and to do research on the various Mongol dialects involved. A second period is designated as a transition period during which the old script will gradually be abolished and the new written language, which corresponds with spoken Mongol, adopted for general use.

This linguistic reform will make the written language of Inner Mongolia the same as that of Outer Mongolia, where a Cyrillic system has been in use since 1946. Whether the use of a common written language will promote closer ties of nationalism between the two major segments of the Mongol people remains to be seen.

Communist China and Outer Mongolia:
New Bonds?

In the twentieth century the status of Outer Mongolia, which has been discussed sporadically in the United Nations, has been very ambiguous in the eyes of the non-Communist world. The Mongolian People's Republic has apparently claimed to be an independent state ever since it was formally established in 1924.[10] For over two decades, however, the Soviet Union was the only state which maintained diplomatic relations with it or recognized it as an independent political entity.

Outer Mongolia was for many years a persisting political and diplomatic issue between the governments of China and Russia. Aside from a short-lived tripartite agreement concluded between Tsarist Russia, China, and Mongolia in 1915, the problem was in diplomatic limbo until the Sino-Soviet Treaty of August 14, 1945, and the subsequent plebiscite, the results of which, to nobody's surprise, were reported as overwhelmingly in favor of "independence." In January 1946, the National Government of China recognized the Mongolian People's Republic as an independent state, but this formal gesture on China's part was not followed by the establishment of diplomatic relations.

Immediately after the establishment of the Central People's Government in Peking, Marshal Choibalsan, then Premier and Foreign Minister of the Mongolian People's Republic, notified Peking, on October 6, 1949, of the decision of his government to establish diplomatic relations with the People's Republic of China and to exchange diplomatic representatives. Chou En-lai, the Foreign Minister in Peking, at once agreed.

The question of Sino-Mongol relations within the Communist bloc had to await a settlement of far more important questions. In February 1950, at the time of the conclusion of the new Sino-Soviet Alliance, the status of Outer Mongolia was formally dealt with in an exchange

10 Gerard M. Friters, *Outer Mongolia and Its International Position* (London: Allen & Unwin, 1951), p. 284.

of notes between Chou En-lai and Vyshinsky. The two governments agreed that the treaty concluded in August 1945 was now null and void, and that "the independent status of the Mongolian People's Republic is fully guaranteed as a result of the plebiscite of 1945 and the establishment with it of diplomatic relations by the People's Republic of China." It is interesting to note that the first step in the new pattern of Sino-Soviet cooperation, a step which affected Outer Mongolia, was arranged directly by the Russians and the Chinese Communists without Mongol participation. This was the agreement, signed in Moscow on March 27, 1950, which provided for the establishment of a Sino-Soviet Civil Aviation Company, one of whose lines was to fly from Peking to Irkutsk by way of Kalgan and Ulan Bator, capital of the Mongolian People's Republic.

It was not until after the outbreak of the Korean war in June 1950 that Peking and Ulan Bator proceeded to exchange diplomatic representatives. On July 3, 1950, Bayaryn Jargalsaihan, the first Mongol ambassador accredited to a Chinese government in the twentieth century, called on Mao Tse-tung. And one week later Chi Ya-t'ai, a Mongol by origin, presented his credentials as the first official Chinese representative to Ulan Bator since 1921.

Since 1950 the pattern of Sino-Mongol-Soviet relations has developed gradually, almost imperceptibly. Many problems are still unanswered; many issues are still in doubt; many basic questions of attitude and orientation are still unclear. But one thing is certain: Outer Mongolia, like all areas in Eastern Asia, cannot be isolated, much less insulated, from the broad implications of the fact of total Communist control on the mainland of China and from the political and strategic implications of Communist China's growing power. A brief review of Sino-Mongol-Soviet relations, as they are now known in the West, may discourage facile conclusions about this remote sector of the Communist world.

In July 1951, the celebration of the thirtieth anniversary

of the "Mongolian People's revolution" of 1921 was attended by probably the most cosmopolitan diplomatic gathering ever held in Ulan Bator. Ambassadors from the Soviet Union, Communist China, and North Korea—the regimes with which the Mongolian People's Republic had exchanged diplomatic representatives—were present, together with special delegations from Communist countries of Eastern Europe. The delegation from Moscow was headed by M. P. Tarasov, Deputy Chairman of the Presidium of the Supreme Soviet of the U.S.S.R., and included the Premier of the Buriat-Mongol Autonomous Republic. Peking's delegation, in contrast, contained no figure of national importance.

When Marshal Choibalsan, the undisputed head of both party and government in Outer Mongolia since about 1939, died at Moscow in January 1952, this event was appropriately marked by both Russian and Chinese Communists. Mao Tse-tung stated that the "death of Marshal Choibalsan, a great leader of the Mongolian people and an outstanding leader and organizer of the Mongolian People's revolution, is a loss both to the Mongolian people and to the world camp of peace and democracy." In February, Peking sent a special delegation to Choibalsan's state funeral. Headed by General Nieh Jung-chen, then Acting Chief of Staff of the People's Revolutionary Military Council, the group also included Ulanfu, Chairman of the Inner Mongolia Autonomous Region; Wu Hsiuch'uan, Vice Minister of Foreign Affairs; and Chi Ya-t'ai, ambassador in Ulan Bator. A special memorial service was held at Kalgan, in Inner Mongolia.

In May 1952, Y. Tsedenbal, another veteran Mongol Communist, succeeded Choibalsan as Premier. His first direct participation in Sino-Soviet-Mongol negotiations brought him to Moscow in September 1952, while Chou En-lai was there to discuss Manchurian and other problems. The Russians accorded full honors to both the Chinese and the Mongols, and Stalin entertained them at a dinner in the Kremlin. Far more significant than the protocol, however, was the fact that at this time the three governments, "with a view to strengthening their mutual economic and cultural ties," worked out a tripartite agreement, only announced two years later, in October 1954, for the construction of a new strategic rail link, across Outer Mongolia, to link the rail systems of the Soviet Union and Communist China.

A few days after leaving Moscow, Tsedenbal arrived in Peking to attend the celebration of Communist China's National Day. This first visit was signalized by the conclusion, on October 4, 1952, of a ten-year Sino-Mongolian Agreement on Economic and Cultural Cooperation, which Tsedenbal described as opening "a new era in the relations between the Mongolian people and the Chinese people." Similar to the February 1946 Soviet-Mongol Agreement on Economic and Cultural Cooperation, this new agreement was significant as the most important agreement concluded by Outer Mongolia up to that time with a government other than the Soviet Union. The Chinese Communist treatment of the visiting Mongol delegation offered two points of special interest: while Mao Tse-tung, Chou En-lai, and other senior Chinese Communists devoted much personal attention to the visitors from Ulan Bator, neither Ulanfu nor any other Mongol important in the Chinese Communist hierarchy participated in the welcome organized by Peking.

For two years after the Tsedenbal mission, relations between Communist China and Outer Mongolia continued to develop slowly. In 1953, Bayanbatoryn Ochirbat replaced Jargalsaihan as representative to Peking, and in 1954 Ho Ying (a Chinese) replaced Chi Ya-t'ai (a Mongol) in the Chinese embassy in Ulan Bator. Carefully worded official announcements by Peking and Ulan Bator informed the world of the "unity of the camp of peace, democracy, and socialism." Annual Sino-Mongolian barter and payments agreements provided for the exchange of Outer Mongolia's livestock, hides, furs, and animal products against Communist China's deliveries of manufactured products (silk piece goods and leather articles), dried and fresh fruits, and other commodities.

It was only in October 1954, during the Khrushchev-Bulganin visit to Peking, that the Communists publicly disclosed one of the most significant recent developments affecting Outer Mongolia. A Sino-Soviet-Mongolian communiqué announced an agreement, actually concluded in September 1952 at Moscow, for the construction of the Tsining-Ulan Bator railway. The Chinese Communists were to lay the section from Tsining (on the railroad between Peking and Paotow, in Inner Mongolia) via Erhlien, to the Sino-Mongolian border, while the Russians and Mongols were jointly responsible for laying the section from Ulan Bator south through Chamuut to the Sino-Mongolian border. The Chinese section, about 210 miles in length, begun in the spring of 1953, was completed at the end of 1954. The Russian-Mongol section was completed during 1955, and various administrative agreements concerning the opening of the railroad to traffic between Communist China, Outer Mongolia, and the Soviet Union were signed at a tripartite conference held in Ulan Bator in September and October 1955. The new line was formally opened to through traffic in January 1956. An inaugural ceremony at the Sino-Mongolian border was attended by Tsedenbal from Outer Mongolia, Ulanfu from the Inner Mongolia Autonomous Region, and the Soviet Minister of Railways.

The new railroad provides an important new interior line of communication between the Soviet Union and its principal Communist ally in the Far East. It shortens by several hundred miles the rail connection between Moscow and Peking, which had formerly been linked only by the indirect, circuitous, and highly vulnerable Manchurian network. At Ulan Bator the new line connects with a railway, completed in 1949, which links that city with Ulan Ude, on the Trans-Siberian line.

The developments of the past few years, especially the completion of the new railroad, may provide Communist China with increased opportunities to expand its political and economic influence in Outer Mongolia. Recalling Mao Tse-tung's reported statement, two decades ago, that, after the general triumph of Communism in China, Outer Mongolia would in due course automatically become a part of the Chinese Communist federation, some observers have suggested that many Chinese Communists have not forgotten that China formerly included Outer Mongolia within its imperial borders. They have noted that Peking sent a strong delegation to attend the Twelfth Congress of the Mongolian People's Revolutionary Party in Ulan Bator in November 1954. This delegation was headed by Ulanfu, who, in his speech to the Congress, laid general stress upon the "unbreakable friendship" of the Soviet Union, Communist China, and Mongolia and also placed specific emphasis upon the development of closer relations between Communist China and Outer Mongolia.

There may indeed be some covert friction between Peking and Moscow over the question of long-term influence in Outer Mongolia. Since 1950, Communist China has had its own representative in Ulan Bator, whereas for about three decades before that Outer Mongolia had been a complete Russian satellite, with no Chinese influence, Communist or other, admitted. Since 1952, Sino-Mongol relations have further expanded within the framework of the Agreement on Economic and Cultural Cooperation. Chinese have gone to study and teach in Ulan Bator, and Mongols from Outer Mongolia have come to visit Communist China. Certain of Mao Tse-tung's writings have been translated into Mongol, and one of the most senior Chinese Communist political figures, Chou En-lai, has twice visited Ulan Bator (in 1952 and 1954, while en route from Moscow to Peking) and talked with the Mongol Communist leaders there. Possibly it is noteworthy that some maps from Communist China show the Sino-Mongolian border as "still undefined."

In broader terms, it does not appear likely that the issue of Outer Mongolia is of sufficient political importance to cause basic difficulties within the Sino-Soviet alliance in the near future.[11] It is doubtful that the Chinese Commu-

11 See Jack Raymond, "Yaks and Yurts, Marx and Mao," *New York Times Magazine*, October 21, 1956, pp. 15 ff. As a correspondent for the

nist leaders are capable of challenging Russian primacy at this time. It is still true, as it has been for many years, that the senior Mongol Communist leaders in Ulan Bator are oriented toward Russia, not China. Their military alignment is delineated in the Soviet-Mongol Treaty of Friendship and Mutual Assistance of February 1946, and Ulan Bator has no comparable treaty with Peking. One *tughrik,* the unit of currency in Outer Mongolia, is still equivalent to one ruble, and the recently completed rail line is Russian-style broad gauge across Outer Mongolia to the Chinese border.

Possibly, therefore, it is more realistic to view the Mongolian People's Republic, not as a major area of immediate political contention between Communist China and the Soviet Union, but rather as an increasingly important geographic area across which the two Communist giants are strengthening their strategic and economic links. Neither Moscow nor Peking has any interest in stirring up potentially disruptive issues of Mongol nationalism or pan-Mongolism, and it appears that the leaders in both capitals are capable of resolving the larger issues involved in their policies toward Mongolia within the general framework of the Sino-Soviet coalition.

Without opportunity for independent investigation in Outer Mongolia itself, it would be presumptuous to attempt to estimate the degree of pro- or anti-Russian or pro- or anti-Chinese sentiment which now prevails among the Mongols there. But the feelings and ambitions of the non-Communist Mongols, no less than the strategic interests of the Soviet Union and Communist China, are still to some extent involved in the politics of the area. The observations of one student of contemporary Mongolia may be pertinent in defining that elusive factor, the Mongol national tradition.

In any case it is remarkable that though faced with powerful neighbors, the individual Mongol has tried to retain one qual-

---

New York Times, Mr. Raymond visited Outer Mongolia in August and September 1956.

ity which is omitted from so-called Marxist interpretations of events—his ardor for independence, which is as much part of his nature as it is that of the eagle.

It befits the Mongol's pride in his past, for it is on his country's earlier history and not on his immediate ancestors (as with the Chinese) on which his heart is set. It falls in with his sturdy, but easy-going nomadic life; with the vast spaces of his land, difficult to control from the center, and with the mobility of his constant companion and other self—the Mongol pony. The Mongol can pitch his tent, i.e., his home, just in front of the imposing new buildings of the capital or move it out of reach of stony walls and officials. (In any case, that is what he would like to do, whatever restrictions may exist as to the moving into or moving out of Ulan Bator.) No wonder therefore that he has always shown a strong aversion to the building of railways in and across his country.

Still more must the many manifestations of Soviet-inspired planning in an economy of scarcity run counter to their individualistic habits. Their breeding and rearing of sheep and other cattle was in fact highly inefficient in the past, but with the coming into being of the Mongolian People's Republic they have been deprived of the right to sell the cattle at the place and in the manner they liked. We realize that they are now protected from the sharp business practices of the Chinese merchants. But even supposing such do not obtain at all in any form under the new conditions, there will always remain some human beings endowed with enough naivety—and the travellers are legion who have testified as to this enthralling characteristic of the Mongols—who prefer being cheated as free men of the plains to being shielded as controlled men of "collectives," "artels," etc.[12]

SINKIANG: COMMUNIST CHINA'S NEW FRONTIER

Far out back of beyond, in the deep interior of Asia, lies Sinkiang, or Chinese Turkestan, ancient and inhospitable. A remote and largely self-contained area, separated from the principal centers of Eurasia by forbidding desert barriers and great mountain ranges, its destiny has been profoundly marked by its geography.

Sinkiang, now comprising about one-sixth of the total

[12] Friters, cited; author's preface to the English edition, pp. vi-vii.

territory of Communist China, is almost three times as large as France. The T'ien Shan range, the loftiest mountain chain in Eastern Asia north of Tibet, runs from the steppes of Mongolia to the Pamirs, roughly bisecting the province from east to west. To the north of this range lies the basin of Dzungaria, which stretches northward to the Altai mountains, on the Russian-Mongolian border. To the south of the T'ien Shan, surrounded by a fertile belt of oases, lies the Tarim basin (Kashgaria), with the desolate and arid Taklamakan desert at the very heart of Inner Asia. Modern Sinkiang looks north and west to the Soviet Union and northeast to the Gobi desert and Outer Mongolia. In the southwest, it looks across the Pamirs to Afghanistan and Gilgit. On the south, it faces the K'un Lun mountains and the high wastes of Tsinghai and Tibet proper. Down a single lane to the east it looks, past Hami, to the Kansu corridor, the Jade Gate, and China.

Sinkiang's indigenous peoples, ethnically distinct from those of China, are predominantly Moslems, related linguistically and culturally to the native peoples of Russian Turkestan.[13] The Chinese comprise only about 10 per cent of the total, estimated by Peking at about 4.87 million in 1953. The Uighurs (estimated at 3.6 million), the principal ethnic group, are a sedentary people, dependent upon small-scale agriculture and oasis-bound. Quite different are the Kazakhs and Kirghiz, nomadic and tribal peoples, Moslems in religion and Turkic in language. The Kazakhs (estimated at 500,000) make up about 10 per cent of the total population of Sinkiang, numerically the second largest group after the Uighurs. The principal Kazakh grazing areas have been the steppes of northern Sinkiang, especially the frontier areas between Sinkiang and the Kazakh S.S.R. on the northwest and between Sinkiang and the Mongolian Peoples' Republic on the northeast. While the Kazakhs are steppe nomads, the Kirghiz (estimated at 70,-000) are alpine nomads, who graze their herds in summer

13 A useful summary of information on the peoples of Sinkiang is given in the chapter by John De Francis in Owen Lattimore and others, *Pivot of Asia* (Boston: Little, Brown, 1950), pp. 103-51.

pastures high on the slopes of the mountains of southwest Sinkiang. The population also includes a significant number of Hui (estimated at 100,000), who are Moslem by religion but Chinese by language, and of Mongols (estimated at 60,000) living outside the borders of the Inner Mongolia Autonomous Region. There are also smaller Moslem groups speaking Turkic languages—Tajiks, Uzbeks, and Tatars—as well as *émigré* Russians and remnants of the Manchus.

This land of mountains and deserts, oases and grasslands, is a region of rich and diverse history. Lying athwart one of the world's great continental highways, Chinese Turkestan was for centuries the channel for cultural and commercial contacts between the ancient civilizations of China, India, and the Hellenized west of Asia. It has seen Arabs, Persians, Turks, Mongols, Tibetans, and Chinese; diplomatic envoys, traders, soldiers, and monks; Buddhists, Moslems, and Christians. In the twentieth century, Sinkiang—its name means the "New Frontier"—continues to combine the color and isolation of a true frontier region with the traditions of a land whose roots go far back into the past. It has preserved a distinctly Central Asian flavor: silks, Khotan carpets, jade, golden Hami melons, deep blue grapes, and donkeys, spread across a dusty stage with walled gardens, dim bazaars, and turreted mosques, against a backdrop of snow-capped mountains, green oases, and rows of poplar trees.

Through this area, with its atmosphere partly Oriental and partly Middle Eastern, Chinese power has ebbed and flowed for many centuries. In periods of vigor like the Han and the T'ang, Chinese power surged relentlessly outward to establish a *pax sinica* in Central Asia. Yet the record of Chinese rule was not one of continuity. While Chinese rulers were able intermittently to subjugate, dominate, and influence Chinese Turkestan, there was no true geographic basis for the extension into the region of the settled, agricultural pattern of life of the Chinese people. Thus, there have been long periods when developments in Turkestan were outside the mainstream of Chinese history.

In the modern period, the Chinese have exercised control over Turkestan with varying success for about two hundred years. In the mid-eighteenth century, military expeditions under the vigorous Ch'ien Lung emperor brought the entire Tarim basin as well as Dzungaria, to the north of the T'ien Shan, under Peking's rule. Following this reassertion of imperial power, there were serious Moslem uprisings in the northwest during the nineteenth century. The most widespread Moslem rebellion (1862-77) caused extensive devastation and was eventually put down only by the determined efforts of one of the ablest Chinese mandarins of the period, the Hunanese general Tso Tsung-t'ang. After his victories Sinkiang became in 1884 the nineteenth province of the Chinese Empire.

Outwardly, the imperial court at Peking continued to govern Sinkiang until 1911. Actually, as the central power of the Manchu regime declined, the government of Sinkiang came, after 1884, to be increasingly controlled by a compact coterie of Chinese families who dominated the local bureaucracy. As in Manchuria, this spirit of regional separatism had considerable significance, for it meant that the Chinese revolution of 1911 had relatively little impact on Sinkiang. The local Chinese officials remained the ruling group in what might otherwise have been a situation of political chaos. When the Manchu governor was deposed in 1911, Yang Tseng-hsin, a Yunnanese official serving in Urumchi, immediately assumed responsibility for administration and continued to govern the province for about seventeen years. While Sinkiang remained under Chinese sovereignty, it was, in fact, quite as autonomous as was Manchuria under the Old Marshal, Chang Tso-lin, during the same period. Yang Tseng-hsin—relatively efficient, shrewd, and autocratic—provided his domain with a consistent and coherent rule during a period when much of China within the Great Wall was in a state of disorganization and disintegration. Like the Old Marshal in Manchuria, Yang dealt with the Russians independently and signed separate agreements with them as *de facto* ruler of an autonomous government. To complete the curious parallelism, Yang Tseng-hsin, like Chang Tso-lin, was assassinated in mid-1928.

The Kuomintang and the new National Government of China, established at Nanking in 1928, had no more success in gaining control over Sinkiang than over Manchuria. For a decade and a half after 1928, Sinkiang continued to go its own way. During these years there were—apart from the Japanese—two major threats to Chinese rule in the province. A bitter and bloody Moslem uprising, led by Ma Chung-ying, the redoubtable "Big Horse" from Kansu, lasted from 1931 until 1934 and nearly overturned the Chinese provincial administration of Chin Shu-jen, the successor of Yang Tseng-hsin. And there was direct Soviet intervention. The Russian intrusion, the principal military factor in suppressing the revolt of Ma Chung-ying, lasted for about a decade, from 1934 to 1943, while Sheng Shih-ts'ai, an adventurer from Manchuria, nominally headed the provincial government in Urumchi.

Strategic considerations were clearly important in the Soviet decision to move directly into Chinese Turkestan. The Russians feared the Japanese might attempt to drive a wedge toward Central Asia; they were disturbed at Japanese intrigues among the Moslems of China which, in conjunction with a Moslem uprising in Sinkiang, might easily spread confusion and unrest across the border to Moslem groups within the Soviet Union. For nearly ten years, with their own military garrison stationed at Hami, the Russians dominated Sinkiang both strategically and economically. Chinese sovereignty was never abrogated, and it is interesting to note in retrospect that the Urumchi authorities' protestations of loyalty to the National Government of China increased in almost direct proportion to the intensification of Russian activity and influence in Sinkiang. This verbal harmony between Urumchi and Chungking lasted throughout the Japanese war, Kuomintang statements on the loyalty of Sinkiang being balanced by

Sheng Shih-ts'ai's avowals of his continued support for the National Government.

In mid-1943, the Russians—doubtless motivated by the military situation in the European theater—withdrew their garrison from Hami, recalled all Russian technical personnel in Sinkiang, and dissolved all Soviet-run enterprises. A year later, in August 1944, Sheng Shih-ts'ai was dislodged, and the Kuomintang set about extending its own political and military influence to Sinkiang for the first time. The pressure of external events, and the spread of civil war in China proper, prevented it from laying a solid foundation for its rule before the Chinese Communist forces invaded the province in 1949. The Kuomintang-Communist struggle for total power in China was reflected in Sinkiang against a tangled local background of political tensions, economic deterioration, and intensified racial antagonisms. The situation was complicated after November 1944 by an anti-Chinese revolt of the native peoples in the Ili region of northwest Sinkiang, adjacent to the Soviet Union. None of the Nationalist governors was able to evolve any generally effective program for dealing with the problems of Sinkiang.

During this period the Soviet posture toward Sinkiang was both cynical and enigmatic. While Moscow continued to maintain diplomatic relations with the National Government of China, it also provided political and military support for the Ili revolt, thus eliminating Chinese authority from an important area of northwest Sinkiang. As late as 1949, the Soviet ambassador in China was negotiating with the National Government over important economic and transportation concessions in Sinkiang. During the very months when the Chinese Communist armies were driving rapidly into the northwest, Moscow appeared intent upon obtaining a special position there.

At the time of the Japanese surrender in 1945, the Chinese Communist Party, like the Kuomintang, had few political roots in Sinkiang. For well over a decade after the establishment of the Chinese Communist Party in 1921, there was no significant Communist activity there. Later, during Sheng Shih-ts'ai's collaboration with the Russians, some Chinese Communist personnel from Yenan entered the province. But, when Sheng broke with the Soviet Union, he imprisoned or executed as many Chinese Communist cadres as he could lay hands on. Ch'en T'an-ch'iu, one of the early leaders of the party in China; Mao Tse-min, Mao Tse-tung's brother; and many others were summarily shot in 1943. From that time until the autumn of 1949, the Chinese Communists had virtually no access to Sinkiang. When they moved into the area, they had neither indigenous roots nor any reservoir of reliable personnel acquainted with the problems of the area.

By the early autumn of 1949 the Chinese Communists were approaching Sinkiang with overwhelming force, and the provincial regime in Urumchi bowed to the inevitable with an action which the Communists termed "peaceful surrender." Late in September, the provincial government, headed by Burhan, a veteran Sinkiang politician, severed relations with the National Government, then located at Canton, pledged its allegiance to the new Communist regime which was being established in Peking, and stated that it would accept the peace terms of Mao Tse-tung and "await reorganization." The Chinese Communist leaders replied at once, approving the "correct" stand taken by the Sinkiang authorities. Early in October, Communist armies entered Sinkiang through the Kansu corridor and moved on to occupy Urumchi, although it was several months later, in early 1950, before Communist forces reached Kashgar, in western Sinkiang, and the outlying districts of northern Sinkiang. At the same time, Peking felt its way slowly in the difficult tasks of political consolidation, during the early period calling upon the advice, knowledge, and influence of Chang Chih-chung, a prominent Nationalist leader who, as governor of Sinkiang, had been closely associated with the postwar negotiations there prior to his defection to the Communists. A new provincial government was established at the end of 1949, with Burhan, durable and amenable, continuing as nominal chairman.

At the very time that the telegraphic surrender of the province reached Peking, delegates from Sinkiang had already arrived there to participate in establishing the new national government of Communist China. The small delegation from Sinkiang was headed by Saifudin, a prominent figure in the insurgent Ili regime.[14] This was a significant development for, prior to the autumn of 1949, there had been no openly avowed connection between the Ili rebels inside Sinkiang and the Chinese Communist rebels outside the region. The Ili group, which had revolted in northwest Sinkiang five years earlier, had for all practical purposes been quite independent of Chinese authority, Nationalist or, so far as is known, Communist. The Russians, interested in fomenting anti-Kuomintang native unrest in Sinkiang, had supported the insurrection. It is not clear who was responsible for the prompt appearance of Saifudin at Peking in September 1949.[15]

The problem of Sinkiang was also one of the issues which Mao Tse-tung discussed with Stalin at the end of 1949. A separate delegation from Sinkiang, led by Saifudin, flew to Moscow in January 1950, to join in the discussions. However, the problem of Sino-Soviet relations in Sinkiang was not within the scope of the published treaty of alliance of February 14, 1950, and was dealt with in separate agreements, signed after the principal Chinese Communist leaders had left Moscow. On March 27, 1950, the Chinese Communist and Soviet governments concluded an agreement for the establishment of two Sino-Soviet joint-stock companies in Sinkiang, one for the prospecting and mining of nonferrous and rare metals, and one for the prospecting, extraction, and refining of pe-

14 Saifudin has since emerged as one of the leading figures in Sinkiang. During the winter of 1949-50 he went to the Soviet Union to participate in the Sino-Soviet discussions there and, upon his return, was formally admitted to membership in the Chinese Communist Party on February 28, 1950.

15 The story of the Ili rebellion and the "East Turkestan Republic" established at Ining is extraordinarily complex and, in many respects, still unclear. Lack of space makes it impossible to attempt to unravel its mysteries here.

troleum. As originally signed, this agreement was to be valid for thirty years, until 1980. An agreement for the establishment of a Sino-Soviet Civil Aviation Company, valid for ten years, until 1960, provided for opening a line between Peking and Alma Ata by way of Sian, Lanchow, and Urumchi.

It is debatable whether these initial Sino-Soviet arrangements in Sinkiang were inspired principally by Russian interest in economic exploitation, by Chinese Communist interest in economic development, or by both. It is, however, reasonably clear that neither exploitation nor development proceeded very rapidly. Domestically, the Chinese Communists were seriously occupied with the problems of military and political consolidation in Sinkiang during the 1950-52 period. Internationally, the prosecution of the Korean war was an objective of far higher priority than the communization of Chinese Central Asia. The Korean war placed increasingly heavy strains upon the domestic economy of Communist China, and the Soviet Union had substantial and continuing commitments to furnish direct military support to the Chinese Communist and North Korean forces. The degree of Russian attention to developments in Sinkiang during this period appears to have been relatively limited. With the cessation of hostilities in mid-1953, however, it became possible to pay more attention to Sinkiang.

In Communist China any significant economic expansion is basically dependent upon the creation of an adequate and integrated system of modern transportation. This problem, important throughout the mainland, is truly acute in the interior of the country. When the Chinese Communists occupied Sinkiang, there were few adequate roads, few airplanes, and no railroads. The norm was still primitive transport—humans and animals, carts and camels—eked out by scattered and antiquated busses, trucks, and jeeps. From the beginning, the Chinese Communists looked to the improvement of communications in Sinkiang.

As early as 1950, the Communists began construction of

the Tienshui-Lanchow railroad, a westward extension of China's principal east-west line, the Lunghai. The Tien-shui-Lanchow section, which runs for over two hundred miles through mountainous terrain, begun in May 1950, was opened to traffic in October 1952. Its completion made possible through rail communication on the Lung-hai line from the Yellow Sea to Lanchow, capital of Kansu province and economic center for the pastoral and mineral products of China's northwest. The long-range implications of the Chinese railroad program became further apparent when, late in 1952, the Chinese Communists determinedly began laying rail on a new Lanchow-Sinkiang line. This railroad, long rumored, is scheduled to extend up the Kansu corridor via the Yumen oil district to Urumchi.

While the Chinese Communists were demonstrating their independent, if limited, capacity for railroad construction, the joint Sino-Soviet companies in Sinkiang were also becoming more active. It appears that during 1950-52, the activities of these companies had not gone beyond planning, geological reconnaissance, prospecting for petroleum and other mineral deposits, and initial training of workers and staff personnel. During 1953 and 1954, Communist reports from Sinkiang indicated that more concrete developments were taking place. Training, with Russian assistance, of Chinese and native Sinkiang technical personnel was pressed. Oil drilling was expanded, and an automatic cracking plant, equipped with Soviet machinery, was completed.

In the autumn of 1954, the Khrushchev-Bulganin visit to Peking marked a new stage in the evolution of the Sino-Soviet coalition. The joint communiqué, issued on October 12, 1954, announced that the Sino-Soviet companies in Sinkiang were to be transferred to exclusive Chinese Communist control. Beginning in 1955, the Russian shares were to be transferred to the Chinese, who agreed to pay for them "over the course of several years" with exports to the Soviet Union. Accordingly, in January 1955, the Sino-Soviet companies were converted to Chinese state-owned enterprises, renamed the Sinkiang Petroleum Company and the Sinkiang Nonferrous Metals Company, and placed under the control of the Ministries of Fuel Industry and Heavy Industry, respectively, in Peking. The Sino-Soviet Civil Aviation Company, which had operated Urumchi-Alma Ata and, after 1953, Urumchi-Kashgar flights, was also transferred to full Chinese Communist control. A new Sino-Soviet Air Service Agreement, providing for flights by Russian and Chinese civil aircraft between the two countries, was signed in Peking at the end of 1954.

The net result is that Peking is now free of the myriad complications involved in operating Sino-Soviet joint-stock companies while it continues to receive Russian economic and technical assistance. Peking is, of course, committed to shipping additional exports—probably including wool, hides and skins, minerals, and other primary products from Sinkiang—to the Soviet Union until the obligation is fully discharged. These agreements indicate a Soviet willingness to recognize Peking's growing stature and, presumably, Peking's willingness to coordinate its policies with those of Moscow.

In October 1954, the Soviet Union and Communist China also announced their agreement for construction of the Lanchow-Urumchi-Alma Ata railroad. The Lanchow-Sinkiang line, which the Chinese had begun building in 1952, is to be extended to Urumchi, and then to the Russian border, where it will connect with a new Soviet line from the frontier to Alma Ata, capital of the Kazakh Republic, and with the Turkestan-Siberian railway. That portion of the line within Chinese territory, some 1,700 miles in length, is to be built by the Chinese with Soviet assistance; the relatively short portion of the line within Soviet territory, from Alma Ata to the Sinkiang border, by the Russians.

When Soviet First Deputy Premier Mikoyan visited Peking in the spring of 1956, a new Sino-Soviet agreement was announced, calling for completion of the railroad by 1960. Prodigious efforts and toil lie ahead, for the projected route lies across some of the most difficult terrain in Asia. The long-range strategic significance of this Lanchow-Urumchi-Alma Ata line is great. When completed, it will provide a third connecting route, and one vulnerable only to long-range aircraft, across the most remote interior regions of both China and the U.S.S.R.

While Peking has, step by step, eliminated the traditional and direct interference by the Russians in the affairs of Sinkiang, it has also been applying an extensive armory of techniques, largely resembling the Soviet model, to consolidate its control over a geographically remote and economically backward area inhabited by a population which is 90 per cent non-Chinese.

The basic instrument of control has been the Chinese Communist armies. While Peking has never released detailed information on the size of its military establishment in Sinkiang, it must be a substantial one, for its garrisons have both a police and an economic role. They bear primary responsibility for maintaining security and for eradicating any "bandit" or "counterrevolutionary" groups which might threaten the total control which the party demands. Elimination of uncooperative elements—people who oppose, or seem likely to oppose, Communism—has, therefore, proceeded with ruthless dispatch. Osman Bator, one of the most vigorous and independent Kazakh chieftains in recent Sinkiang history, was publicly executed in Urumchi in the spring of 1951, and many other local non-Communist leaders, including certain members of the former Ili regime, have been killed or imprisoned by the Communists.

The Chinese Communist forces in Sinkiang also fulfill a major economic function. From the outset, they have planted and harvested food for their own sustenance. They also provide a basic, disciplined source of labor for general agricultural development in Sinkiang. Chinese military units, aided by Soviet seed, equipment, and technical assistance, have been utilized to establish mechanized farms, collective farm villages, and machine-tractor stations. They have been mobilized for road construction and repair, land reclamation, irrigation projects, reforestation, animal husbandry, mining, and construction of new buildings, dams, reservoirs, and other installations required by the regime. All indications are that the Chinese armies stationed in Sinkiang will continue for many years to be a major factor in its agricultural and industrial development. This policy is being pursued consciously as part of a general political and social program of promoting large-scale, planned Chinese immigration to the far northwest. The Chinese Communist troops in Sinkiang serve both as military colonizers and, through their reclamation work, as advance elements preparing the way for the increasing numbers of nonmilitary cadres, technicians, and other Chinese who are being moved from China proper to work and settle in Sinkiang.

Sinkiang is, of course, too large and complex an area to be governed solely by military units and through military coercion. During the past six years, the Chinese Communists have also given close attention to political measures, both repressive and persuasive, which would be useful in creating a reasonably solid base for their control of Sinkiang as an integral part of the national administrative structure of Communist China.

The evolving pattern has been quite consistent: control from the center, participation at the periphery, and—most significant in the long run—the increasing immigration of Chinese into the area. The principal goal in the political reshaping of Sinkiang—organization and mobilization of the non-Chinese peoples under the authority of the Chinese Communist Party—was indicated as early as January 1950 in Sinkiang's first Peking-directed statement of its local "administrative program." And the tactics employed have, in general, been similar to those used in Inner Mongolia. Peking's intention is, in the short run, to encourage local participation, under Communist direction and control, in local political affairs and, in the long run, to train local non-Chinese personnel who, as administrative cadres and party members, will carry out the aims of the Chinese Communist Party in Sinkiang.

The great physical distances involved pose difficult practical problems, but the theory is clear. Peking transmits its basic political directives to Sinkiang through the local apparatus of the Chinese Communist Party and its military orders through the local apparatus of the Chinese Communist military organization. The planners in Peking have regularly indicated that the rehabilitation and development programs in Sinkiang are a part of the general effort of economic expansion. In 1951, the local Sinkiang currency was abolished and replaced by a new note issue, printed in Uighur, which has since been part of the national banking and financial system of Communist China. And Peking maintains total control of communications media in Sinkiang. It prints the works of Mao Tse-tung, textbooks, magazines, and the official newspaper, the *Sinkiang Daily,* in Uighur, Kazakh, and Mongol, as well as Chinese, and has even devised a system for the transmission of local telegrams in Uighur. In August 1956, Peking announced that the Cyrillic alphabet used in the Soviet Union had been adopted for the Uighur language in Sinkiang.

The political climax of Chinese Communist efforts to deal with the difficult minorities problem in Sinkiang came late in 1955, after three years of studies and steps. From 1952 to 1955, Peking slowly felt its way through the tortuous maze of native peoples in Sinkiang, establishing fourteen separate autonomous areas below the provincial level, for the Kazakhs, Kirghiz, Hui, Mongols, Tajiks, and other non-Chinese groups. Finally, in September 1955, it formally established the Sinkiang-Uighur Autonomous Area—unique in that it is at the provincial level in Communist China's administrative hierarchy—with the Uighurs, who make up about three-fourths of the population of Sinkiang, recognized as the principal ethnic group. Chairman of the new regime is Saifudin. Burhan, nominal provincial governor of Sinkiang from 1949 to 1955, continued his active but still secondary role in the new regime in Urumchi.

On this occasion Peking issued a statement of its general

policy toward the Sinkiang-Uighur Autonomous Area. Speaking at Urumchi, Tung Pi-wu, senior member of the Political Bureau of the party, lauded the establishment of the new regime as final proof of the "invincibility of the nationalities policy of the Chinese Communist Party and Chairman Mao formulated on the basis of Marxism-Leninism." Sternly he advised the non-Chinese cadres in Sinkiang to recognize their continuing responsibility to assist and cooperate with the Chinese cadres in order to carry out the great tasks of "Socialist construction" and the plans of the Central People's Government for Sinkiang. Tung Pi-wu's theoretical implication was clear: with the general victory of Communism in China, there is no longer any basis for restless, assertive, separatist nationalism on the part of the non-Chinese peoples in Chinese Central Asia. Practically, Sinkiang's new "autonomy" is designed to bind the area closer to Communist China.

In the late nineteenth and early twentieth centuries, Sinkiang was a focus of friction for the great powers—China, Russia, and Great Britain—whose actual or presumed interests impinged upon it. Russian and British sparring in the Central Asian arena was, in a broad sense, an aspect of their general rivalry in Europe and Southwest Asia. Basic geographic factors made it simpler to find a temporary solution in Central Asia than in some other parts of the world. Once the two powers were assured that there was no easy invasion route between Russia and India, their national interests permitted them to view Sinkiang as an intermediate buffer area in which no active military intervention was required.

Sino-Russian rivalry in Chinese Central Asia has had a long and distinctive history. Russian thinking appears to have been dominated by both strategic and economic considerations. Moscow has regularly shown concern over any possible political disturbances which might, directly, pose a threat to or, indirectly, arouse unrest in its Central Asian territories. And, with the movement of so much of Russian industry to areas east of the Urals during and after the second World War, the Soviet leaders have continued to hold a major strategic interest in Sinkiang, based on its potential importance in an age of air power. Of secondary, but nevertheless significant, concern has been the economic relation of Sinkiang to Russia. The growth of Russian commercial interests in Central Asia during the late nineteenth century spilled over into Sinkiang, and this economic interest was revived after the Russian revolution of 1917. Soviet domination of its economic life was greatly facilitated by the facts of physical geography: the natural economic relations of Chinese Turkestan have been with Russian Turkestan across a political border which is largely artificial, from the standpoint of human geography. Indeed, the richest agricultural and mineral resources of Sinkiang are found in the far northwest, directly adjacent to Soviet Central Asia and within easy access to the Turkestan-Siberian railway which was completed in 1930. However, the primary resources of Sinkiang, while of some regional importance to Central Asia, are not of major significance to the Russian national economy as a whole. Sinkiang is not a vital link in the expansion of Russian industry in either Central Asia or Siberia, nor are its resources necessary to the growth of the Soviet economy.

The present pattern of Sino-Soviet cooperation in Sinkiang is a relatively new phenomenon, one which has emerged from the extension of Chinese Communist control to the area. Russian strategic and economic interests appear to be adequately served by the establishment of a firm and cooperative Chinese Communist-dominated regime in Sinkiang. Increasingly since the death of Stalin, the Soviet leaders have been willing to work out a joint approach to the area which leaves primary political control to Peking and limits direct Russian activity to the sphere of economic and technical assistance. The general gain through consolidating the Sino-Soviet coalition far outweighs, for Moscow, any minor local gains which might be achieved through more active intervention in the complex affairs of Sinkiang. Accordingly, the Russians acquiesced in the liquidation by the Chinese Communists of the insurgent Ili regime, which had been born in 1944 with Soviet influence and assistance, and agreed to the dissolution of the Sino-Soviet joint-stock companies.

From the standpoint of Peking, the political situation is still basically similar to that which has prevailed in Sinkiang over the past eighty years, ever since the reconquest of the area by Tso Tsung-t'ang in the late Ch'ing period. Chinese Communist control of this enormous area must rest upon Peking's ability to manipulate diverse congeries of non-Chinese peoples, predominantly Moslem and directly related to the Turkic peoples of Soviet Central Asia. A mixture of resolute harshness and calculated moderation, as well as a balancing of immediate requirements against long-term ambitions, has accompanied the vigorous extension of total Chinese military and political authority to Sinkiang. Peking is probably realistic enough to know that Sino-Soviet economic and technical cooperation in Sinkiang will, for many years to come, remain an essential prerequisite for the development of the region.

In Sinkiang, at the far western end of the long Sino-Mongolian-Soviet border, there appears to be sufficient mutuality of general interest between Peking and Moscow to overcome, or at least to contain, the local frictions which may well continue to arise from time to time. Control of Sinkiang is of great symbolic significance to Peking. Viewed realistically, Sinkiang is neither the pivot of Asia nor even an important center of gravity within the present Sino-Soviet alliance. Its basic importance, to either Communist China or the Soviet Union, is relatively small so long as it remains securely anchored within the general Communist realm. Communist China, without serious controversy with Moscow, can be expected to retain primary responsibility for working out the Marxist-Leninist destiny of modern Sinkiang.

THE BORDERLANDS AND THE MOSCOW-PEKING AXIS

If the situation in the Sino-Soviet borderlands is similar to human situations elsewhere, there will presumably continue to be some degree of friction between the Chinese, the Russians, and the indigenous population. It is, however, doubtful whether, in the foreseeable future, any local problems within these areas will be permitted to become, in and of themselves, of sufficient importance to give rise to major difficulties in Sino-Soviet relations. In the event of war, the immense area stretching from Manchuria through Mongolia to Sinkiang would be of great strategic importance to the entire Communist bloc. And both Moscow and Peking share a considerable common interest in curbing minor, regional squabbles in favor of maintaining the general advantages which each partner now obtains from the alliance.

Peking's basic purposes—political centralization, economic and industrial expansion, and increased military power—are clear, and the impact of these purposes upon the northern borderlands is not different, except in detail, from their impact upon the life of all mainland China. And, because Peking is pursuing these objectives in close cooperation with the Soviet Union, the borderlands are doubly important because of their sensitive relationship to Russia.

Any Chinese government which aims to unify China must also exercise full control over the borderlands. During the period of the National Government the policy of the central government toward the non-Chinese peoples was either oppressive or apathetic. Its Mongolian and Tibetan Affairs Commission, for example, was never a vital organ of political action. Since 1949, however, the Chinese Communist leaders in Peking have bound Manchuria, Inner Mongolia, and Sinkiang to China proper more tightly than these areas have ever before been bound in this century. In implementing the firm control which Peking exacts, the Chinese Communist authorities have been relatively imaginative in their political and psychological approach to the peoples of the borderlands.

Since 1949, Chinese Communism has made vigorous attempts to organize, mobilize, and indoctrinate the non-Chinese peoples living within the borders of the People's Republic. In many areas Peking has judiciously made use of local leaders, familiar with local conditions, to gain initial support and to speed the extension of Communist political domination. It has seen to it that non-Chinese cadres go to Peking, not Moscow, for their training. It has facilitated the expansion of cultural activities among the minorities, permitting and actually stimulating the use of the native languages. Yet, all texts, for Chinese and non-Chinese alike, are edited and produced in Peking, and the native peoples, while they may now have an opportunity to learn to read in their own languages, are permitted to read only what the Chinese Communist Party desires them to read. Further, it is made readily apparent that any non-Chinese youth who hopes to make his way up the ladder of power in Communist China must, as the first essential, learn Chinese and learn it well.

In carrying out its minorities program, Peking has gradually woven a complex fabric of so-called "autonomous areas" for non-Chinese peoples. In a highly unified state such as Communist China, "autonomy" is, of course, in no sense equivalent to genuine self-rule. It represents formal rather than substantive autonomy. It permits local minority groups to participate in Communist-directed political activities and, to a certain extent, to assume responsibility for local administrative problems, or, more often, for the local enforcement of general policies laid down by Peking. In most cases, the relatively small and widely dispersed autonomous areas can have only a very minor sphere of activity. Where larger autonomous areas have been created, as in Inner Mongolia and Sinkiang, the reins of power are held in dependable Chinese Communist hands. The broad aim of Peking's policy is to facilitate the manipulation and control of the minority peoples by the Chinese Communists, not to generate or encourage any ambition for independence among the native peoples whom they rule.

In retrospect, it is apparent that the principal domestic problem which the Chinese Communists have encountered in dealing with the borderlands is essentially the same one which the Chinese have always faced there: that of mutual suspicion and distrust. The deep feeling of contempt which the Chinese normally hold for the non-Chinese has, in modern times, been matched only by the deep feeling of contempt which the non-Chinese normally hold for the Chinese. In the pre-Communist period—even within the circle of enlightened Chinese who could state, with bland confidence and genteel condescension, that some of their best friends were Mongols—it was clear that the Chinese usually regarded the Mongol as a greasy and rather simple-minded oaf who ate mutton with his fingers and neglected to wash his clothes.

It is doubtful whether these psychological attitudes have yet been purged on either side by the general commandments of Marxist-Leninist-Stalinist nationalities policy or by the specific statement in the constitution of the People's Republic that "all nationalities are equal; that there shall be no national discrimination or oppression of any kind." The Chinese Communists still regard the native peoples as picturesque children who must be controlled with a firm hand. They invite the minority peoples to Peking to exhibit their native dances and to stand, as colorful decorations, on the rostrum at T'ien An Men at the great Communist celebrations on May Day and October First. But the rulers in Peking, both as Chinese and as Chinese Communists, are still confident of their own innate Sinic superiority. When the occasion demands, they do not hesitate to make it clear that some nationalities are more equal than others and that Chinese guidance and leadership are still essential to the development of the borderlands.

The requirements of political consolidation in the outlying areas have also led to significant economic changes. Peking has done much to expand trade in minority areas which, in earlier years, had been backward and economically depressed. Increased production, as well as more efficient utilization of manpower and natural resources, has accompanied the broad emphasis upon national economic expansion and industrialization. As part of its general program of developing transportation facilities in all parts of the mainland, Peking has been responsible for building new roads—and in some cases railroads—into and across many areas inhabited by non-Chinese peoples. Improved transportation has been very important in aiding the rapid extension of national authority into areas which have been politically isolated for many years, and in facilitating economic development programs.

Peking has also made clear its long-range plans for land utilization. Its aim is to carry through the widespread reclamation of wastelands in Manchuria, Inner Mongolia, and Sinkiang in preparation for enlarging the flow of Chinese, both peasants and demobilized military personnel, into the borderlands as workers and settlers. This program of migration and assimilation, if pressed, will represent a significant attempt to transform the basic economic and social pattern of life in the borderlands. The pre-Communist record in China suggests that the Chinese have, on the whole, never been very eager voluntarily to pursue the frontier westward, and it is still not certain that Communism, or Communist duress, will be successful in changing their predispositions.

In the strategic sphere, Peking's policy toward its northern borderlands has been implemented in accordance both with the general spirit of its foreign policy and with the specific requirements of the lengthy Sino-Russian border and the Sino-Soviet alliance. Mao Tse-tung's basic anti-Western framework of policy, whether stated in "lean-to-one-side" or any other terms, has, in a real sense, turned Communist China's face away from the sea and inward toward its continental ramparts. The development of new, interior lines of communication with the Soviet Union— through Mongolia and, by 1960, through Sinkiang— will be of great importance in determining China's future position in world politics. Already the new links have greatly increased Communist China's orientation toward, dependence upon, and vulnerability to the Soviet Union.

Certainly Moscow recognizes these implications, aware as it is of the strategic importance of the Eurasian heartland in any future military clash with the West. Prior to 1949, Soviet policy toward the Chinese borderlands was primarily concerned with strengthening Russia's national defenses and extending Russian-oriented Communist influence into Inner Asia. Since 1949, Soviet policy toward the Chinese borderlands has been increasingly concerned with the wider role of the Sino-Soviet alliance as an instrument for expanding general Communist influence throughout Asia. Recognizing the strong role of Chinese nationalism in Peking's policy, the Soviet leaders appear to have taken particular care to avoid direct conflict or unnecessary competition with the Chinese Communists in the borderlands and have gradually retracted their own sphere of activity in them. Within the alliance as a whole, with all the general advantages which it brings to both partners, the Russians have far more to gain from reasonably good behavior along the frontier than from minor local attempts at direct intrigue or interference in the politics of these areas.

The basic arrangements relating to the borderlands appear, in general, to have been worked out in a spirit of cooperation. With Peking's acquiescence—indeed, at Peking's request—Moscow continues active in the sphere of economic and technical assistance, designed to encourage the planned development of these areas within the confines of the Communist bloc. There has been no serious attempt to integrate Chinese industry, either in Manchuria or in Sinkiang, where development is still primitive, with that of Soviet Asia. On the contrary, Peking has demonstrated its determination to integrate these areas and their resources into a unified Chinese economy.

There is also an internal aspect to the problem, one which is commonly overlooked. The borderlands and the border peoples continue to possess some intrinsic importance, apart from their subordination to the power interests of Moscow and Peking. Perhaps the most outstanding common denominator found among the native peoples of these areas is the desire for true autonomy, for freedom to handle their own affairs without external interference. This characteristic has been notable for many years in Manchuria, where the Manchurian Chinese, while Chinese in speech and culture, have nurtured the hope of handling their own problems more or less independently of their countrymen to the south of the Great Wall. Similarly, strong localism has been expressed in the political attitudes of the Mongols of Inner Mongolia and the native peoples of Sinkiang, most of whom have long yearned for autonomy. It is doubtful whether many of the borderlands peoples are deluded by the theoretical equality now offered them by Communism, for Communism, as an operating political system, has no place for their regional ambitions. Whatever their feelings regarding modernization may be, they appear to harbor a deep, instinctive distrust of both the Chinese and the Russians.

The peoples of Inner Asia today seem doomed by the facts of political geography. Now caught and held securely between the Chinese and the Russians, between the pressing requirements of the industrialization and militarization programs of both Communist China and Communist Russia, the minority peoples on the frontier can have little hope and see no alternative. In a broader sense, their present situation is symptomatic of the fact that not even the heart of Asia, with its deeply frozen habits of life, can escape the impact of the modern world. Even if Chinese Communism had not come to the Chinese borderlands, the patterns of life of the native peoples there would gradually be rendered obsolete by the process of technological change, of which the airplane, the tractor, and the truck are only the apparatus. Secularization, centralization, urbanization, and nationalization—as well as the political ideology and the political organization of Communism—are gradually intruding into these remote areas. The individualistic mounted mobility which has long been the hallmark of the nomad is now being progressively immobilized by the rigid demands of the Communist system. It is doubtful whether the Chinese Communists will be successful in converting the borderland peoples, except for a portion of the youth, to Marxism-Leninism and Maoism, but it is increasingly clear that they are accelerating the general trend toward modernization in the borderlands. An English observer has aptly summarized the trend:

The consolidation of Russian and Chinese authority over all Central Asia has had one momentous consequence. It has ended the importance of nomad peoples as the makers of history. For many centuries the nomads had hung threateningly on the outskirts of the settled land empires. . . . But today it seems most unlikely that nomad hordes will ever again be on the move. Much of the pasture land is being ploughed. The children of the nomads will presently be assimilated by the rival civilizations. One of the main historic ways of life is thus being ended in our time.[16]

The politics of the northern borderlands of China are based, essentially, upon relative power. In periods when the central political authority in China was weak and unstable, other powers have been able to expand their influence into these regions. And when the national authority of China has been strong, aggressive, and effective, the Chinese have been able to reassert their ascendancy in these hinterlands. The pendulum is still swinging today, although the international environment has undergone a basic change, expressed in the total victory of Communism on the mainland of China and the emergence of a strong Chinese Communist regime in Peking allied with a much stronger Russian Communist government in Moscow. The growing strength and increasing self-confidence of the People's Republic of China have penetrated the borderlands of the nation and have led to the consolidation of Peking's overriding authority and to the gradual reduction of Moscow's influence. The agreement, formally set forth in the Sino-Soviet Treaty of February 1950, for "noninterference in the internal affairs of the other contracting power," has practical meaning only in a situation in which both Communist powers are strong domestically and confident of their indigenous energies and capabilities.

From the standpoint of the Sino-Soviet axis today, the

16 Guy Wint, *Spotlight on Asia* (Harmondsworth, Middlesex: Penguin Books, 1955), p. 159.

borderlands, as geographic areas, are important, while the inhabitants of the borderlands, as human beings, are of relatively little significance. In areas where the same groups live on both sides of the border—for example, the Turkic-Moslem peoples of Chinese Turkestan and Russian Turkestan, or the Mongols of Inner and Outer Mongolia—the human factor is of some relevance. If notable differences between the Russian and Chinese Communist spheres should become apparent, they might be accompanied by local political tensions. Significantly different political treatment, variations in social and cultural development or in rates of economic growth, might result in frictions which could have major repercussions upon the Sino-Soviet entente. These trends, however, are not apparent today. In the foreseeable future, it appears more likely that Peking and Moscow will continue to devise solutions to local problems of the borderlands in cooperation and without subjecting the Sino-Soviet alliance to any unmanageable strain.

CHAPTER FIVE

THE MOSCOW-PEKING AXIS IN WORLD POLITICS

by Philip E. Mosely

WORKING IN CLOSE cooperation since October 1949, the Moscow and Peking centers of Communism have been firmly linked together by a shared system of political values and aims and by a shared interpretation of the movement of history which, they believe and proclaim, will bring about the triumph of Communism throughout the world. They have taken great risks together, navigated difficult twists and turns of policy in outward harmony, and chalked up a number of important gains, though less than they aimed for. Moscow has not received from Peking, and probably has not demanded, the automatic response to its commands which it has until recently been able to exact from the satellite leaderships in Eastern Europe.

Since 1949, Moscow and Peking have presumably had to negotiate out a large number of concrete decisions, and between them there may well have been divergences in detail over the advantages and disadvantages of specific steps. They have also had to work closely together in the field of economic cooperation. In doing so, the traditional Communist primacy of politics over economics has led them to accept some important disadvantages and even some substantial sacrifices. The cement which holds together their alliance and makes it one of the two most powerful blocs in the world is primarily a shared system of political ideas and aims, and behind these aims, whether immediate or of longer range, is the basic purpose of expanding Communist power politically, militarily, industrially, and territorially.

Perhaps the ideological community between the two leaderships has not been complete at all times. The paths which non-Soviet Communist leaderships have to tread are not always simple or safe. Hints of past divergences over dogma have been expressed somewhat more plainly since the dethroning of the Stalin-image in Khrushchev's partially published speech, on February 25, 1956, to the Twentieth Congress of the Soviet party. After the close of the Congress, the Chinese leadership, without attacking Stalin head-on, spoke out strongly against ". . . some of our comrades mechanically applying Stalinist formulas in the Chinese Revolution" from 1927 to 1936, and their "dogmatic error." [1] Some further hint of continuing controversies in Moscow inner sanctums over the path followed by the Chinese Communist Party, of disputes over its Leninist purity, may perhaps be detected in the speech at the Twentieth Congress by Dimitri T. Shepilov, who, at the end of May 1956, was appointed Foreign Minister:

The progress of the socialist revolution in China has been even more unique. . . . From the point of view of pedant Marxists such an approach to the question of transforming exploitative ownership into socialist ownership almost amounts to slighting the principles of Marxism-Leninism. But in reality this is creative Marxism-Leninism in action, a masterly application of Marxist dialectic to the specific conditions of China, boldly and wisely carried out by the heroic Communist Party of China. (Stormy applause.) [2]

In mid-1956 rumors began seeping out from satellite capitals of a speech which Khrushchev had made to party

[1] "Concerning the historical experience of dictatorship of the proletariat," editorial in *Jen Min Jih Pao* (People's Daily) (Peking), summarized in *Pravda*, April 7, 1956; cited from *Current Digest of the Soviet Press* (New York), May 16, 1956, p. 5.

[2] *Pravda*, February 17, 1956; cited from *Current Digest*, March 28, 1956, p. 19.

circles in Warsaw in March 1956.[3] He was quoted as having attacked Stalin for subjecting the Kremlin's relations with Peking to a dangerous strain, particularly through his insistence upon establishing Soviet-controlled joint-stock companies. These devices, which seemed to many in Peking to constitute an unexpected revival of imperialism, were abolished only some months after Stalin's death.

The increasing emphasis, at least on paper, by Khrushchev and Bulganin on Moscow's new toleration of "different paths to socialism" seemed designed to reduce or eliminate the likelihood that ideological divergences would place an intolerable strain upon the alliance. Perhaps Peking is satisfied with Moscow's formal recognition of its ideological autonomy and, therefore, as in the dramatic events of October and November 1956, it is content to affirm its support of Moscow's grudging acceptance of the Nagy path for Hungary. At the end of December, at an extraordinary session, the Chinese Politburo reaffirmed its unequivocal support of Soviet policies toward the East European satellites and denounced Tito for following a course which "can only lead to a split in the Communist movement." [4]

Certainly, by acknowledging Peking's autonomy in matters of Communist ideology, the present Kremlin leadership runs less risk of alienating Mao and his followers than they would by insisting on Moscow's sole right to determine what constitutes true Communist dogma and to define the "correct path" to socialism. And conceivably Peking's underwriting of Soviet policies toward the satellites in Eastern Europe, reaffirmed in the declaration of January 18, 1957, may have its counterpart in Moscow's leaving to the Chinese party the direct responsibility for "guiding" several of the Communist parties and regimes in Asia.

Perhaps the growing emphasis since 1953 upon the enhanced stature of Peking as an autonomous center of Communism reflects, in the ideological sphere, the reality

3 New York Times, June 4, 1956.
4 Peking broadcast, December 28, 1956; summarized in New York Times, December 29, 1956.

of a self-contained and self-propelled system of power, a center which has been built up from within by the Chinese Communists and which is fully capable of dealing on a basis of independent decision, if not true equality of power, with the Moscow center. Granted that Moscow will retain for several decades a great superiority of industrial and military power, and that this inequality of strength will continue to influence profoundly the manner and the speed with which Peking pursues its purposes, the fact also remains that the Soviet leadership must henceforth pursue its vast goals in Asia with and through the new Chinese regime, not without it or against it.

Shared political and strategic objectives provide the strongest incentive for both partners, senior and junior alike, to bridge over even major conflicts of ideological outlook or economic interest. Those who believe that the Moscow and Peking centers can be separated from each other must, it would seem, prove either that their goals are incompatible or that each of the two centers may judge itself better able, in separation or even in conflict with the other, to achieve its own goals. The evidence of their visible actions indicates, thus far, that each partner sets a high value on their close cooperation and will make great efforts to assure its continuation.

THE RANGE OF PEKING'S AIMS

Judging by the policies which the Chinese Communist regime has followed ever since 1950, it has a definite range of immediate and longer-term objectives. Peking is intensely interested in overthrowing the Nationalist Chinese regime on Taiwan and thus in rounding out its victory in what both it and the Nationalists regard as a civil war between opposing Chinese forces. The Nationalist occupation of the offshore islands, in the view of the Communist Chinese regime, impinges even more directly upon its security.

The fact that the United States regards its strategic frontiers as including Taiwan and the Pescadores, and as involving the protection of the offshore islands against attack, raises this issue to a level of power politics which makes it impossible for mainland China at present to resolve it by its own military strength. Obviously, without the active military backing of the Soviet Union, Peking cannot undertake to force a military decision against the main strength of the United States. Peking now counts on undermining the Nationalist regime by attrition. Even the desultory United States-Communist Chinese negotiations at Geneva, during 1955 and 1956, were utilized in Peking's propaganda to imply that the Americans were negotiating a "deal" to scuttle the Nationalists.[5]

The Chinese Communists have not abandoned their desire to see the two halves of Korea united under Communist control, and presumably under Chinese hegemony. Similarly, they have pressed constantly for reuniting the two parts of Vietnam, of course, only under conditions which would, they believe, assure Communist control. Beyond that, Communist China looks to strengthening its influence—and, presumably, establishing ultimately its dominance—over the countries of Southeast Asia, and over Burma and Indonesia. For the near future, it prefers to see India and Indonesia pursue their "neutralist" role. It is encouraged that those countries' leaders constantly criticize non-Communist alliances but seldom, if ever, mention the most massive and ominous bloc of all, the Sino-Soviet bloc.

Communist China is interested in fostering the spread of "neutralism" and "de-commitment" to Pakistan and Thailand, to Japan and the Philippines, and it favors the "liberation" of Malaya. Both Soviet and Chinese Communist propaganda make it clear that neutralism and non-commitment are policies recommended as the way of salvation for countries outside the periphery of Communist control, but not to be encouraged or tolerated within the Communist bloc. If new evidence of this double standard were needed, it was provided by Moscow's ruthless

5 Chou En-lai, "The Foreign Policy of the Chinese People's Republic and the Question of the Liberation of Taiwan," *Pravda*, July 18, 1956.

suppression of the Imre Nagy government's attempt to proclaim the neutrality of Hungary. All these aims of Peking, if they can be achieved without involving the Soviet bloc in a major war, are enthusiastically endorsed and promoted by the Soviet leadership. Divergences, which are apparently resolved by frequent and secret consultations between the two leaderships, relate not to aims, but to questions of means, timing, and judgment of the risks involved.

Let us assume, on the other hand, that Communist China were to seek to cooperate or even to coexist in permanent harmony with the nations which have joined together to resist the expansion of the two major Communist powers. In this case, Mao's government would have to abandon all present goals of its foreign policy. It would have to accept the indefinite existence of the "two Chinas" and abandon any threat to take Taiwan by force. It would have to agree to the reunification of Korea and Vietnam through free elections. It would have to tolerate the American alliances with Formosa, Japan, Korea, the Philippines, Australia and New Zealand, and the continued existence of SEATO, at least until such time as its own mild demeanor had persuaded China's neighbors that the danger of a future renewal of Communist expansion was gone forever.

In brief, Communist China would have to concentrate its efforts entirely on its domestic reconstruction and pursue an exclusively peaceful competition for the future leadership of Asia. Presumably, it would also have to accept whatever economic terms could reasonably be secured from the major free-world powers. While trade barriers would be relaxed promptly, Peking could not expect any large economic sacrifices by the West or Japan to help it along in its program of industrialization. By contrast, the Soviet leadership wishes to see China achieve its far-ranging ambitions, both at home and abroad, though it may well differ in estimating the costs and risks involved in any specific action. Divergences over means may grow into friction and strain, but in practice they are likely, for the sake of larger and shared goals, to result in compromises rather than in a rupture.

Perhaps the basic strain in Sino-Soviet relations arises from the question of the range of power to be applied in any given situation. So long as Peking and Moscow subordinate their disputes over means to the achievement of shared goals, China is not likely to tear itself loose from Russia. In addition, when an issue moves toward the risk of using large-scale military power, and particularly when it increases the risk of involving the United States and its allies in a direct military struggle, the responsibilities and the risks of the Soviet partner are drastically enhanced, together with China's dependence on Moscow's backing. So long as primarily political, ideological and economic means can be employed to promote the cause of "liberation" Communist-style, Peking probably enjoys a wide range of initiative and autonomous responsibility.

Moscow apparently prefers to remain in the background except at points of major crisis. When the Chinese Communists' intervention in the Korean war fell short of its goal of conquering South Korea and expelling the influence of the United States from the Asian continent, the Soviet regime took upon itself, in June 1951, the major responsibility in seeking to bring about negotiations for a cease-fire. The wearisome negotiations over the terms of the truce were, however, left primarily to the Chinese Communist negotiators. In March and April 1955, when the Chinese Communists' preparations for seizing the off-shore islands had reached a threatening stage, and American opinion seemed to be sharply divided over the question of whether or not to use force to defend them, Moscow, it has been widely surmised, exerted its influence to deter Peking from pressing the issue to a military showdown and thus prepared the way for the Geneva Conference between East and West, held in July 1955.

Are there potential or actual divergences of interests between the two partners? Or is there merely a division of roles within the alliance? Have Moscow and Peking agreed on assigning to one or the other regional priorities or spheres of influence in their dealings both with governments and with Communist parties in the various countries of Asia? Are there divergences in their respective estimates of the risks which any given course may involve? Because of the extreme secrecy which surrounds Communist policy-making, any answers to these central questions are bound to be highly speculative and tentative, but, even at a more than normal risk of being refuted by future events, the questions cannot be evaded.

TAIWAN AND THE OFFSHORE ISLANDS

Do Moscow and Peking believe that the conquest of Taiwan can conceivably be carried out without involving the United States? The refusal of Peking, during the prolonged Sino-American discussions at Geneva in 1955 and 1956, to renounce the use of force against Taiwan, and its persistent demands that the United States renounce the use of force to defend Taiwan, indicated clearly its insistence on maintaining its right, at some future opportunity, to use force to overthrow the Chinese Nationalist regime. Since the crisis in the spring of 1955, however, Moscow and Peking have presumably agreed that the direct use of force by mainland China would, at this stage, seriously undermine Peking's claim to support the policy of coexistence and that destructive American reprisals might leave China in a weaker position than it now enjoys.

Both Peking and Moscow now assume that Taiwan may fall to mainland attack either as one segment of a much vaster program for driving the United States from all of Eastern Asia, in other words, through a major and decisive war, or, more likely, through American naval and air forces being withdrawn from the Western Pacific to parry a Soviet threat to Western Europe or the Middle East, or both. In any case, the acceptance by Peking, and Moscow, perhaps not without some severe friction, of the fact that it was not worth risking a direct and presumably unsuccessful engagement with the United States over Taiwan was followed by a new emphasis on political rather than military pressure against Taiwan. Of course, as part of this political pressure, the Chinese Communists have carried through an intensive build-up of air and land power and supporting facilities on the mainland opposite Formosa. In the future, if the Soviet leaders should conclude that an early showdown with the United States was both unavoidable and desirable, a mainland attack on Taiwan would be a convenient initial move designed to pin down a large part of available American forces in a war in which a quick local decision would be unlikely.

The policy of coexistence, proclaimed by Chou En-lai at Bandung in April 1955, has promised Peking increasing opportunities to extend its influence and has opened the way for more active relations with many countries of Asia and the Middle East. Thus, in November 1956, Peking hastened to offer Nasser contingents of Chinese "volunteers." Each time that a new government extends recognition and establishes relations with Peking, the Nationalist regime loses ground, politically and morally, even though its immediate security remains unimpaired. As a consequence of Bandung, followed up by the Soviet campaign, dramatized by the Geneva Conference of July 1955 for a "relaxation of tensions," Peking, for some time to come, will have to be satisfied with extending its political influence by the normal channels of international negotiations and propaganda. It hopes thus to place its claim to Taiwan on a stronger footing, if or when it should decide, at a later stage, to revert to the use of force.

The Soviet and Chinese Communist campaign, waged persistently since late 1949, to secure for Peking China's seat in the United Nations, would, if successful, greatly strengthen its claim that the future of Taiwan is an internal, purely Chinese, question and that in using force to prevent the conquest of Taiwan by Mao's forces the United States would be guilty of "aggression." The seating of Communist China in the United Nations, if accomplished by Moscow and Peking without some action by the West to consolidate Taiwan's separate international status, would tend to promote the disintegration of Nationalist hopes of survival and might eventually make it unnecessary for Communist China to conquer Taiwan by force. The "peaceful" subversion of Taiwan would almost certainly inhibit the United States from using force to defend it. If, as is possible, Moscow was not really eager in 1950-53 to see Peking actually seated in the United Nations, since 1953 and particularly since 1955, they have both been pressing, with increasing prospect of success, for this major accretion of prestige and freedom of maneuver.

The period of relaxation of strain, which followed the crisis of March and April 1955, offered an opportunity for new political thinking and action. Peking has utilized the lull intensively to extend its political influence and to continue its campaign for discrediting the Nationalists and attempting to undermine their morale. British policy has supported the "two Chinas" proposal. American policy has been to stand pat.

Even if Peking and the Soviet bloc remain adamant in refusing to recognize the permanent existence of the Taiwan regime, it has been suggested that United States policy could gain a valuable initiative by taking up the advocacy of the "two Chinas" solution. This step, while disheartening to any remaining Nationalist hopes of re-covering control of the mainland, would perhaps rally the backing of many active supporters in the free-world coalition, and would win the approval of many uncommitted states. India, for example, recognizes Peking's claim to sovereignty over Taiwan, but strongly opposes any use of force to seize it.

A mainland attack on Taiwan, coming after a strong United States effort to secure the adoption of the "two Chinas" solution, would probably result in India and other uncommitted countries throwing their weight against this act of aggression. The present American policy in this question tends to lend plausibility to the Communist-propagated image of Taiwan as being of interest to the United States primarily as a potential springboard for mounting an invasion of mainland China.[6] Active American advocacy of a "two Chinas" policy, without changing the strategic outlook in any essential respect, would put the Communist bloc on the political defensive.

The question of the Chinese offshore islands is in quite a different status. Almost everywhere outside the United States and Taiwan, there is a general assumption that Quemoy, Matsu and the lesser offshore islands have no historic connection with Taiwan and are constituent parts of the nearby mainland territories. Here a local military attack by the Chinese Communist forces would almost surely be successful, unless the United States intervened with strong military force against mainland air bases. An American declaration in advance that it would use its strategic power to resist their seizure through retaliation against the mainland would most probably serve as a deterrent. But if this failed and the United States retaliated, by atomic bombardments of the mainland, against the Communist seizure, without using atomic weapons, of the offshore islands, this step would profoundly alarm public opinion throughout the world. It might well result in mobilizing a great many countries, including many of the best friends of the United States, behind political efforts to put a stop to hostilities before they had caused serious damage to the mainland government or had forced it to break off its aggressive action. Under these circumstances, tremendous political and moral pressure, backed by Soviet atomic threats against Japan and Western Europe, would be organized to halt the American retaliation in midcourse. As one result, the offshore islands would probably remain in Communist hands and the military resources and political prospects of the Nationalist regime would be seriously damaged.

In the second half of 1955 and throughout 1956, the attention of the world was seldom drawn to the offshore islands, but the Communist military build-up has pro-

[6] For a fuller statement of the alternatives, see Arthur H. Dean, "United States Foreign Policy and Formosa," *Foreign Affairs*, v. 33, n. 3 (April 1955), pp. 360-75.

ceeded apace. By carrying on its intensive campaign to promote "coexistence" and the "five principles," the mainland regime may now have put itself in a stronger political position to undertake a seizure of the islands. If successful, this action might shatter the morale of the Nationalist forces, of whom some 40 per cent have been concentrated in the offshore islands. It might drive a wedge between the Nationalists and the native Taiwanese. And it might induce a serious panic among America's allies in Eastern Asia and a panicky flight to "neutralism." Although the United States government has officially reserved the right to determine for itself whether or not it would take direct military action to protect the offshore islands, the passage of time, the massing of American-supplied equipment on the islands, and the presence there of American military advisers have tended to link American prestige, as well as the ambitions of the Chinese Nationalist leaders, to the maintenance of Nationalist possession of them.

So long as the Chinese Nationalists claim, and most of the world believes, even though mistakenly, that the offshore islands are primarily of importance as a staging area for invading the mainland, the United States government, through its policy of deliberate ambiguity, leaves itself open to a political flanking attack. Perhaps the United States would be better advised to utilize the period of quiescence in this question to decide definitely, and without immediate pressure on it, how it can best defend Taiwan over a long, perhaps an indefinite, future.

Would it be wiser to support a plainly defensive posture, such as would be forcefully advertised to the world by its adopting the "two Chinas" policy, even if it were not accepted by either Chinese government? A corollary to this would be to induce the Nationalists to withdraw their forces intact from the offshore islands, to secure wide political support for Taiwan as a "second China," and perhaps to place Taiwan under a United Nations guarantee prior to its giving up possession of China's permanent seat in the Security Council of the United Nations. The other alternative appears to be for the United States to wait passively, to see what may happen next. Meanwhile, the prospects for the Nationalists to control the offshore islands indefinitely can be expected to worsen, and Taiwan's political isolation to be deepened, while Peking continues to push home its propaganda advantage.

KOREA, VIETNAM, SOUTHEAST ASIA

It is hardly necessary to linger over the Chinese Communists' persistent ambition to unify Korea under their control. As a consequence of the serious setback administered to this ambition in the Korean war, the issue has been subordinated since 1953 to a wider pattern of Communist-bloc interests.

Can United States striking power be jockeyed out of its bases in Japan? Can the defense partnership between the United States and Japan be undermined by Soviet-bloc blandishments and Japanese Communist pressure, thus eventually depriving the United States of the use of a base system in Japan? Without a strong partnership with Japan and the use of strong bases in Japan, can American power again protect South Korea against a new local attack launched by the re-equipped Chinese Communist forces, except by the threat of all-out retaliation against both Russia and China? And would an American withdrawal from Japan, and perhaps Okinawa, weaken decisively the threat of retaliation? One final question is whether the United States will continue for as long as may be necessary to assist the economic development of South Korea, and whether it will succeed in stabilizing its economy at a viable level. For the time being, any Chinese Communist action against South Korea is subordinated to the longer-range questions of the degree of the American determination to strengthen South Korea and its ability to maintain its defenses in Japan.

During the current partial relaxation of tension, Peking's attention has been centered primarily on its ambition to complete the Communist conquest of Vietnam.

Ever since the Geneva Conference on Indochina, of May-July 1954, it has been clear that the Communist bloc has strong hopes of being able to take over South Vietnam, Laos and Cambodia by peaceful and gradual means. During the first year following the partition, the Communist bloc must have been extremely hopeful that South Vietnam would fail to achieve inner stability and external security and would fall sooner rather than later under Communist control. While it is hazardous to make long-range predictions in these matters, South Vietnam has certainly achieved major successes since mid-1955. With American military support and economic assistance, its new government has done far more than many had predicted was possible to solve its political, military and economic problems.

It must not be forgotten that, despite similar predictions of domestic collapse, South Korea had also begun, between 1948 and June 1950, to achieve a more satisfactory level of stabilization, and that it was at this time that the Sino-Soviet bloc, presumably at the lengthy Moscow consultations of January and February 1950 between Mao and Stalin, decided to resort to direct force in order to conquer it. With respect to South Vietnam, the degree of certainty over the extent of United States commitment is today substantially greater than it was concerning South Korea in June 1950. Through SEATO the United States has joined with several allies to declare South Vietnam within the area to be defended by that organization. While the United States has no forces, aside from an advisory group, in South Vietnam and has no direct military commitment toward it, the intensive efforts which it is making to strengthen South Vietnam should be adequate, for some time, to deter the Communist bloc from a direct resort to military force and from yielding to any temptation to turn the North Vietnamese army loose for a march south.

The Moscow-Peking axis has been relentlessly pressing its political warfare against South Vietnam, ceaselessly denouncing United States military and economic aid as a new form of "colonization." Taking advantage of the frictions between South Vietnam and Cambodia, both Moscow and Peking have showered attentions on the latter. In 1956 Prince Norodom Sihanouk, temporarily out of the government but still powerful, paid lengthy visits of state to both Russia and China, both of which have extended aid to Cambodia in the form of long-term credits and grants, technical assistance and scholarships. Isolated Laos, still partitioned since the abortive Geneva agreement of July 1954, has also carried out exchanges of ceremonial visits and signed agreements with Peking, as gestures designed to assert its status of "noncommitment."

Despite the plain fact that neither South Vietnam nor the United States is bound by the Geneva Convention to support the holding of nation-wide elections which were scheduled under that agreement for July 1956, the Soviet-bloc press and radio never tire of denouncing them for their obvious unwillingness to have South Vietnam participate in some sort of elections to "reunify" the country. Both Communist China and Soviet Russia have gone to great lengths to secure from many other governments endorsements of their claim that elections must be held at once throughout Vietnam to elect an all-Vietnamese government. For example, during their visit to India and Burma, Khrushchev and Bulganin succeeded in pocketing joint declarations in support of elections, without any hint that genuinely free elections, if difficult in South Vietnam, would be entirely out of the question in North Vietnam under the control of the Vietminh. In addition, the slightly larger population of North Vietnam, when marched to the polls under Communist discipline, would be able to vote a Communist regime into power over the entire country, even if South Vietnam was completely opposed to it.

Through these and other steps Moscow and Peking are laying the groundwork for a strenuous political campaign against the United States on this issue, within and outside the United Nations, accusing it of "increasing tensions" and "violating agreements." While this campaign may not actually bring about elections, whether free or not, its

persistence and its vehemence do a great deal to keep opinion uncertain and fearful in South Vietnam, Laos and
Cambodia. After all, China is an ancient and close neighbor of the peoples of Southeast Asia. The United States, on
the other hand, is far away, has been involved only recently
in the affairs of the region, and may not be presumed to
have an equally persistent interest in its future, especially
in view of the many claims on its attention and resources in
other parts of the world. At the very least, then, the Soviet-
bloc agitation for elections serves to encourage uncertainty, fence-sitting, and secret currents of timorous
pro-Communist appeasement within South Vietnam, and
thus to make the efforts of the Free Vietnamese and the
United States less fruitful. And all this, at the cost of mere
words!

United States policy need not remain on the defensive
in this issue, which is being made a touchstone of the
good faith of its concern for the future of the peoples of
Southeast Asia. It can accept the general proposal for an
election in both North and South Vietnam, provided it
is first satisfied that genuinely adequate safeguards for a
free choice will be determined in detail and then enforced. It can go further. It can insist that genuinely free
elections be held simultaneously in all three partitioned
nations—Germany, Korea and Vietnam. This stand, in
clear support of a basic principle of liberty, would compel
the Soviet bloc to explain why it urges "free" elections in
Vietnam and rejects them in Germany and Korea. Again,
a stand taken on broad principle would clarify the basic
contrast between Communist and democratic attitudes toward freedom of decision by the peoples directly concerned and would rally wide backing outside the Soviet
bloc for this basic principle.

Communist China seems to have assumed not only a
priority of political direction, but also the principal burden of economic aid, with respect to both North Korea
and North Vietnam. Itself a recipient of large-scale Soviet assistance for its development programs, Peking has

extended, or has promised to extend, substantial aid of a similar type, based only in part on China's own production, to assist in the reconstruction and development of its two satellites. Presumably, the provision of supplementary Soviet aid to both areas still leaves the Chinese Communists with the principal position of influence. Similarly, Peking has taken on substantial obligations for training and equipping the armed forces of the two regimes, although, obviously, aircraft and other heavy equipment, which have been reported in large numbers in North Korea, are of Soviet origin. To what extent North Korea and North Vietnam are able, through exports, to compensate mainland China for its military and economic support remains highly obscure.

Within the countries of Southeast Asia, the Communist Chinese must reckon that they possess substantial and growing assets. Most important of these, perhaps, is the large Chinese population.[7] As Communist China has grown in political and military strength, the national pride of the overseas Chinese and their resentment of the inferior position to which they have generally been relegated by the nations among which they reside, have tended to focus their loyalties on mainland China, now admired as a major power.

Peking has also undertaken to build up its economic relations with the area. Since a great deal of both local and international commerce is in Chinese hands, this in turn provides an additional channel for the expansion of Communist Chinese influence, both directly, through their dealings with governments, and indirectly, through stimulating and financing the efforts of the local Communist parties. In Thailand, for example, Peking has engaged in an extensive campaign to sell its new manufactured goods, including small electric motors, sewing machines and bicycles, as a demonstration of its rapid economic growth. In June 1956, Peking signed an economic assistance agreement with Cambodia, reportedly providing an

[7] cf. Walter H. Mallory, "Chinese Minorities in Southeast Asia," *Foreign Affairs*, v. 34, n. 2 (January 1956), pp. 258-70.

unconditional grant of aid for purchases in China during 1956-58. The ability of Communist China to absorb some of the traditional exports of the region, particularly rice and rubber, works in its favor. The slow recovery of Japanese trade in Southeast Asia and the almost complete breakdown of its trade with Indonesia also tend to leave open wide channels of commercial penetration for the trade of mainland China.

Above all, there is the power factor. Traditionally, a strong China, prior to the early nineteenth century, exerted a strong influence—political, commercial and cultural —within these countries. During the nineteenth century China lost its position, but its present recovery of strength tends to reactivate both the fears and the attractions of superior power among the peoples of Southeast Asia. In many ways, their bonds with each other are weaker than their traditional bonds with China, and, unfortunately, they show little desire to take a common stand. Certainly, over the next several years the Chinese Communist aim will be to deal separately with each of them, to encourage "noncommitment" and to undermine SEATO, which they attack as a "Trojan horse" for the "reimposition of the white man's imperialism."

Much criticism has been leveled at SEATO because it has only two members—Thailand and Pakistan—on the Asian mainland. To this, the only reply is that, in their present view of the world, neither India nor Burma would be willing or able to join in an intraregional grouping, even a neutralist one which excluded non-Asian powers, for their mutual defense. Of the island states in the area, the Philippines belong to SEATO, and Indonesia takes a neutralist position, patterned on that of India. Therefore, SEATO, even in its present form, is merely the best grouping that can be worked out among those states which are willing to combine their efforts for their common defense. Against SEATO, it has been argued that its very existence tends to drive the nonmembers to search out reasons for opposing it and to justify their abstention by praising Communist China and Soviet Russia. Whether Burma's recent experience in attempting to persuade Peking to withdraw its troops from the contested border areas will make its leaders more happy or less happy about entrusting its entire security to China's good will remains uncertain.

SEATO exists. Its disbandment would be a serious blow to future attempts to organize resistance to a renewal of Communist expansionism and would be generally interpreted as a withdrawal of American interest from the mainland countries of Southeast Asia and a reversion to the peripheral strategy of building its defense on the island chain. The only choice, then, is to make SEATO work as well as possible, so that the advantages of belonging to it will become clear to both members and nonmembers.

The proponents of SEATO also urge, and rightly, that the SEATO concept must be enlarged beyond the military sphere, to provide the basis for geographically wider nonmilitary programs of economic and cultural development. These programs are necessary in themselves and they may serve to make clear to present nonparticipants in SEATO the basic values of national independence and democratic progress which it is designed to safeguard. How far nonmembers may prove willing to take part in its nonmilitary programs is at present not at all clear. In any case, economic and cultural progress in Southeast Asia requires confidence in the future security of the area. As Communist China becomes more powerful and more active, the only potential barrier to its pressure is represented by SEATO. It is a hopeful concept which must grow in strength or else wither on the vine.

THE CHOICES BEFORE PEKING

Is Communist China likely, in the near future, to resort to direct military force in order to extend its power throughout the arc from Burma to Vietnam and Indonesia? Probably not, for at least two other and less risky paths are open to it. It can continue its present campaign,

launched at Bandung, to win over the governments in the
area, binding them more closely through trade agreements, playing on their memories and fears of Western
and Japanese imperialism, and discouraging them from
seeking military support or economic aid from the non-
Soviet world. Peking may come to believe that it can
achieve its negative aims of excluding United States and
Western influences from Southeast Asia without resorting
again to force, especially as its growing strength carries
with it the increasing ability to use the threat of force as
a political weapon.

By following this path, the Chinese Communists would
avoid arousing fear and resentment in India. While the
Indian government has shown a definite interest in securing and exchanging promises of nonintervention and non-
resort to force, it does not possess the political or economic
strength to provide a counterforce of attraction, in resistance to the pull toward China. So long as independent
though weak governments were voluntarily pursuing policies of ever closer cooperation with China, India would
have no grounds for mobilizing opinion at home or abroad
to resist this pull. The main risk to Communist China in
pursuing this path is that at some stage the governments
of Southeast Asia and Indonesia might prefer to form a
larger noncommitted bloc under Indian leadership, and
in opposition to both major power blocs. To Peking, this
risk must seem slight, for India has gone far to underwrite
China's benevolent intentions in Asian eyes and India itself would be the last to feel the direct consequences of a
Chinese policy of indirect and gradual expansion over its
smaller neighbors.

A second path, which is also available to China, is not
incompatible with the first and may even run parallel
with it. This involves the building up of Communist parties and pro-Communist movements, working toward the
establishment of "united front" governments, within
which the Communists would aim to gain control of several "commanding heights," such as defense, information
and education. The elections of 1956 in Burma and Indo-

nesia showed substantial gains for the Communists, and in Indonesia they have won many concessions from other parties.

When Khrushchev and other Soviet leaders referred, at the Twentieth Party Congress, to the possibility of a "peaceful and even parliamentary path to socialism," it was presumably countries like Indonesia, Burma, Ceylon and even India which they had in mind. As Khrushchev pointed out, in some countries the "working class" may gain "a firm majority in parliament and transform it from an organ of bourgeois democracy into an organ of true popular will. *(Applause.)*" "Of course," he went on, "in those countries where capitalism is still strong, where it has in its hands an enormous military-police apparatus, there the serious opposition of the reactionary forces is inevitable. There the transition to socialism will take place in conditions of sharp class, revolutionary struggle." [8] In other words, if the opponents of Communist totalitarianism are willing to surrender power peaceably, the revolution will take place with little or no bloodshed, at least prior to the establishment of Communist rule. If they resist, they will by that very fact be declared solely responsible for the Communists' having to resort to methods of violence in order to seize control.

To those governments which are committed to resisting cooperation with the West and yet are unable to build strong defenses and progressive economies by their own means, Soviet and Chinese Communist offers of "aid-through-trade" present an attractive and seemingly harmless alternative. In addition to the Soviet aid-through-trade agreements with India, Burma, Cambodia, Indonesia, Afghanistan, Syria and Egypt, Communist China, in June 1956, concluded its first agreement for the outright granting of aid to a non-bloc country, Cambodia, and was reported to have made offers to Burma, Ceylon and Egypt. Soviet and Chinese programs usually include provision for educating increasing numbers of young engineers in Russia or China, which can easily appear to young and im-

[8] *Pravda*, February 15, 1956, p. 4.

pressionable Asian intellectuals as representing the acme of social and economic progress. The hosts in Moscow and Peking hope that their guests will return home to reinforce the idea that cooperation with Communists at home against the "imperialists" and their local "hirelings" is as harmless as cooperation with Communist governments.

A third path, one which cannot be excluded from calculation, is that, after a more or less prolonged period of intensive wooing and softening up both at the governmental and "united front" levels, the Communist parties in Southeast Asia would be ready to revert, this time with greater prospects of success, to the strategy of the violent seizure of power which they tried out in each country, except Thailand, between 1948 and 1951. Following a "trade-union conference" at Calcutta, in 1948, and obeying the "tough" line which had been promulgated by Moscow at the founding conference of the Cominform, in September and October 1947, each Communist party in Asia scrapped its previous gradualist program and embarked on a fierce struggle to seize power through armed uprisings and extensive sabotage.

Were these bloody campaigns, which raged on into 1951, designed to assist the Chinese Communists in the final stage of their conquest of the mainland? Or did Moscow believe that, with the departure of the Western "imperialists" from India, Pakistan, Ceylon, Burma and Indonesia, the time was ripe for the Communists to seize power, before non-Communist nationalist regimes had time to consolidate their control and embark on positive programs of social and economic progress? Whatever the estimates of Moscow, the militant parties had pretty much burned out their strength of revolt by 1951, although they returned fully to the "peaceful" path only in 1955 and 1956.

Today the Communist bloc probably reckons that the prospects of success through violent tactics would be much greater several years from now, particularly if the Western ability to work with the governments of the area had been increasingly blunted in the interim. The past history of the alternation of the Communists between "hard" and "soft" tactics suggests that the major Communist powers can order, and the local Communists parties will carry out, a revival of violent methods whenever the prospects of early success seem favorable to Moscow and Peking, or whenever it suits their political strategy. Whichever tactic, "soft" or "hard," may seem more promising is the one which will be applied.

PEKING AND JAPAN

Since 1951 and particularly since the return, in 1955, of the Japanese Communist Party to the "lovable," gradualist policy of Nosaka, Peking seems to enjoy a certain priority of interest over Moscow in the development of close relations with Japan. Chinese spokesmen, who formerly insisted that the Japanese government must withdraw its recognition from the Taiwan regime if it hoped to establish relations with Peking, now imply, unofficially, that the establishment of relations between Tokyo and Peking can be effected without requiring this step as a precondition. Aside from the question of Japan's enforcement of the trade controls against mainland China, there are now no difficult questions pending between Japan and Communist China, in contrast to the profound differences which have so long delayed the conclusion of a peace treaty between Soviet Russia and Japan. In general, Japanese opinion, traditionally distrustful of Russia, places great confidence in the ability of the Japanese to work well with the Chinese, whom it regards as primarily "Chinese" rather than Communists. While many of the more optimistic estimates of the value of a revived China trade with Japan have been revised downward of late, Japan's difficulties in opening up markets in other parts of the world would make even a modest revival of trade with China an attractive addition to its economic opportunities.

Peking and Moscow share a common desire to see Japan detached from its alliance and defense agreement with the United States—the alliance concluded in September 1951, and the defense agreement in February 1952. In January 1951, Stalin sent a resounding message "to the Japanese people" urging them to throw off the yoke of their American conquerors, and the theme of "Japan, an American colony" is played up continuously by Peking and Moscow. Since all Japanese parties had promised to negotiate the re-establishment of relations with Russia and mainland China, the Soviet government was able, in the agreement of October 1956, to stand pat on its refusal to discuss the Japanese claim to recover some of the Kurile Islands, even though it agreed to give up the Habomai and Shikotan Islands, long recognized as part of Hokkaido Prefecture, after the conclusion of a peace treaty.

Did Communist China press the Soviet Union to complete its negotiations with Japan? There is certainly no suggestion that Peking would think of urging Moscow to abandon any territorial claims, but probably Peking welcomed the Soviet compromise proposal, of May 1956, for establishing diplomatic relations without a prior settlement of conflicting territorial claims. The reopening of relations, even in this truncated form, between Russia and Japan opened the way for an eventual restoration of relations between Peking and Tokyo and for the further broadening of Chinese Communist contacts with various groups and interests within Japan. Both Peking and Moscow place their hopes in the emergence of a parliamentary majority in Japan committed to bring about the withdrawal of United States forces and installations from Japan, and in a consequent rapid decline in United States diplomatic and economic support for Japan. This, they believe, would make political and economic cooperation with the Communist powers even more attractive and perhaps indispensable for Japan, which would then be more vulnerable to military and economic blackmail by the Communist powers.

Whether the Japanese Communist Party is more directly influenced by Peking or Moscow remains obscure and may have tactical rather than strategic importance.

Peking and Moscow are both working hard to bring Japan over to a neutralist and "de-committed" position, a shift which might be effected more readily through Chinese Communist blandishments rather than through Soviet pressures. If this can be achieved, the growing strategic threat of the Soviet Union, multiplied by the new and rapid advances in military technology, would in turn make Japan even more vulnerable to a sudden revival of political and military pressure from the mainland. If there is a potential rivalry between Peking and Moscow for dominant control over the Japanese Communist Party, this is not likely, short of a victory of Communism in Japan, to prevent them from sharing out the appropriate roles in striving to achieve their common objective.

MOSCOW, DELHI, PEKING

In India, the first impact of the Chinese Communist revolution was to strengthen the extremists among the Communists. Under the Ranadive leadership, the Communist party resorted to methods of violence, and to all-out denunciations of the ruling Congress party. Large-scale railroad and industrial sabotage was practiced, and an attempt was made to build up "Yenans" in several regions of the country. In a sharp reversal of the party's previous "line," Gandhi and Nehru were demoted to the ranks of "hirelings of the imperialists."

The return to peaceful methods was proclaimed with some waverings as early as 1951, more clearly after 1953, and the new line was fully spelled out at the Communist party conference of 1956, following the Khrushchev-Bulganin visit. Since then, the Communist Party of India has secured the release of many political prisoners from custody and has proclaimed its support for Nehru's policy of "noncommitment." The Communists now concentrate their attacks on Western enterprises and investment in India, while wooing the "national bourgeoisie," and glorifying Soviet and Chinese Communist achievements as models for India to follow. It has been suggested, but not

confirmed, that from 1948 to 1951 the Communist Party
of India fell within the sphere of direction of the Chinese
Communists, who pressed it to launch a civil war against
India's "Chiang Kai-shek," and that today the Soviet Communist leadership has asserted its direct interest in the
movement in India, brushing to one side the traditional
channel of contact, the Communist Party of Great Britain.

India is involved in both cooperation and rivalry with
Communist China, and many Indians see the next five
to ten years as a decisive period in which either India or
China will "prove" the superiority of its methods of economic progress. If this is so, then why should Soviet Russia extend economic support to the Indian Five-Year Plan
of 1956-60, especially when China has a better claim to all
assistance that Moscow can spare? The Soviet support
given to India may conceivably be a long-range hedge, designed to build up Russia's influence in India as a potential offset to the preponderant role which China is
assuming in Southeast Asia.

Burma, lying uncomfortably close to Communist China
and still plagued by Communist insurgents at home and
by Chinese pressure and encroachments along an ill-de-
fined frontier, may feel that a direct Soviet interest, as
expressed in the Khrushchev-Bulganin visit of 1955 and
the subsequent trade agreements, may serve to offset any
direct pressure from China. Whether or not an attempt to
play off Moscow against Peking, if it is in Burmese thinking, is likely to succeed is doubtful. In a crisis, it is more
likely that any influence exercised by Moscow over governments or Communist parties would be used to serve the
common aims of both major Communist powers.

For the time being, since neutralism is designed solely
for export beyond the periphery of the Soviet bloc, the
negative purpose of the axis in strengthening the attach-
ment of India, Burma, Cambodia, Laos, Indonesia and
perhaps of Ceylon to their status of "noncommitment" can
be best served through programs of political, economic
and cultural cooperation. The prestige of India, which
gives approval to many Soviet and Chinese Communist

demands made in the name of "peace" and of opposition to "blocs," tends, in many parts of Asia and Africa, to underwrite a vague popular trustfulness in the peaceful intentions of the Soviet bloc.

PEKING, MOSCOW, AND THE "ZONE OF PEACE"

At the Twentieth Party Congress, Soviet spokesmen stressed again and again the great importance of building up cooperation between the "peace bloc" of the Soviet-led "one-third of mankind" and the "peace zone," exemplified by India, which influences another one-third of mankind, in order to isolate the "imperialist-controlled" remaining third. Both Moscow and Peking affirm on every occasion their support for Prime Minister Nehru's "five principles," although Nehru himself has frequently denounced the Indian Communists as "strangers" who "love Russia more than India." In contrast, he has repeatedly endorsed the "peace-loving" purposes of the two major Communist partners. Even the Soviet suppression of the revolt in Hungary, in November 1956, was denounced by Nehru more in pain than in anger. While he complains frequently against Western-inspired alliances and blocs and, less frequently, has chided Russia for its Warsaw bloc, he apparently has no public misgivings about the powerful Sino-Soviet alliance.

In the Soviet view of political strategy, the "peace bloc" has an important role to play. It can help to restrain the resistance of the non-Communist world to any Soviet actions short of all-out war, and discourage any political or military prepartions for facing up to or forestalling such an eventuality. And in the meantime it may serve Moscow's and Peking's purposes by winning away a number of countries from the "imperialist" camp and bringing them over to the ranks of the uncommitted and defenseless nations. Probably the Soviet government now estimates that, despite the trend toward nuclear stalemate, any serious military clash would increasingly run the risk of expanding into an all-out struggle between the United States and the Soviet bloc. Possibly it has decided that it is in its own vital interest to avert or, at least, to postpone such a stupendous conflict and to avoid enlarging its risks beyond politically manageable limits for the next few years, or until the outcome of the present race for superiority in long-range aircraft, atomic power and guided missiles has been resolved.

In the meantime, while minimizing the risk of all-out war, Moscow hopes to make important political gains through cooperating with the "peace zone," particularly, as in the case of Egypt and Syria, by supporting its members against the "imperialists." If its new and more conciliatory tactics work well, it may hope to weaken or even eliminate the political influence of the non-Soviet bloc from the mainland of Asia. It hopes that the attractions of noncommitment will bring Thailand and Pakistan to abandon their commitments to SEATO, as Ceylon has done with respect to the British bases there. If this should come about, partly through domestic pressures within the two mainland allies of SEATO, it is doubtful that the Indian government would see any purpose to be served by organizing a defensive bloc of its own within the "peace zone." Accordingly, with SEATO's counterpressure removed, each individual country of the "peace zone" would be increasingly vulnerable to the pressures and blandishments, combined or alternated, which can be exerted by Russia and China. Presumably this policy is compatible with the primary short-run aim of the Soviet bloc, to destroy the Western system of alliances and thus to bring about the retraction of United States political and military commitments from the mainland of Asia.

Finally, it must not be forgotten that both in Moscow and Peking policies are shaped by basic Marxist assumptions. Relying on Marxist reasoning, the Communist leaders undoubtedly reckon that methods of development based upon liberal institutions and upon cooperation with the timid venture capital of the West cannot solve the problems of internal economic and social development in the underdeveloped and newly independent countries. It

is only a question of time, they believe, before the failure
of the liberal-democratic path will be made clear, thus
opening the way for these peoples to adopt, peacefully or
through violence, the alternative path of modernization,
represented by the Soviet model of compulsion and dictatorship.

During a period of violent action, from 1945 through
1951, the Communist leaderships drove their own forces
to the limit and consolidated their territorial gains in Eastern Europe and China, only to overreach themselves in
Greece, Berlin, Yugoslavia and Korea. From 1951 to 1955
they were occupied in disengaging their forces from coun-
terproductive adventures and testing out a variety of tactics, some of them contradictory to others. Since Bandung
and Geneva, in 1955, the Soviet leadership, seconded somewhat clumsily and perhaps reluctantly by Peking, has gone
all-out for peaceful cooperation with any governments
which are or may become hostile to its principal adver-
sary, the United States, and its close allies. Similarly, it
has ordered the Communist parties to woo into "united
fronts" the parties and regimes they had previously promised to destroy. The broad smile of Moscow and the less
gracious grimace of Peking are alike expressions of these
new or refurbished "soft" tactics.

Cooperating with any and all regimes for shared goals,
tapping a reservoir of resentment against recent colonialism and fear of the "white man's imperialism," the Moscow-Peking axis is actively engaged in extending its
political, economic and cultural influence beyond the
periphery of the bloc, while respecting outwardly the existing regimes and cultivating their favor. Parallel to their
diplomatic efforts, Moscow and Peking are working for
the emergence of new "united front" alliances and coalition governments, within which superior Communist discipline and organization may, they hope, effect a further
enhancement of Communist power.

As Moscow and Peking look out on Communist Asia,
they feel confident that, in a more or less prolonged period
of relaxed tension, their growing political, economic and

military strength will bring great gains, especially through their efforts to monopolize the emotions released by the waves of anti-imperialism, national liberation, and modernization. If this results in the extension of the area of neutralism, in the retraction of United States and free-world commitments and in a diminished willingness of the United States and its allies to make sacrifices or run risks, their immediate purposes will be fully served. The expectation of Moscow and Peking is that, after a period of "peaceful competition," their axis will be stronger, and its opponents weaker, than they now are.

By the Bulganin-Chou En-lai declaration of January 18, 1957, the two major Communist powers proclaimed again "the unbreakable unity" of their countries and their determination to cooperate fully in striving for "victory in the common struggle for triumph of Communism."

For the next few years, the primary challenge of the Moscow-Peking axis is likely to be political, economic and cultural in character, while the two partners go on building up their military power at top speed, to prepare for future contingencies and opportunities. This means that programs for the strategic consolidation of the free world must be backed up flexibly through imaginative programs of political, economic and cultural cooperation, programs which can win the sincere support of the peoples of both committed and uncommitted areas. At the same time the countries of the free world cannot afford to drop their guard or be lulled into falling behind in the race for military power and political cohesion. In Asia, the free world has both handicaps and advantages. It must examine both realistically if it is to meet successfully the new challenge of the Moscow-Peking axis.

INDEX